ACHIEVING ANEW

ACHIEVING ANEW

How New Immigrants Do in American
Schools, Jobs, and Neighborhoods

Michael J .White and Jennifer E. Glick

Russell Sage Foundation ♦ New York

The Russell Sage Foundation

The Russell Sage Foundation, one of the oldest of America's general purpose foundations, was established in 1907 by Mrs. Margaret Olivia Sage for "the improvement of social and living conditions in the United States." The Foundation seeks to fulfill this mandate by fostering the development and dissemination of knowledge about the country's political, social, and economic problems. While the Foundation endeavors to assure the accuracy and objectivity of each book it publishes, the conclusions and interpretations in Russell Sage Foundation publications are those of the authors and not of the Foundation, its Trustees, or its staff. Publication by Russell Sage, therefore, does not imply Foundation endorsement.

Library of Congress Cataloging-in-Publication Data
White, Michael J., 1953–
Achieving anew : how new immigrants do in American schools, jobs, and neighborhoods
    / Michael J. White and Jennifer E. Glick.
        p.   cm.
    Includes bibliographical references and index.
    ISBN 978-0-87154-920-4 (alk. paper)
    1. United States—Emigration and immigration.   2. Assimilation (Sociology)—
United States.   I. Glick, Jennifer E.   II. Title.
    JV6465.W45 2009
    305.9′069120973—dc22

                                                                                  2008050965

The paper used in this publication meets the minimum requirements of American National Standard for Information Sciences—Permanence of Paper for Printed Library Materials. ANSI Z39.48-1992.

Text design by Suzanne Nichols.

RUSSELL SAGE FOUNDATION
112 East 64th Street, New York, New York 10065
10   9   8   7   6   5   4   3   2   1

CONTENTS

ABOUT THE AUTHORS

MICHAEL J. WHITE is professor of sociology and director of the Population Studies and Training Center at Brown University.

JENNIFER E. GLICK is associate professor of sociology and associate director of the Center for Population Dynamics at Arizona State University.

ACKNOWLEDGMENTS

WE OWE a substantial debt of gratitude to several organizations and individuals for help in bringing this effort into print. The Demographic and Behavioral Sciences Branch of the Eunice Shriver National Institute of Child Health and Human Development (R01 HD37054 "Immigration and Early Life Course Transitions") supported our work with the analysis of High School and Beyond and the National Educational Longitudinal Study. The National Science Foundation (SES-9975126 "Advancing Segregation Measurement") supported our work on residential segregation. The Population Research Infrastructure Program award (R24 HD041020) to Brown University's Population Studies and Training Center further supported our efforts.

We owe much to our home institutions, Brown University and Arizona State University, and our colleagues and students there who provided a sounding board for our ideas. Several colleagues collaborated with one or both of us on related immigration work. We happily subjected colleagues at seminars and colloquia to our ideas, and they responded with constructive criticism. Within and beyond our own institutions, colleagues gave us valued and often provocative feedback on the arguments and evidence we were presenting. Among colleagues who helped us rethink or refine our arguments we would like to thank Calvin Goldscheider, Frances Goldscheider, Michael Fix, Dennis Hogan, Joseph Hogan, Ann Kim, David Lindstrom, Cecilia Menjivar, Jeffrey Passel and Scott Yabiku. Students Joshua Biber, Te-Ping Chen, Orly Clerge, Erica Mullen, and Weiwei Zhang helped provide research assistance at Brown. Kelley Alison Smith and Katelyn Clary provided incomparable help in putting the manuscript together in coherent form. Littisha Bates, Bryndl Hohmann-Marriott, Stacey Ruf, Chunyan Song, and Yun Zhou provided research assistance at Arizona State University.

The Russell Sage Foundation has played a particularly instrumental role. From foundation president Eric Wanner through the production staff we have benefitted from a steady progression of helpful input and assistance. We are particularly indebted to our editor Suzanne Nichols, who has been encouraging and patient. She has gently nudged us, always with enthusiasm, for which we are most grateful. We are thankful to anonymous reviewers who generously offered informed criticism and, in so doing, inspired some new analyses. We trust that this volume is stronger and more readable for these efforts.

Last, we would like to thank our families, who have stood by us even as we added this task to many others. White thanks Jane Desforges for her support and for her continuing discussion of the immigrant story and life out there beyond academia's walls. Glick thanks Dave Highfield for his continual encouragement and company on the journey.

Chapter 1

Introduction

THE FACES of new arrivals to our shores, ports, and cities reinforce the self-image of the United States as a country of immigration. At the same time, this newest wave of immigrants brings challenges and opportunities. In the eyes of some observers, it challenges key values of American society. For others, it reinforces those values. For some, it strengthens the economy; for others, it limits the economic opportunities of residents and raises the prospect of a mass of unskilled newcomers on the bottom rungs of society. Unquestionably, recent years have witnessed one of the largest flows of immigrants in U.S. history. Such a volume raises questions about the absorptive capacity of American society.

Immigration is contentious territory. In large part this is precisely because immigration brings new faces and new voices to the destination country. Historically, immigration flows to the United States have been from diverse origins. The recent period is no exception. Typically, immigrants have been less skilled than their American resident counterparts, though the universality of this generalization holds better in mythology than it does in fact. All told, the cultural distance, the demographic distinction, and the vagaries of economic absorption raise questions about how well immigrants and their children do in their new environment. This book examines that issue. Our objective is to look at the assimilation of immigrants in school, the workforce, and in residential communities. Where possible, we take an explicitly longitudinal view. This is of course not the only way to look at contemporary immigration, but it is a crucial vantage point from which to see how well the first and second generation are faring and what the future may hold.

Immigration is also controversial political territory because it is one of the few aspects of national population change that is seen as totally appropriate for the government to regulate. Nation-states may decide who may legitimately enter. Even the phrase *control of our borders*, so often invoked in U.S. political rhetoric, is built on this assumption. Note also the asymmetry in this population regulation. Although the United Nations Universal Declaration of Human Rights (Article 13) asserts the right of freedom of movement within a state and includes a right of departure, there is no corresponding right of arrival and settlement into other sovereign nations. There are certainly examples of governments trying to influence natural increase; these are mostly indirect and limited in scope. Indeed, direct intervention to increase birth rates (such as in some European countries now) has met with at best modest success, and direct intervention to decrease birth rates (such as China's one-child policy) is met with deep concern about draconian policies used to achieve targets. Throughout, states are seen as totally within bounds to limit immigrants and return undocumented migrants to their origins. Hence, regulating the flow and composition of immigrants is totally up for grabs in the policy arena. In the U.S. context, everything from the national identity to the economic prospects for the nation in the twenty-first century global economy is fodder in the debate about how many get in and who they are.

Our efforts in the following chapters are designed to speak to this widening debate about U.S. immigration. Among recent academic writers, Samuel Huntington has engaged the debate most vividly with his publication of *Who Are We?* He argues precisely that immigration challenges American identity, even referring to a contemporary crisis of national identity, a crisis linked in large part to the arrival of new faces from distinct and nontraditional origins. This, in Huntington's view, is not an entirely new phenomenon, and even the assimilation process itself is implicated: "The ethnic component of American identity gradually weakened as a result of the assimilation of the Irish and the Germans who came in the mid-nineteenth century and the southern and eastern Europeans who came between 1800 and 1914" (2004, 17).

Huntington goes on to weave his argument, examining both historical patterns and contemporary trends. He is careful not to privilege Anglo-Saxon persons, but clearly worries about the loss of Anglo-Saxon values in American society. In his chapter on assimilation, Huntington tendentiously questions whether assimilation is still a success: "The great American success story may face an uncertain future" (2004, 184). Our aim here is not to set up Huntington as a straw figure, and several of his points about the changing immigration landscape are well taken, but rather we see him as an academic representative of a line of thought questioning features of the current U.S. immigrant stream. This line of thinking—questioning the size, pace, and composition of immigration to the United States—has many adherents.

The economist George Borjas has contributed extensively to the literature on the adjustment of immigrants in the United States. It was his early work that challenged the notion of immigrant super-achievement in the post-1965 period. The outset of Borjas' book-length treatment of the immigrant experience, *Heaven's Door*, raises the same basic question about immigrant assimilability: "And there's the traditional concern over assimilation: Will today's immigrants find it harder to assimilate than earlier waves? . . . Will the presence of hard-to-assimilate immigrants further balkanize the country, leading to undesirable social, economic, and political consequences in the next century?" (1999, 4).

Borjas takes up a number of economic issues regarding the arrival and absorption of immigrants. Some focus on the labor market impact of immigrants on those already here; others view the relative success or failure of immigrants in the U.S. economy. In his treatment, Borjas raises concerns about the declining skill levels of recent immigrants and offers a very dour assessment of their prospects: "There is little hope that they will reach economic parity with native workers during their lifetimes" (1999, 38). Borjas is quite concerned with policy, as are we. His analysis leads him to recommend that the stream of immigrants should be smaller and more skilled. We will take up some of the same policy questions, though our overlap with Borjas will be more focused on the aspect of the adjustment of immigrants themselves.

The prominence and centrality of the immigration issue has attracted the attention of the U.S. National Academy of Sciences (NAS) on multiple occasions. In 1997, it published a synthesis of research on immigration that gave a generally favorable review of immigration but concentrated on the economic impacts: overall economic growth and native workers (Smith and Edmonston 1997). This is unquestionably a key window on the effect of immigration. The volume, however, was relatively silent about the progress of the foreign born specifically, and on the assimilation process generally. It is our view that immigrant assimilation is very much a part of the debate about immigration, sometimes at the surface and sometimes beneath it. Indeed, Huntington and Borjas raised questions on both economic and cultural grounds about whether new immigrants will adapt and play the same role as their counterparts of a century ago.

The arrival in the contemporary period of so many immigrants from a single country (Mexico) or world region (Latin America) speaking the same non-English language has exacerbated the concern about assimilability. Whereas in the past the cacophony of foreign languages hastened the adoption of the core tongue, there is—so the speculation goes—less prospect for quick linguistic assimilation now. This critical mass of those speaking another language, compounded further by the illegal arrival of many across the southern land border, has shed particularly strong light on Latino migration.[1] This too has attracted the attention of the NAS, which formed a Panel on Hispanics in the United States. After acknowledging the size, growth, and diversity of the Hispanic population of the United States, the NAS panel's volume *Multiple Origins, Uncertain Destinies* examines several aspects of the accommodation and position of this major ethnic group (Tienda and Mitchell 2006).

Trends in wages, household income, wealth, and home ownership across time and generations point to the gradual ascension of many U.S.-born Hispanics to the middle class. But, as a group, Hispanics are losing economic ground relative to whites because of the weak economic position of the many low-skilled immigrants, large numbers of whom are undocumented, which lowers the population averages on numerous socioeconomic measures. Several important features distinguish the Hispanic experience from those of other ethnic and minority groups. Understanding these differences is essential to appreciating the opportunities that the growing numbers of Hispanics represent for their communities and for the nation, as well as for alerting policymakers of potential risks to the nation's economic and political life (Tienda and Mitchell 2006, 5).

In measured prose, the Panel on Hispanics identifies similarities and differences of the Hispanic experience to that of earlier ethnic and immigrant groups. One can also detect in that report the challenge inherent in separating ethnicity and immigration, given that immigration so often generates or reinforces ethnic diversification. In this volume we examine, when possible, both ethnicity and generation, assessing the degree to which the progress of immigrants and their descendants is separable from their racial and ethnic category.

The Panel on Hispanics authors came to doubt the movement of the United States toward becoming a two-language nation as generations of Hispanics adopt English. More somberly, however, the authors point out that the U.S. economy has changed and may not provide the upward economic escalator that assisted previous waves of immigrants and their descendants. They also call attention to the educational differentials—high-school dropout rates and lagging postsecondary attendance—that characterize the current Latino population. Educational attainment is prominent in the NAS discussion and we shed light on the school as a locus of achievement for immigrants and ethnic groups.

These two NAS panels have generally seen immigration in a more positive light than some of the critical or worrisome views cited. Other scholarship is also more optimistic about assimilation. Richard Alba and Victor Nee, in their discussion *Remaking the Mainstream* (2003), see positive trajectories for immigrants, on balance. Philip Kasinitz, John Mollenkopf, and Mary Waters, in focusing specifically on the experience of New York, paint a portrait of a highly variegated second-generation experience, but one that ultimately seems to accord with successful adaptation: "By and large, these young people are joining—while also profoundly reshaping—the economic, cultural, and social mainstream" (2004, 396).

The interplay between assimilation and policy is dynamic and feeds a policy circuit. If immigrants are perceived to fail in social or economic life, or cause excessive stress to the receiving society, the cry is one of restriction. If immigrants succeed, however we think of success, then there is call for maintaining the current flow, a call for tolerance and acceptance. Our approach, which we describe in more detail later, is to focus on differentiating starting point and trajectory where possible. Thus, we look at how achievement unfolds within the lives of individuals and across generations. We also give particular attention to timing of arrival, noting the case of the 1.5 generation—those who are in the first generation but arrived in time to receive almost all their schooling in the United States.[2] We can exploit this level of resolution in our analysis of schooling and the labor force. We also look at residential patterns, because the intermingling of neighbors—immigrants, ethnics—provides a crucial window on the fabric of American society. It is our view that by better understanding how well immigrants do, and how they compare to members of their own age cohorts, we can better develop policy for addressing immigration.

THE PLAN OF THIS BOOK

In this first chapter, we attempted to introduce broad issues that frame the immigration debate. In chapter 2, we look more carefully at the flow of immigration, to better understand its historical scale and the change in its composition over time. We take a demographic view of the relative size of contemporary U.S. immigration compared to other periods and other countries now receiving substantial numbers of immigrants. We also look at the changing composition of immigrants over time.

Chapter 3 looks at theory surrounding assimilation. The new great wave of immigration has ushered in a corresponding backwash of theoretical discussions about assimilation. These theories become the frameworks on which the empirical results of the scholarly community hang. The concepts and paradigms of assimilation influence our interpretation of results. In particular, recent thinking among social scientists has come to challenge the orthodox notion of gradual but inexorable assimilation. The conventional long-standing presumption of upward socioeconomic mobility has been replaced, in the eyes of some, by a world of alternative paths—some more successful, some less.

Chapter 4 turns to policy. Given that immigration is one area in which government can intervene to dramatically change future population size and composition, we review some of the key changes in U.S. immigration policy with concentration on the period since legislation in 1965 removed national origin quotas. Policymaking, of course, has been extensive in this area over the history—even just recent history—of the nation. We try to provide the reader some of the key policy events of the last century, with particular attention to those that bear on assimilation. We also distinguish immigration policy (rules about how many get in and who they are) from immigrant policy (rules and provisions for the foreign born residing in the United States). These policy shifts not only determined the demographic structure of immigration itself, they also placed in relief the historical policy and social context for earlier immigration and attendant views of assimilation. This context in turn provides the backlighting for present discussions of immigrant assimilation.

Chapter 5 begins the presentation of our empirical results. We first examine schooling, for schools are the crucible of socioeconomic achievement. We analyze, in turn, national cross-sectional data from the U.S. Current Population Survey and two longitudinal surveys spaced about a decade apart, High School and Beyond (HSB) and the National Educational Longitudinal Study (NELS). The two surveys have the virtue of following nationally representative cohorts of individuals through high school and into young adulthood. These longitudinal data also have the advantage of containing relatively rich information about family background and performance within school. Our approach incorporates the emphasis on distinguishing starting point and trajectory, as we discuss in chapters 3 and 4. Our results indicate that generation status (birth outside the United States or membership in the second generation) is not an obstacle in and of itself to advancing in the U.S. educational system.

In chapter 6 we examine economic progress data for age and entry cohorts of immigrants, comparing them to U.S.-born age cohorts, again drawing on the Current Population Survey. Then we turn to analyzing the same longitudinal data sources as in chapter 5, examining economic outcomes beyond school. Here, too, we can take advantage of the longitudinal nature of the data and include earlier schooling information in our analysis of labor market performance. Again, we find that immigrants, and often the second generation, do no worse than others, once we adjust for their socioeconomic origins. We also find that overall, the second generation looks much more like the third and subsequent generations in occupation and economic status than the first generation.

Chapter 7 turns to a different playing field—the neighborhood—and examines patterns of residential segregation for immigrants and ethnic groups. We rely on decennial census data from 2000 to gain insights into the degree to which residential intermingling (or segregation) is linked to length of

U.S. residence or to national origin. Residential or spatial patterns are seen as part of the assimilation process in contemporary scholarly writing (see Massey 2008). Much interest has arisen in new destinations, that is, the overall spread of immigrants across the United States. We extend this spatial analysis to looking within metropolitan regions and ask about proximity of urban neighbors. Based on our empirical results and a wider body of literature, we argue that time, both within and across generations, is clearly associated with residential mixing, but that national origin (thus, ethnic) differences continue to show through. These results for residential patterns provide a valuable counterpoint to the inferences made solely from socioeconomic data. The degree to which immigrants (and their ethnic descendants) are intermingled with persons of other generations, ethnic groups of different immigrant vintages,[3] and other Americans provides an alternative assessment of assimilation.

In chapter 8, which concludes this volume, we return to the themes that motivate us here at the outset. We look back on our empirical results and review additional research to discuss how well immigrants do. Our goal is to shed light for both social science knowledge and policy practice on the consequences of the arrival of these new faces.

Chapter 2

A Tidal Wave of Immigration? The Scale of the Contemporary Immigration Flow

THE UNITED States is typically characterized as a nation of immigrants. More than 70 million people were counted as immigrants to the United States between 1820 and 2005 (U.S. Department of Homeland Security 2005). But how large is the current immigration flow to the United States, and how does it compare across historical periods? This chapter examines the trends in immigration to the United States and places the most recent wave of immigration in demographic, historical, and geographic context. The problem one faces in an exercise of this sort is finding useful and appropriate points of comparison. Absolute numbers suggest one thing, proportions another. More detailed statistical analysis may suggest still another viewpoint. All these aspects may reflect part of the demographic reality. In the national debate about the size and composition of immigration to the United States, proponents of one view or another may draw selectively on these statistics. Discussions of assimilation, or assimilability, in particular invoke concerns about scale or about the way in which the present immigration experience does or does not mirror the past. Accordingly, we present a few key demographically informed vantage points on the scale of contemporary U.S. immigration.

Absolute numbers for the late 1990s and early 2000s approach one million immigrants annually, and perhaps exceed that number, depending on the estimate of undocumented immigrants. Contemporary commentary, from the floors of the houses of Congress to the reports on the evening news, frequently notes this large influx through the proverbial golden door. Comparisons to history, to other contemporary societies, and some demographic analysis can help inform us on this point. As we argue, the contemporary flow of immigrants to the United States and its contribution to U.S. population growth is not out of demographic scale with experience.

In trying to get a handle on the scale of immigration, we look, successively, at the absolute and proportionate numbers, then demographic dynamics (comparing immigration to other sources of American population growth over the twentieth century), and then to the distribution and national origin composition of immigrants. Finally, we turn to a wider geographic framework, examining U.S. immigration in light of global population movement. These four views offer a different take on contemporary U.S. immigration, one suggesting that the contemporary experience of immigration is not at all unprecedented.

According to statistics compiled by the Office of Immigration Statistics, recorded immigration amounted to 9.1 million people in the 1990s, up from 7.3 million in the 1980s and eclipsing any decade of the twentieth century (U.S. Department of Homeland Security 2005). The previous peak came between 1901 and 1910, when about 8.8 million immigrants were admitted. Official statistics necessarily omit the flow of undocumented migrants to the United States. Demographic estimates put the undocumented immigrant population in the United States at 11.1 million in 2004 and the pace at about 500,000 per year since 2000 (Passel 2005). This level is in line with earlier estimates.[1] Barry Edmonston and Jeffrey Passel earlier developed demographic estimates that placed the total arrivals during the 1980s closer to 10 million (1994).

It is useful to step back and look at the broad historical flow of immigrants to the United States, in terms of both the absolute numbers of people arriving and the number of immigrants per U.S. resident. Figure 2.1 presents this information (U.S. Department of Homeland Security 2005). The solid line (axis on left) presents the well-known pattern of official immigrant admissions to the United States since 1820. The dashed line (right scale) expresses this number as a ratio to the U.S. population at the beginning of the decade—immigrants per resident.

In the trend of absolute numbers of immigrants, we see the significant rise in immigration throughout the nineteenth century peaking at 5 million for the 1880s, before falling to slightly under 4 million in the 1890s. The first decade of the twentieth century brought 8.8 million new faces to the United States in a flow commonly seen as the great wave of Ellis Island immigrants. After this initial peak, increasing legal and administrative restrictions, the economic setback of the Great Depression, and two world wars brought the number of immigrants down substantially through the mid-twentieth century. The final decades of the twentieth century saw another sweep upward in the flow of immigrants to the United States. The story of this last upturn is fairly well known because it followed on the 1965 lifting of national origins quotas, bringing in increasing diverse arrivals through the golden door. These recent decades also witnessed substantial undocumented migration, a controversial flow itself linked partly to historical patterns of labor recruitment.

Between 1995 and 2005, immigration levels fluctuated considerably. Official admissions ranged from 916,000 legal immigrants admitted in fiscal year 1996, down to 645,000 in 1999. This was followed by a return to more than 1 million in 2001 and 2002, a decline to 704,000 in 2003, back up to above 1.1 million in 2005. These fluctuations are attributable to the repercussions of changes in immigration law dating back to 1986 and 1990, and somewhat to the aftereffects of the September 11, 2001 terrorist attacks. In certain years, a substantial proportion of so-called immigrants were individuals who had already lived in the United States for a considerable time and whose legalization, dating to the 1986 law that included amnesty, had been processed. The terrorist attacks of 2001 resulted in more restrictionist policies for some time, evident in the declines in admission during 2003 and 2004, but soon after, recovery to the previous level of around 1 million annually is visible.

The absolute numbers do not tell the whole story about the scale of immigration. The dashed lines of figure 2.1 (right vertical axis) present an alternative view: the number of immigrants over the decade per 1,000 U.S. residents at the start of the decade. This ratio gives us some sense of the relative size of the immigrant flow and, at least intuitively, the demographic challenge of absorbing these new faces into American society. This line gives us a different picture than the first. The recent influx has not reached the relative scale either of earlier in the twentieth century or at many points during the nineteenth. In the 1990s, America's 9 million documented arrivals represented 3.4 immigrants per 1,000 U.S. residents. Estimating undocumented migration over the decade at about 5.8 million (after Passel 2005) would bring that ratio to 5.3, about 50 percent higher. Even including the estimate for undocumented migration, this falls far below the ratio seen between 1901 and 1910, when the value exceeded ten immigrants per 1,000 residents. Although the scale of Ellis Island migration has been seen again in absolute numbers, in relative terms it has not.

It would be entirely too rudimentary to suggest that the issues of immigrant assimilation are captured simply by this ratio. Nonetheless, the simple figure does provide powerful insight into the relative impact—or at least presumptive impact—of immigration in U.S. society a century ago compared to today. The economy, public provision of services, and ethnic relations are different issues now than then, all influencing the manner in which new arrivals will adjust to American society, yet the issue of how this host society can (or can best) absorb a large influx of new residents remains part of the public discussion.

Figure 2.1   U.S. Immigration Trends, 1820 to 2010

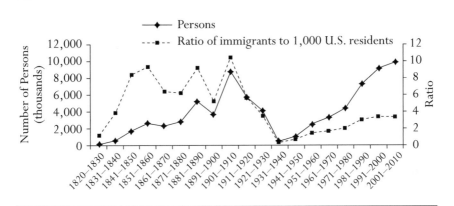

Source: Authors' compilation from U.S. Department of Homeland Security, various years, and U.S. Bureau of the Census 2007a.
Note: 2001 to 2010 projected on basis of 2005.

DEMOGRAPHIC DYNAMICS

Statements about the impact of immigration and immigrants on the United States can be difficult to evaluate without keeping other demographic changes in perspective. To get some sense of the context into which the discussion of immigration has been inserted, consider three decades in the twentieth century as represented in table 2.1. The apparent scale of immigration depends very much on the scale of natural increase (excess of births over deaths) during each interval of time. Between 1901 and 1910 (first row), the United States added a number of births equal to almost 30 percent of the population at the start of the decade, and about another 11.6 percent from immigration. In the 1950s (second row), during the baby boom era, the fraction added through births was about the same as between 1901 and 1910, but the immigration proportion had dropped to under 2 percent. The 1990s (final row) were different from the 1950s at least as much for the declining fertility rate as for any immigration changes. The birth contribution is 16 percent of the population in 1990, only about half that in the two earlier decades. The documented migration contribution is 3.7 percent. Undocumented migration, of course, also contributes to this population change. When we add in the estimate of 6 million undocumented migrants the decade proportion grows to just under 6 percent.[2]

This simple demographic scale comparison suggests that the new immi-

Table 2.1   Relative Contribution of Fertility and Immigration to U.S. Demographic Change

Decade	Starting Population	Births	Immigrants
1901 to 1910	75,994,575	21,980,000	8,795,386
		28.9%	11.6%
1951 to 1960	150,697,361	41,146,000	2,598,214
		27.3%	1.7%
1991 to 2000	248,791,000	39,785,000	9,095,417
		16.0%	3.7%

Source: Authors' compilation from U.S. Immigration and Naturalization Service 1996, U.S. Bureau of the Census 2007, and U.S. Department of Homeland Security 2003.
Note: Births and immigrant percentages are of initial population.

grant flow to the United States is not abnormally large when compared to previous flows, especially the historic wave of a century ago. The bigger story is the decline in birth rates. The fall in the fertility rate to historically low levels has helped increase the share of overall population growth attributable to immigration. In the 1990s, the immigration share amounted to about 19 percent of the population increase over the decade.

Baby boom fertility peaked in 1957 at a rate (total fertility rate, or TFR) equivalent to 3.8 children per woman (Anderton, Barrett, and Bogue 1997). By the early 1960s, this had declined slightly to about 3.4. Had these rates persisted from the 1950s into the 1980s, and the experience of immigration remained identical, the total U.S. population in 2000 would have been much larger. Consider fertility remaining at baby boom levels: by 2000, the population would have grown to 346 million.[3] The exercise, which this clearly is, underscores the dramatic influence fertility shifts can have on population outcomes. Table 2.1 and figure 2.1 both demonstrate that despite the concerns about the impact of immigration on overall population growth, its impact can be readily dwarfed by swings in rates of natural increase.

One final element of demographic composition helps fill out the picture of the scale of immigration. Immigrants generally join the workforce, and concerns naturally arise that immigration may reduce both the chances of employment and wages for native workers. To be sure, millions of immigrants have been added to the U.S. workforce since 1960, and, as of about 2003, some 14.3 percent of the labor force was foreign born. Consider, though, women in the labor force. The growth in the female proportion from 36 to 58 percent between 1960 and 2000 brought an enormous addi-

tional stock of workers into the labor force. A back-of-the-envelope calculation suggests that the U.S. labor force in 2000 included about 22 million
more workers than it would have had women had remained at 1960 labor
force participation rates. This number is just about the same size as the foreign-born civilian labor force in 2000 (U.S. Bureau of the Census 2007a).
Paths into the labor force differ of course, but this exercise provides one more
window on the relative scale of recent immigration in the United States.[4]

URBAN CONCENTRATION: THEN AND NOW

Immigrants have tended to set their sights on major cities. For most of the
twentieth century, major cities were home to disproportionate shares of the
foreign born. For much of the century also, these larger metropolitan cen-
ters offered the most economic opportunity. Thus urban areas tended to
have larger concentrations of immigrants than the country as a whole. But
more recent observations of the growth in immigrants in new destinations
have attracted considerable attention (Kandel and Parrado 2005; Massey
2008; Singer 2004). Douglas Massey and Chiara Capoferro, after acknowledging the pattern prevailing for much of the twentieth century, observed,
"during the 1990s, however, something dramatic happened—there was a
marked shift of immigrants away from global cities and the states or regions
where they are located toward new places of destination throughout the
United States" (2008, 26). Massey and Capoferro (and others in the same
volume) pointed to examples of new destination areas for immigration and
some possible reasons for the shift. These reasons include, not surprisingly,
coincidental shifts in the regional demand for labor, especially low-skill
labor. Massey and Capoferro also argued that new laws and regulations, such
as Proposition 187 in California and, more generally, increased border enforcement, have shifted labor market opportunities and the attractiveness of
various potential destinations.

Nevertheless, a walk today down major avenues or a ride on public transportation in New York, Los Angeles, Chicago, Houston, and other large
American cities reveals a diversity of faces, many of them new immigrants.
In this sense the streetscape at the turn of the twenty-first century would appear to be as diverse as that of the early twentieth century, though the exact
composition of that diversity does differ. Given the historical cityward
movement of immigrants, and the more recent suggestion that immigrant
destinations are diffusing, it is useful to review the pattern of immigration to
urban areas then and now.

When immigrants enter the United States, they are asked for their intended destination. The reports of these destinations are overwhelmingly
urban, and furthermore, are disproportionately the largest metropolitan
areas. Table 2.2 shows the distribution of the U.S. population by major met-

Table 2.2   Distribution of Foreign-Born and Total Population, 2000

Metropolitan Area (2000 Census Rank)	Population	2000 Arrivals (INS)	U.S. Foreign Born	Metro Foreign Born
1. New York	7.5	10.1	16.0	26.7
2. Los Angeles	5.8	8.3	15.2	30.3
3. Chicago	3.3	3.8	4.1	16.1
4. Washington, D.C.	2.7	3.5	3.1	14.2
5. San Francisco	2.5	1.9	6.3	31.1
6. Philadelphia	2.2	1.5	1.8	9.4
7. Boston	2.1	1.9	2.3	13.8
8. Detroit	1.9	1.3	1.4	8.0
9. Dallas-Ft. Worth	1.9	1.7	2.9	17.3
10. Houston	1.7	2.1	2.2	15.6
U.S. total	31.6	36.1	55.3	—

Source: Authors' compilation from the Current Population Survey, December 2001 (weighted) and U.S. Department of Homeland Security 2000.
Note: All figures in percentages. First three columns take U.S. totals as base. Final column takes Metro population as base.

ropolitan area, the distribution among reported destinations of immigrants, the fraction of the U.S. immigrant population in each metropolitan area, and the proportion of each metropolitan area population that is foreign-born.

Immigrants move within the United States after arrival, of course, because for many the intended place of residence reported to the U.S. Immigration and Naturalization Service (INS) is only the location of a sponsoring relative or employer. Although some immigrant groups do exhibit mobility that exceeds that of natives (Bartel and Koch 1991; Donato et al. 2008), they still remain more concentrated in metropolitan locations.[5] As the second column of table 2.2 indicates, 36 percent of recent immigrants headed to the ten largest metropolitan areas, but only 32 percent of the U.S. population lived there. Even more striking, about one-tenth of immigrants in 2000 headed to the New York region. An individual year's statistics exhibit the particular fluctuations of the economic, political, and administrative forces that bring people to the United States at that time, but this pattern of concentration holds for immigrants in general.

The fourth column of table 2.2 demonstrates that the foreign born overall are much more concentrated than the most recent (2000) immigrants. More than half of the foreign born live in these ten largest cities. This concentration is evident at the very top of the urban distribution: 31.2 percent of the U.S. foreign born lived in the New York and Los Angeles metropolitan areas, whereas only 13.3 percent of the overall U.S. population did. By contrast, about 18 percent of immigrants in 2000 identified one of these two metropolitan areas as a destination.

The scale of immigration to major metropolitan areas has been such that it offsets net population declines in some metropolitan regions. The U.S. Bureau of the Census data in table 2.3 indicate the scale of this impact in the 2000 to 2006 period (2007b).[6] The New York metropolitan statistical area experienced a domestic out-migration rate of more than 1.4 million people, equivalent to nearly 8 percent of the 2000 resident population. By domestic out-migration, we mean migration of initial residents to other locations in the United States outside the New York metropolitan region. The metropolitan area also received more than 1 million new international migrants. International migration then compensated for about three-quarters of the loss of residents through internal migration. Given that New York experienced positive natural increase (more than 700,000), the overall change in the region was positive at 2.7 percent.

The experience of the second- and third-largest metropolitan regions, Los Angeles and Chicago, was similar, despite their varying geographic location and industrial base. In Los Angeles, immigration (almost 800,000) offset 85 percent of the loss through internal migration; in the Chicago region, 377,000 immigrants counterbalanced nearly 90 percent of the loss through internal migration. Table 2.3 summarizes this analysis of the components of population change for the twenty largest U.S. metropolitan areas. In eleven of the twenty areas net domestic migration was negative, yet international migration was enough in seven of these areas to turn the overall net migration picture positive. More comprehensively, in the largest ten areas taken together, a loss of 2.6 million residents through internal migration was more than compensated by a gain of 3.8 million immigrants. For the full set of twenty metropolitan areas, 2.3 million people moved out (internally) in the 2000 to 2006 period, but some 4.8 million people arrived from outside the United States. All told, this flow was enough to place international migration at a level of 62 percent of population growth in these metropolitan territories.

This replenishment of domestic population loss by international migration has been going on for some time. Again, Census Bureau data indicate the impact in the three largest metropolitan areas: New York, Los Angeles, and Chicago for the 1990s. Across these three areas (primary metropolitan statistical areas), the natural increase between 1990 and 1997 was 1,944,874, and the net international migration was estimated at 1,690,930. The growth in the metropolitan population from these two sources was over 3.6 million, also enough in that period to offset domestic internal migration loss, estimated at 2.9 million.[7] For the 1970 to 1980 period, Alden Speare

Table 2.3 Components of Population Change for U.S. Metropolitan Areas, 2000 to 2006

| Geographic Area | Population Change | | | | Net Migration | | |
	Metro Population	Number	Per-centage	Natural Increase	Total	Inter-national	Internal
Metropolitan statistical areas							
New York-Northern NJ-Long Island, NY-NJ-PA	18,818,536	495,154	2.7	724,190	−379,700	1,067,539	−1,447,239
Los Angeles-Long Beach-Santa Ana, CA	12,950,129	584,510	4.7	763,585	−140,033	797,652	−937,685
Chicago-Naperville-Joliet, IL-IN-WI	9,505,748	407,133	4.5	446,678	−44,019	377,134	−421,153
Dallas-Fort Worth-Arlington, TX	6,003,967	842,449	16.3	401,526	454,652	286,171	168,481
Philadelphia-Camden-Wilmington, PA-NJ-DE-MD	5,826,742	139,601	2.5	131,974	24,511	92,889	−68,378
Houston-Sugar Land-Baytown, TX	5,539,949	824,547	17.5	360,770	405,518	259,428	146,090
Miami-Fort Lauderdale-Miami Beach, FL	5,463,857	455,869	9.1	137,722	327,418	409,426	−82,008
Washington-Arlington-Alexandria, DC-VA-MD-WV	5,290,400	494,220	10.3	287,867	159,015	239,246	−80,231
Atlanta-Sandy Springs-Marietta, GA	5,138,223	890,211	21.0	295,216	454,758	177,843	276,915

Detroit-Warren-Livonia, MI	4,468,966	16,409	0.4	129,067	−102,736	89,296	−192,032
Boston-Cambridge-Quincy, MA-NH	4,455,217	62,877	1.4	130,182	−101,638	163,546	−265,184
San Francisco-Oakland-Fremont, CA	4,180,027	56,285	1.4	170,559	−104,920	244,752	−349,672
Phoenix-Mesa-Scottsdale, AZ	4,039,182	787,306	24.2	225,951	563,286	165,088	398,198
Riverside-San Bernardino-Ontario, CA	4,026,135	771,314	23.7	209,193	569,904	95,283	474,621
Seattle-Tacoma-Bellevue, WA	3,263,497	219,612	7.2	126,384	92,298	102,447	−10,149
Minneapolis-St. Paul-Bloomington, MN-WI	3,175,041	206,224	6.9	164,053	49,260	71,745	−22,485
San Diego-Carlsbad-San Marcos, CA	2,941,454	127,621	4.5	158,614	−20,168	99,468	−119,636
St. Louis, MO-IL	2,796,368	97,696	3.6	67,135	3,233	26,682	−23,449
Tampa-St. Petersburg-Clearwater, FL	2,697,731	301,718	12.6	9,946	299,212	57,179	242,033
Baltimore-Towson, MD	2,658,405	105,411	4.1	66,818	16,572	31,891	−15,319
Largest three metro areas	41,274,413	1,486,797	—	1,934,453	−563,752	2,242,325	−2,806,077
Largest ten metro areas	79,006,517	5,150,103	—	3,678,595	1,159,384	3,796,624	−2,637,240
Largest twenty metro areas	113,239,574	7,886,167	—	5,007,430	2,526,423	4,854,705	−2,328,282

Source: U.S. Bureau of the Census 2007b.

and William Frey calculated that immigration was generally enough to offset net losses due to internal migration for the nation's metropolitan areas. In fact, the magnitude of net immigration was nearly double that of net internal outmigration (Frey and Speare 1988). For the 1985 to 1990 period, Frey and Kao-Lee Liaw determined that large metropolitan areas (with populations exceeding 1 million) continued to lose people through net internal migration (−0.5 percent), but that this loss was substantially offset by immigration (+2.7 percent). In the 1990 to 1995 period, immigration continued to offset internal losses for large metropolitan areas. Smaller metropolitan areas gained both immigrants and internal migrants between 1985 and 1990 and again between 1990 and 1995 (Frey and Liaw 1998).

These demographic dynamics are not lost on observers, especially those in public office. Some view immigration with concern or alarm. Others, predominantly those in northern, slower-growing areas of the country, have been more welcoming. Consider the views expressed in 1996 by then New York City Mayor Rudolf Giuliani: "Immigrants are exactly what America needs. They're what we need economically, and I think they're what we need morally . . . Immigration revitalizes America and gets it back to its sense of confidence . . . All of these immigrants that come here help us with the work they do, they challenge us with new ideas and new perspectives, and they give us perspective" ("Excerpt from Address on Immigration," New York Times, October 1, 1996).

This more receptive stance is attributable to the potential offset to population decline that immigration can provide, coupled with the long history of receiving immigrants in older, industrial areas.[8] It comes as no surprise that population redistribution of this sort brings on its coattails some other demographic changes, most notably shifts in age and ethnic composition, the changing balance of population in cities and suburbs, and some alterations in the occupational and income distribution of urban residents. The more receptive stance is not limited to officeholders, however. More positive sentiment toward immigration is expressed in such places by the populace at large (De Jong and Tran 2001).

Just how concentrated are cities with immigrants nowadays compared to the great immigration wave at the turn of the century? Figure 2.2 provides some insight. Here we array the ten most populous cities in 1910 and metropolitan areas in 2000 and chart the fraction of immigrants in each.[9] Where in 1910 the proportion of foreign born was about 40 percent, in 2000 it was about 25 percent. Similarly, the second and third ranked cities contained appreciably higher immigrant proportions in the early part of the century. In almost every comparison, the impact of immigration in 1910 outscores, even swamps, that of 2000. Of course, the mix of cities has changed. Only five of 1910's top ten cities remain among the top ten by 2000 (New York, Chicago, Philadelphia, Detroit, and Boston). Among the remainder (St.

Figure 2.2   Foreign Born Concentration in Major Cities, 1910 and 2000

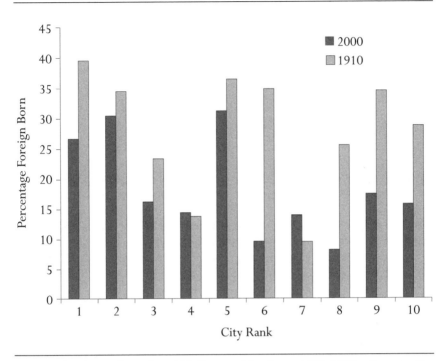

Source: Authors' compilation from U.S. Bureau of the Census 1976, 2006, referencing Decennial Census data from U.S. Bureau of the Census 1910, 2000.

Louis, Cleveland, Baltimore, Pittsburgh, and Buffalo), the shift in immigrant fractions is even more dramatic. In 1910, this group, except Baltimore, had immigrant fractions exceeding 25 percent of the population. By 2000, all had dropped to under 6 percent (U.S. Bureau of the Census 2007b, table B4).

This companion shift is no accident. Immigrants tend to head for the places with the most opportunity. As slower economic growth has dropped some of these cities from the top ten, so too have immigrants passed them by. On the other hand, the foreign born are well represented in the more rapidly growing metropolitan areas: Los Angeles, Dallas, Houston, and Washington, D.C. Beyond this, analysts have identified some emerging gateways for immigrant metropolitan areas such as Atlanta, Raleigh-Durham, and even Salt Lake City (and smaller places) which have begun to attract increasing amounts of immigrants (Singer 2004). Whereas a century ago low-skilled immigrants often found employment in burgeoning industrial metropolises, contemporary immigrants may find employment in smaller metropolitan areas or even rural communities. In this vein, Daniel Lichter and Kenneth Johnson demonstrated the spatial dispersion of the new immigrant population (2006), and Emilio Parrado and William Kandel called attention to the link between low-skilled labor demand (particularly in construction and meat-packing) and new Hispanic growth areas often far from major metropolises (2008).

In sum, as the Ellis Island wave of immigrants was arriving into a rapidly industrializing 1910 America, these ten largest cities collectively held about 14 percent of the U.S. population and had 32 percent of its foreign born. About 65 percent of the population of these leading cities was either first or second generation. By contrast, in 2000 the ten largest metropolitan areas represented in table 2.2 ranged from 8 percent to 30 percent immigrant, most exceeding the proportion in 2000 of about 11.1 percent, but still smaller than a century ago. Only metropolitan Miami, with 50.9 percent foreign born in 2000,[10] exceeded the proportion in New York City in 1910 (39.4 percent). No matter how one cuts the population numbers, it is difficult to see the current urban impact of immigration as grossly out of line with historical precedent.

SHIFTING NATIONAL ORIGINS

One aspect of recent U.S. immigration that inevitably draws commentary is the shift in the national origins of the immigrants. Whereas Europe accounted for more than half of the immigrant population between 1955 and 1964, this share declined to less than 15 percent by the 1990 to 1999 decade. Over the same period, the proportion of Asian immigrants almost tripled, and the proportion from other American origins has risen from about 30 percent to more than 50 percent, with about 25 percent from Mexico alone.

In most accounts, this apparently dramatic shift in national origins of the immigrant flow is attributed to the Immigration and Naturalization Act of 1965 and the act's removal of the national origins quotas established earlier in the century. At least some observers, however, have argued that the regional shift was well under way before 1965 and that the impact of the quotas may be overstated (Massey 1995; Rumbaut 1994a). What is true is that abolition of quotas, international marriage (spouses of armed forces personnel stationed overseas), international student training and job recruitment, and, to some degree, the aftermath of undocumented migration, have served to shift the complexion of new faces in the United States.

Contemporary discussion of this phenomenon would make it seem that the experience of shifting national origins is something new for the United States. In fact, previous waves of immigration have also served to change the

Figure 2.3   Immigrant and Ethnic Composition, 1790 to 2005

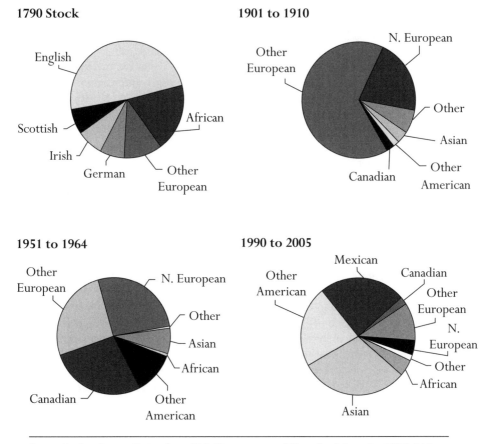

Source: Authors' compilation from U.S. Department of Homeland Security 2005, Lieberson and Waters 1988.

complexion of new arrivals. Consider figure 2.3, which compares the ethnic background of the stock of the population in 1790 and the composition of the immigrant flow at three subsequent periods: 1901 to 1910, 1951 to 1964, and 1995 to 2005.

At the founding of the American republic, almost all the nonindigenous population traced its origins either to the African continent (20 percent), or to the British Isles (70 percent) (Lieberson and Waters 1988). Much of the remainder came from other parts of northern Europe. If we now consider northwestern Europe the reference point, much as present-day accounts use

Europe in toto as the reference, we see another apparently dramatic shift. Whereas in the early period immigrants from northwestern Europe (England, Scotland, Wales, Ireland, Scandinavia, France, and Germany) were the vast majority of U.S. immigrants, that proportion shrank as the docks of Ellis Island and other locations received thousands upon thousands of new arrivals from Italy, Greece, Poland, the Balkans, and other locations in southern and eastern Europe. By the first decade of the twentieth century, two-thirds of new arrivals were from southern, central, and eastern Europe. Indeed, this shift was so dramatic at the time that students of immigration such as Stanley Lieberson referred to the first set of origins as the "old" immigrants, and the second as the "new" immigrants (1963, 1980).[11]

The different physiognomy and cultural background of these new immigrants gave rise to concerns—nay, fears—that they could not be assimilated into American society. Early commissions, political debate, and ultimately legislation were themselves responses to these concerns. The discussion of the 1980s and 1990s is in many ways a replay of that heard in the 1920s and before. (Chapter 3 recounts key aspects of these debates.) Even though the United States is and has been a country of immigration, the assimilation issue continues to play itself out over and over again. Even in the seventeenth and eighteenth centuries, the old and established groups (Puritans and Quakers) expressed concern about newcomers, not always welcoming those from elsewhere in Great Britain (Fischer 1989). The immigration field is understandably one of historical comparison across waves. The reference point and whether it shifts is central, of course, to the comparisons that result. Several recent synthetic scholarly treatments take note of this, and in particular, identify the late nineteenth–early twentieth century, or Ellis Island wave, as the touchstone of immigration comparisons (Hirschman, Kasinitz, and DeWind 1999; Kasinitz, Mollenkopf, and Waters 2004; Massey 2008; Perlmann 2005).[12]

In the 1951 to 1964 period, just before the signal event of the passage of the 1965 Immigration Act and during a period of relatively low immigrant flow into the United States, we observe that European origins accounted for about half of the flow, with a slight majority from the north. Canada, interestingly, accounted for about a quarter of new arrivals during this period. Although the proportion was large, the net flow was still modest. An upswing in Latin American and Asian migration can be seen as well, questioning the contention that all the late twentieth century shifts in immigration are fallout from the 1965 act. In this period, Latin American migration was aided somewhat by the lower restrictions on entry from elsewhere in the Western Hemisphere. Also operating in this period, the Bracero program supplied temporary labor to U.S. agriculture; equally important perhaps, it also set in place the information and personal networks to inaugurate and sustain subsequent permanent migration when the temporary migration program was curtailed. Asian immigration, although less than 10 percent of the total flow at this time, was engendered partly by refugee movement, war brides, and other social connections traceable to the U.S. presence in the Pacific during this time.[13]

During the 1991 to 2002 period, the well-known shift in origins was complete, with immigration from elsewhere in the hemisphere accounting for about half of all documented entrants. Of these, the largest proportion is Spanish-speaking, and about half of that Mexican. Next is Asian (30.8 percent), and after it European (less than 10 percent).

Although the picture of immigrant origins differs somewhat depending on what year's numbers are used (and whether then or now one includes undocumented migrants), the overall pattern is clear. The substantial shift in migratory patterns away from European origins has been recounted many times. Less often considered, however, is how this redistribution fits into a two-century pattern of shifting origins of the people who choose to (and are allowed to or are forced to) make the United States a new home. Whereas once the vast majority embarked from England, this origin point gave way to other portions of northern Europe, then other portions of Europe, then to other areas in the Western Hemisphere, and now increasingly to Asia and Latin America. Even within these broad groups, there is a shift of national origins as well. The more recent admonitions about shifting origins, such as those found in Huntington's *Who Are We?*, can be seen in another light, that of a long term shift as in figure 2.3. These shifting origins are nothing new, nor are the social concerns and political tensions that arise when newcomers arrive.

THE GLOBAL CONTEXT

Perhaps the global village has arrived. News media in other regions of the world regularly carry information about the United States and Europe. Technological advances in transportation and communication have integrated the world economy in a way that was not possible in the nineteenth century and early twentieth century. It has been observed repeatedly that this integration has increased the movement of people across borders. Two important additional considerations exist for our analysis, however.

First, international communication and transportation technology make long distance movement relatively more feasible than short distance movement. Evidence that overall distance is less of a barrier is abundant. For instance, although overall migration rates in the United States shifted only modestly between 1940 and 2000, the long-distance proportion changed substantially (White and Mueser 1994; U.S. Bureau of the Census 2007a). This finding suggests that the same holds true on a global scale. This in turn suggests that international migrants may be less likely to settle long-term in their initial arrival community, and some recent evidence indicates considerable internal migration among the foreign born (Donato et al. 2008). The ease of movement and retaining communication between origin and destination underscores the movement toward transnational communities, in which migrants and their networks are simultaneously connected to multiple countries. This phenomenon has begun to attract increasing attention from scholars (Levitt 2007).

Second, closer global links shift the economic calculation regarding international migration as well. The lower cost of international transportation and communication provides both the means and the incentives to arbitrage wage differentials through migration. That is, a modest wage differential between an origin labor market and a potential destination labor market might be enough to set people in motion. On the one hand, communications technology will make it more likely for the resident in the origin country—say, Mexico, China, or Morocco—to learn about opportunities in the potential destination—say, the United States, Australia, or France. On the other hand, the decline in transport costs and the relative ease with which the migrant can stay in touch with those in the origin country make it easier to undertake the move and manage the separation.

Although the United States has long been a country of immigration, a roster of higher-income nations have over time joined its ranks as destination countries. Figure 2.4 displays recent data for the immigrant proportions of several high-income countries. In the United States and Sweden, this stands at about 11 percent. For some countries, such as the Netherlands, the high proportion can be traced in part to high-skilled migration through the European Union; in many other cases, the immigrants are from outside the EU and are workers in the domestic economy. Canada and Australia have immigrant proportions about double the American figure.

Globally, international migration has been on the upswing for decades. The reasons are many. War and civil strife induce movement themselves, and furthermore alter political and ethnic boundaries. Still, labor migration remains a huge worldwide flow. The United Nations population division has estimated that in 2005, some 191 million people were living outside of their country of birth (United Nations 2006). That is on the order of 3 percent of the world's population. According to the UN, the volume of movement has more than doubled since 1960, but that alone would not produce an appreciable change in the global population of international migrants. What there has been is a shift over time in the destination (or host) countries. The UN found that "in 1960, 57 per cent of all (international) migrants lived in the less developed regions but by 2005, just 37 per cent did so" (2006, 2). Thus the south-north or third-world-to-first-world migration that is so much a part of the American scene, has picked up pace, not only for the United States, but for a number of other major receiving countries as well.

Figure 2.4   Foreign Born as a Percentage of Total Population, Selected Countries, 2000

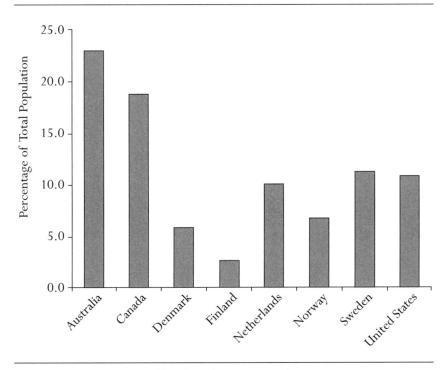

Source: Authors' compilation of data from the Migration Policy Institute, 2008.

Figure 2.5 presents a broader historical look at this global context and the approximate proportion of the world pool that migrates to the United States in each of the four time points.[14] Such calculations give us quite a different perspective on the migratory phenomenon. Whereas U.S. migration nowadays absorbs more of the world pool than it did around 1950 (an ebb tide in migration), the rate is actually comparable to that in the mid-nineteenth century. By contrast, the rate of world population migration to the United States at the end of the twentieth century was one-third the rate than at the beginning.

CONCLUSION

Immigration is high—but not extraordinarily high—by historical standards. We have argued that three key elements have changed since the earlier

Figure 2.5   Rates of World Immigration to the United States

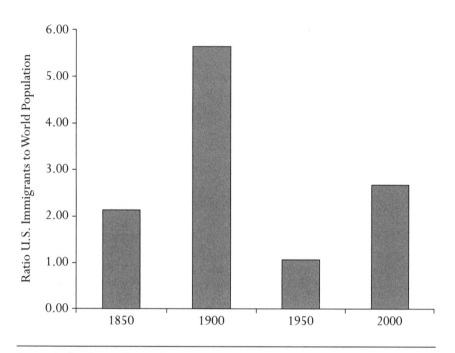

Sources: Authors' compilations from Demeny 1986, U.S. Bureau of the Census 2007a, and U.S. Department of Homeland Security 2003.

waves of U.S. immigration: the increase in population growth attributable to immigration can be traced in part to declines in fertility rates, immigrant origins have shifted away from Europe, and the world's population is much larger and more connected technologically.

As in earlier periods, that immigrants are new groups generates apprehension, concerns about assimilability, or even outright hostility. Expressions of these points of view now are echoes of similar expressions heard in the early part of the twentieth century, before the immigration doorway was narrowed by various restrictions. Whereas once southern Europeans were a source of concern in the public debate, Asian and Latin American arrivals now are, implicitly or explicitly.

If we compare the United States to other major industrialized countries, the proportion of immigrants in the current U.S. population is not extraordinarily high—11.1 percent in the 2000 Census, an estimated 12.5 percent in the 2006 American Community Survey. In fact, the share of immigrants in the American population today is demonstrably lower than in other countries of immigration, such as Australia and Canada. Rates of world immigration to the United States were much higher earlier in this century. But more recent declines in birth rates and shifting origins of immigrants reinforce perceptions of a current tidal wave of immigration. Present-day cities packed with immigrants are contemporary versions of the turn-of-the-century view of eastern seaboard and midwestern industrial metropolises. Our perceptions derive from certain pointed references, such as a period of ebb tide in immigration and a long era of European-centered origins. There are many new aspects to the contemporary American immigration experience. New origins alter the countenances of new arrivals. Technology makes it easier for potential migrants to learn about the United States and to stay in touch with their origins. These developments take place in a context that, in terms of the volume of immigration, is not out of scale with historical experience or the experience of some other contemporary immigrant-receiving societies. In the two chapters that follow we provide context for our empirical analysis, discussing theories of immigrant assimilation and some major shifts regarding policies that govern immigration and immigrants.

Chapter 3

Revisiting Assimilation Theory

EVEN AS the United States has continued to admit substantial numbers of immigrants in recent decades, scholarly discussion has raised questions not only about how well these new arrivals are doing, but also what theoretical framework would best underpin our understanding of their relative success. In this chapter we examine this discussion about the progress of immigrants and their descendants in the United States.

Assimilation theorists and policy analysts, while acknowledging that assimilation or adaptation is a process bound in time, often conduct their discussion at an aggregated level (Alba and Nee 2003; Brubaker 2001), and therefore have not been sufficiently attentive to the frame of reference for tracing individuals of the first, second, and subsequent generations. We offer a framework for doing so. Although most notions of assimilation incorporate some aspect of change over time, ours rests on the chronology of the individual (using longitudinal individual data when we have it) and generation. Our approach emphasizes the socioeconomic progress of immigrants and the second generation, as seen in educational, labor market, and residential settings. We refer to this as structural assimilation.

We examine first the differing terminology and its interpretation by asking what researchers and scholars mean by immigrant adaptation or assimilation. Current writing cuts a broad swath, and certainly differs both in theoretical framework and in interpretation of outcomes for policy. We then examine in more depth the recent social science frameworks under the rubric of assimilation theory. Recent writing has moved far from the conventional notions of assimilation that characterized some of the theorizing of the 1960s and 1970s. These new contributions capture well the complexity of diverse immigrant origins intersecting with diverse settlement contexts. Yet even these alternative formulations leave something to be desired, either in capturing the variegated experiences of recent arrivals or in generating empirically testable propositions about the fate of immigrants in major host societies.

The vernacular notion of immigrant adaptation reflects the expectation of convergence: immigrants and the host society somehow become more alike with the passage of time. Most scholarly writing incorporates convergence, but includes more complicated changes over time. Alternatively, the notion of segmented assimilation (Rumbaut and Portes 2001a), which we review in more detail, allows for varying paths over time in the host society. To be sure, this adaptation is multidimensional, and immigrants may become more like their hosts at different rates and in different ways.

In particular, we stress the importance of several features of the contemporary U.S. pattern of immigrant arrival and change within and across generations. Contemporary thinking about paths of assimilation and the dynamic interplay between host society conditions and the experience of the immigrants are valuable for incorporating the very different experiences of migrants. But in our view, the very lively academic discussion under way about paths of assimilation still comes up short.

Of course, the process is likely to be multilevel, given that the experience of individuals is both aggregated to the group and conditioned by group experience. We argue that it is important to keep distinct the starting point and subsequent trajectory in understanding the experience of immigrants—the second and later generations. This matters for theory, empirical analysis, and policy. It is our view that the discussion has sometimes been clouded by too little attention being paid to the distinction. We argue that cohort change and individual achievement are often confused and conflated. Our empirical analysis in this volume concentrates on demonstrating the value of inferences from individual-level data.

One caveat to our discussion is a truism—that assimilation proceeds at different rates in different realms of social life. Immigrants can adapt to the host society along multiple dimensions. Milton Gordon's classic exposition, *Assimilation in American Life*, laid out several domains of assimilation and, though the temporal and causal connection among them was unresolved at the time of his 1964 writing, it is certainly clear that these domains are interrelated (Gordon 1964). To simplify for the sake of exposition, but in keeping with others (Alba and Nee 2003; Bean and Stevens 2003; Brubaker 2001; Smith and Edmonston 1997), we can think of immigrant and ethnic group assimilation as proceeding on these dimensions. We are most interested in structural assimilation because these domains tie in more directly to policy considerations. By structural assimilation, we mean the patterns of adaptation linked most directly to socioeconomic position in society. We examine several of these: achievement within school and overall attainment; employment, occupation, and income; and residential patterns. We follow Alba and Nee, who in turn interpret Gordon, in distinguishing structural assimilation or conditions from acculturation (1997, 2003). Acculturation, by contrast, emphasizes the immigrant (or presumably another minority) group's adoption of the cultural patterns of the majority. In a recent review, Mary Waters and Tomás Jiménez (2005) identify four key benchmarks of assimilation: socioeconomic status, spatial concentration, language assimilation, and intermarriage. Our approach concentrates on the first two, analyzing schooling and labor market as windows on socioeconomic status, and residential segregation as a window on spatial concentration. Both perspectives offer some view of the more structural parts of immigrant incorporation into the United States. In the section that follows we discuss these interpretations and debates surrounding assimilation, and then turn to identifying our approach to the concept.

ASSIMILATION CONTESTED

The very word *assimilation* is a lightning rod. To some observers, assimilation seems to imply that immigrants come to assume all the characteristics of the host society. It can also connote the abandonment or loss of social and cultural traits that characterized these individuals in their countries of origin. We will for the most part speak of movement toward socioeconomic parity and residential intermingling with the host society. All the while we recognize that these dynamics involve movement of both host and new arrivals along multiple dimensions. We will at times use the term *adaptation* to connote the broader set of changes that the immigrants experience. We do so because conventional usage for assimilation has tended to connote movement of the new arrivals toward the mainstream (Alba and Nee 2003).

The intellectual territory of assimilation is surely contested. As Frank Bean and Gillian Stevens have pointed out, for some there is a normative component to assimilation or adaptation to the host society mainstream—newcomers are the ones obliged to make this transition (2003). Other criticisms of the notion of assimilation emphasized a culture-specific teleology that assimilation, especially acculturation, was defined by movement toward the dominant group's norms and values (Alba and Nee 2003). Some have seen assimilation in terms of a project undertaken by the host society to incorporate newcomers and, perhaps in the process, to remove premigration cultural practices. An indication of this debate is how Waters and Jiménez described the current state of scholarship, specifically when speaking about Alba and Nee, who "rehabilitate the sometimes controversial term *assimilation*" in their work on immigrants moving into the mainstream (2005, 107).

Rogers Brubaker has chronicled the very different stances of France and

Germany toward assimilation (1992). In an article tellingly titled "The Return of Assimilation?" Brubaker offered a more recent interpretation of the shifts in the ideology: "Assimilation has acquired such a bad name in many American differentialist circles that it has come to be associated, as a kind of automatic reflex, with the narrowest understanding of Anglo-conformity or the worst excesses of Americanization campaigns" (2001, 533).

Brubaker concluded with an enumerated summary of a revised concept of assimilation. Several of these items refer to the active role (now) perceived for the new arrivals and their descendants and the aspect of growing similarity rather than complete absorption. Among Brubaker's items, two help indicate where our work is situated: a shift in the analytical focus from cultural to socioeconomic matters, and a shift from a holistic and monodimensional approach, which assumed and implicitly examined movement toward a core culture, to a multidimensional approach across different domains (2001, 542–44).[1] Even in such varied circumstances as France, Germany, and the United States, Richard Alba's empirical analysis of assimilation is organized around the framework of movement toward parity (Alba 2005).

These alternative conceptions—holistic versus multidimensional, cultural absorption versus socioeconomic achievement—still have resonance in social science writing and policy. Indeed, they are sharply articulated in some recent debate in contemporary receiving societies. Emily Greenman and Yu Xie also called attention not only to the multidimensional aspect of assimilation, but also to its multidirectional nature (2008). Echoing observations of others, they pointed out, first, the diversity of immigrants and their socioeconomic traits: some arrive with appreciable skills, some with limited skills. Some processes of adaptation, improved education for instance, would generally be regarded as beneficial and advantageous, and others, such as taking on oppositional youth behaviors or poor health habits, would generally be regarded as deleterious. These deleterious outcomes then might be manifestations of assimilation.[2] This variety of origins and possible trajectories resurrects old questions about any teleology of assimilation; for example, to what are immigrants and the second generation assimilating? In recent writing, Barry Chiswick, who has looked extensively at immigrant labor market outcomes, even develops a model (with coauthor Paul Miller) of negative assimilation (2008).

Many immigration scholars have now commented on the possible disjuncture between socioeconomic assimilation and full acculturation. Most important may be the degree to which identificational assimilation occurs (Gordon 1964; Bean and Stevens 2003). One may observe parity in income or education levels, yet also a society in which ethnic differences are highly manifest in other domains, such as marriage, friendship ties, or neighboring (Alba and Nee 1997; Bean and Stevens 2003; Gordon 1964). In other words, we may not be able to predict socioeconomic position from knowledge of ethnic group (even knowledge of the second or third generation), yet social separation remains. To verify the extent to which social proximity varies by generation status, other domains of assimilation beyond individual educational or economic mobility are worth considering.

Notions of ethnic pluralism, symbolic ethnicity (Alba and Nee 2003), selective assimilation (Bean and Stevens 2003), and selective acculturation (Rumbaut and Portes 2001b) all involve structural incorporation in the face of less-than-full cultural assimilation. Most notable of these is the selective acculturation path Portes and Rumbaut identified, that the immigrant-ethnic group achieves upward (socioeconomic) assimilation in the presence of ethnic and racial discrimination. Social capital (family and community support, social networks, and the like) operate to buttress the second generation, offering a route to economic success but maintaining cultural distinctiveness. For groups who face less prejudice and discrimination from the majority, distinctiveness may be less apparent in all realms. Their context of reception allows them the benefits of the racial majority with relatively few obstacles. Here, ethnic and generational identity may be expressed, but it is more in the mode of symbolic identity (Alba 1990; Bean and Stevens 2003). Such a route, and the implicit realm of choice that it allows, is more likely the province of light-skinned socioeconomically advantaged immigrants (Bean and Stevens 2003).

All this is to say that the notion of what constitutes assimilation may mean different things to different observers looking in from the policy sphere or social science research. For our work, we focus on observable educational, labor market, and residential outcomes. There is less controversy about interpreting relative progress of immigrants and the second generation in these realms. Consequently, we leave aside some of the more cultural aspects of absorption and reflexive change in the host society itself.

Our focus on structural assimilation certainly does not preclude attention to the relationship between immigration, its diverse national origins, and ethnicity. The definition of ethnicity itself is somewhat problematic, but common definitions emphasize a shared identity based on descent (See and Wilson 1988). Perhaps even more disruptive to the idea of a simple immutable classification, ethnic identity can been seen as part of a process of boundary construction, by both human actors and institutional actors such as states (Lamont and Molnar 2002). Immigration generates ethnic diversity, to be sure. The immigrants of one era (or more precisely, their descendants) become the ethnic groups of subsequent eras. But the transformation is anything but routine, nor is it identical for all groups. Many immigration scholars have now commented on the possible disjuncture between socioeconomic assimilation (movement toward parity in socioeconomic status) and full acculturation (often taken to mean abandonment of origin society identity). Most important may be the degree to which the immigrants and their children adopt the identity of the host society, producing what in conventional terminology is termed identificational assimilation (Alba and Nee 1997; Gordon 1964). Rumbaut has even raised the specter of segmented identificational assimilation, questioning the expectation of linear or inevitable adoption of the dominant group ethnicity (Rumbaut 1994b).

Acknowledging that structural assimilation may not proceed evenly across groups, we separate immigrant status (or generation status) and ethnicity. Although highly correlated in empirical work, these are conceptually distinct. This distinction is all the more important for several contemporary models that argue for a continuing, strong, even deterministic role for race and ethnicity in American society. Here one would find that generation may matter relatively little, but that racial and ethnic background introduce an overriding determinacy. We discuss this in more detail as we deal with the notion of segmented assimilation, a paradigm that has garnered increasing adherents in recent years. In other words, a statistical analysis does not predict socioeconomic differences from knowledge of ethnic group (even knowledge of the second or third generation), yet social intermingling is not complete.

For us, assimilation is the decline in the predictive power of nativity and generation. Evidence for assimilation thus grows when labor market earnings are predicted by family background and educational achievement, but not by the fact that the worker is first or second generation. The connection between immigration and ethnicity does produce a complication, however. Another perhaps more comprehensive view of assimilation would argue that after family background and educational achievement are controlled (for instance), ethnicity should not matter. Roger Waldinger spoke similarly, arguing for a concept that involves the reduction of ethnic group prediction and the convergence around the reference population average (2003, 23–25). It is in this way—relatively weak predictive power in the face of other key traits—that we will speak of assimilation.

We generally restrict our use of the term assimilation to these structural traits we have described. Our more general use of adaptation includes any changes that immigrant groups experience to make their way in the host society. Typically these include adopting traits (language, food, education) that make the immigrants (and their children) more like the hosts, but it need not be so. Adaptation may involve developing entirely new identities in the host society—such as the panethnic characterizations Asian or Latino—that span more than one national origin group and are themselves an outcome of the melding of diverse origins.

We recognize, as do others, that adaptation strategies could include developing traits that move the group away from the host society. Criminal behavior as a response to blocked opportunities could be one such pattern. Oppositional behavior in school settings could be the manifestation of another adaptation that involves divergence from the host society. Such outcomes could be classified as negative assimilation, as could behaviors that indicate more similarity with the host society, but which are perceived (like risky sexual behavior) as negative (Greenman and Xie 2008).[3] Richard Alba critically extended thinking along these lines. In comparing France, Germany, and the United States, he challenged several conventional notions of negative or segmented assimilation. Whereas some analysts attribute segmented assimilation to the unique racial history of the United States, Alba raised the specter that downward assimilation may exist for other societies without this historical precondition (2005).

The receiving society, of course, also changes in the wake of substantial waves of immigration. Documenting how the host society is changed by immigration is beyond our scope here, but understanding the ways in which immigrants adapt, and as part of that, the ways in which host country traits change, can help shed light on the bidirectional nature of immigrant absorption.

Bean and Stevens argued that "most observers think that . . . immigrant group movement to parity in education and earnings is practical and worthwhile" (2003, 94). We share this view, especially because it aligns with our wish to understand structural assimilation. Despite the contentiousness of the notion of—even the word—assimilation, improvement of relative position in these areas of human capital and level of well-being, including access to integrated neighborhoods, are important outcomes to observe. They will be important for us, because our subsequent empirical chapters deal directly with these spheres. Our focus is mostly on the first and second generations, often referred to as the foreign stock in the classic literature. We are particularly concerned with examining how well such individuals do in school and in the labor market when considering their family background and ethnic heritage as well as their generation status. We are also concerned with the degree to which they mingled with others outside their own generational and ethnic groups, because local environments provide important opportunities for socialization and access to geographically allocated public services.

We begin by laying out some of the theory guiding historical and contemporary discussion of adaptation. We then offer some refinements to conventional discussion. Our approach emphasizes the path of structural progress and considers it net of origin. This starting point and trajectory view of assimilation dynamics helps frame contemporary policy concerns regarding ethnic relations, social stratification, and immigration itself.

MELTING POT, STEWPOT, OR SOMETHING BETWEEN

Perhaps the most overworked metaphor for the experience of immigration and immigrants in the United States is the *melting pot*. The notion flew in the face of turn-of-the century notions of the adaptability of new immigrants (Hirschman 1983). Charles Hirschman quite tellingly recounted the strong, prevailing view of inevitable and permanent differentness that prevailed in the first half of the twentieth century. The social science parallel to the melting pot is seen in the processes of accommodation and assimilation expected among ethnic groups in urban industrial society. Robert Park hypothesized, in an often-quoted passage, a process of "contact, competition, accommodation, and eventual assimilation" (1950, 150). The processes of urbanization and industrialization, so evident and dramatic in the early twentieth century when Park was writing, produced meritocratic forces to help drive assimilation.

The assimilation perspective later received an elaboration in the work—now dated but still a touchstone in many discussions—of Milton Gordon. Gordon leaned quite heavily on cultural aspects of assimilation, even entertaining a discussion of acculturation as a process similar to assimilation, but favoring a term used by anthropologists rather than sociologists. He described seven "assimilation subprocesses or variables" (1964, 71). These subprocesses and the stage of assimilation they are associated with are the change of cultural patterns to those of the host society (acculturation), the entrance into primary social groups (structural), intermarriage (amalgamation), development of a sense of peoplehood (identificational), absence of prejudice (attitude receptional), absence of discrimination (behavior receptional), and absence of value and power conflict (civic). Despite the broad reach of this paradigm, conceptual representation of these elements for contemporary empirical analysis and their temporal (even causal) sequencing was left relatively underdeveloped by Gordon. As might be expected, then, subsequent empirical work has taken off in multiple directions. Contemporary theory, too, has moved beyond Gordon's terminology, but certainly owes a debt to his formulation.

Key issues in assimilation theory are the degree to which there is a core culture, the attributes that constitute the manifestation of the core culture, and whether minority groups and immigrants must shift their orientation to that core culture for assimilation to take place. In the writings of Gordon and many others of the time, the core culture had a distinct ethnoreligious character: "If there is anything in American culture which serves as a reference point for immigrants and their children, it can best be described, it seems to us, as the middle class cultural patterns of, largely, white Protestant, Anglo-Saxon origins" (1964, 72). The articulation here is one of Anglo-conformity, for it presumes that aside from "minor reciprocal influences," the new arrivals do the shifting in the direction of the dominant group (Gordon 1964, 72–73).

The melting pot is the archetypical alternative to Anglo conformity. In the melting pot paradigm, the culture evolves into some sort of admixture of the various ethnic groups within it. The underlying notion, however, is that there is still a single culture—"a new cultural product with a single consistency," in the words of Gordon (74). Rather than reflecting only the prior dominant group (Anglo-conformity), mutual change has taken place, and all members, at least eventually, are presumed to adopt the new cultural whole. The melting pot perspective has been adopted widely, with Hirschman going so far as to dub it "the primary theoretical framework for sociological research on race and ethnic inequality" (1983, 401). The treatment of assimilation by Alba and Nee certainly gives a nod to the paradigm (2003). Of major concern to these authors is the degree to which there is convergence to the mainstream.

A more recent twist on adaptation or assimilation is offered by the cultural pluralism framework. Although not quite precisely defined, advocates of the cultural pluralism approach take note from the apparent persistence of ethnicity—even among earlier immigrant groups—well into the twentieth century (Greeley 1974; Lieberson and Waters 1988; Novak 1996). Here the notion is that although immigrants and their ethnic descendants achieve some measure of structural integration (or success) in the host society, ethnic groups (or ethnics) retain their distinctiveness along many dimensions. The notion of complete convergence to a melting pot of common culture is rejected. Peter Salins called this ethnic federalism (1997). Even while granting some persistence of ethnic identity, other scholars have noted an often selective residue of ethnic traits that persist from one generation to those who come much later (Alba 1990). As these cases illustrate, more recent thinking has clearly moved far away from a model of ineluctable progression toward a core social grouping (Alba and Nee 2003).

Although useful from the perspective of identifying orientations to the adaptation of ethnic groups in American society, these frameworks still leave us short in many respects. They do not precisely identify workable dimensions of assimilation, beyond the various subprocesses offered by Gordon and those who succeeded him. Furthermore, the degree of adaptation experienced or exhibited by a specific group is an empirical question. The ultimate objective would be to identify the causal connections, if any, between the various dimensions of adaptation. Such a task is Herculean, but in what follows we try to set out some key features of the present-day landscape.

DIVERGENT ASSIMILATION PATHS?

Present-day thinking about immigrant adaptation has moved well beyond the melting pot notion and the initial criticism of it. At the same time, there does not appear to be a ready new consensus (Alba and Nee 2003, 1). There has been much effort at revision of older notions of how immigrants and their descendants come to find their way in a new society. Contemporary theories often incorporate more nuanced features of the basic outlines of other concepts and typically offer a more active role for host society conditions. The *context of reception* is one such phrase invoked to capture the view that the host society—in our case, the United States—can treat origin groups differently. This scale of this context can range from the national, such as formal government policy or national public opinion (Cranford 2005), to the local, such as neighborhood reaction. Of course, the reception itself can range from welcoming to hostile (Portes and Borocz 1989). The host society shapes outcomes for immigrants and their descendants, sometimes in very different ways depending on the immigrants' own ethnicity or human capital. Contemporary research on new arrivals acknowledges this. At the same time, however, we argue that research needs to grapple more directly and specifically with the matter of the starting point for immigrants and their subsequent trajectory as they move through their new structural and cultural landscapes. This is necessary to capture the extent to which outcomes really differ and what characteristics are associated with these differences.

Although much discussion—including that in circles consequential for public policy—turns on cross-sectional comparisons of immigrant-native differences at a point in time, both theory and good policy demand a more dynamic view. To help develop that sense, we review some of the most active discussions in social science regarding assimilation. This will both help situate our contribution to come and provide an interpretative framework for our results. We draw from some of the current thinking and discussion across the social sciences, most notably from the sociology of immigration and ethnicity, and from the labor economics of immigrant adaptation.

The simple straight-line assimilation model suggests that a group, say a particular national origin group, experiences steady improvement in socioeconomic outcomes (and/or cultural proximity) over time. Again, time is not always precisely reckoned here, but cross-generation improvement is generally implied. We argue that strict adherence to the straight-line model posits improvement both within and across generations toward proximity to the average or reference group population. The framing of this concept is critical. Many writings on assimilation—from whatever perspective— express the process and the observable outcomes in term of broad, aggregate characterizations. Because we will deal with individual data in a multivariate framework, we need a theory and hypotheses that offer more precision in terms of time and competing factors.

Probably the most actively discussed contemporary theory of immigration adaptation is segmented assimilation. Constructed in contradistinction to the model of straight-line assimilation, segmented assimilation accepts the unevenness of the road traveled by immigrants and their descendants. In many ways it builds on and expands the notion of bumpy-line assimilation that Herbert Gans offered (1992). Moreover, the concept of segmented assimilation brings in the context of reception of the immigrant group and emphasizes the experience of a group across generations. Particular attention is paid to the experiences and outcomes of the second and third generations (Rumbaut and Portes 2001b).

A substantial scholarly literature now draws on segmented assimilation, yet the model implied by segmented assimilation is not always precisely or narrowly defined. The clearest contemporary statement of segmented assimilation is probably given by two of its architects. Rumbaut and Portes expressed the difference from conventional uniform and straightforward assimilation this way: "Instead the present second generation is better defined as undergoing a process of segmented assimilation where outcomes differ across immigrant minorities and where rapid integration and acceptance into the American mainstream represent just one possible alternative" (2001a, 6).

The authors identified several factors as bearing on the assimilation path of the group. Key among them is the interplay between group characteristics and treatment in the host society. Barriers linked to ethnic discrimination or cultural distance play a role, as would the pre-arrival and on-arrival characteristics of the immigrant group.

Min Zhou offered three scenarios for contemporary immigrants within this framework of segmented assimilation. One path traces classic assimilation and acculturation into the middle class. A second is a move to the underclass and long-term disadvantage. A third sees more rapid economic progress buttressed by immigrant community social structure and perhaps social capital (1999). Zhou explored how immigrants and their ethnic descendants seek to achieve in American society, but emphasizes how the assimilation path varies in how structural and cultural factors interact (1999). These three scenarios are further refined in the notions of dissonant, consonant, and selective acculturation that Rumbaut and Portes laid out (2001b, fig. 10.1). All three forms involve outcomes across generations, with conditions in the first generation interacting with conditions in the host society (namely, external obstacles) to generate the outcomes.

In our interpretation, the context of reception helps set the conditions for the trajectory—and sometimes the starting point if reception helps determine who gets in—and is detectable in the differential paths traced by groups of immigrants. Host society racial and ethnic relations form one critical prong of the context of reception. Host populace ethnocentrism, or more explicitly targeted discrimination against immigrants, could limit opportunities for the new arrivals and their descendants. The number and composition of the immigrants by admission category (especially regarding skills) and national origin provide the second prong of context. The conscious element of context determines how many and which types of immigrants get in; the composition of the flow in turn is likely to influence the social environment—whether supportive or not—within residential communities, schools, and the workplace. Several immigration analysts have pointed to the potentially important consequences of both the overall size and continuation of the flow of immigrants for influencing the changes of new arrivals (Lieberson 1980; Waters and Jiménez 2005).

The negative or downward path for immigrants or their descendants, so provocatively raised by segmented assimilation theory, is noteworthy because it offers such a strong and pessimistic alternative to the usual optimistic upward trajectory in most conventional assimilation writing. The segmented assimilation model reminds us that the socioeconomic or acculturative path traced by any immigrant or national origin group may be negative as well as positive.

Crucial to segmented assimilation is the role of race and ethnicity in the American setting. American ethnic stratification, especially that based on skin color, sets the conditions for the assimilation path. Proponents of segmented assimilation argue that the combination of host society racial discrimination and the absence of countervailing social capital can drive the trajectory toward downward assimilation with attendant inferior socioeconomic outcomes. Oppositional behavior (Zhou 1999) can arise in this circumstance as opportunities are (genuinely or apparently) blocked for the second generation. The notion of oppositional behavior, especially for historically disadvantaged minority groups, may offer an explanation that is attractive on its face.

Not all the evidence is supportive, however. As an alternative to an oppositional stance, consonant acculturation may track a path of upward assimilation, where social capital and family resources counteract the discrimination and potential negative subcultural influences on the second generation. In this vein, Katherine Neckerman and her coauthors suggested a somewhat distinct middle-class minority culture of mobility, a model that would incorporate response to unique features of the social landscape faced by members of minority and many immigrant groups (Neckerman, Carter, and Lee 1999). Mario Small and Katherine Newman, in reviewing research on urban poverty, questioned the applicability of the oppositional culture thesis and argued that it lacks empirical evidence (2001). In research that followed the academic paths of minority and majority group students at highly competitive colleges, little evidence emerged to support the notion of oppositional behavior among minority group students[4] (Massey et al. 2007). In their examination of youths' risky behaviors, Greenman and Xie found evidence for convergence and assimilation, though they also called attention to the heterogeneity of outcomes across groups (2008). After noting the prospect of oppositional culture promoting at-risk behaviors, they examined rich lon-

gitudinal data on youths that includes information on ethnicity and generation. They found that duration in the United States is associated with both
some deleterious behaviors and some advantageous schooling and psychological outcomes.

Selective acculturation sees a constructive role for social capital and family background, with a stronger role perhaps for community social capital
operating through ethnic networks. Bilingualism has been repeatedly found
to be associated with higher achievement, but there is some debate about
the nature and depth of the association. According to Portes and Rumbaut,
upward assimilation and biculturalism are predicted from a combination of
factors (2001). Others would argue that bilingualism is a proxy for the operation of ethnic networks (and their social capital) or that the influence of
bilingualism is only transitional (Mouw and Xie 1999).

Bean and Stevens also argued for the variability of outcomes across the
several nativity and origin groups. They invoked more explicitly the role of
skin color in determining outcomes, particularly as skin color intersects
with background socioeconomic status (2003, 109). Their approach draws
particularly on the experience of the Mexican origin population but is not
limited to that ethnic group. They found that lighter-skinned groups experience favorable trajectories in assimilation—straight-line assimilation for
middle-class and even lower-class individuals. It is for darker-skinned individuals that the greater variation is seen, with high-SES origin translating
into selective assimilation, middle-class to bumpy line assimilation, and
lower-class to reactive ethnicity. This last and unsuccessful trajectory incorporates notions of discriminatory environments and oppositional behavior,
which are also elements of the standard segmented assimilation exposition.
This view is not merely speculative. A body of empirical evidence indicates
that skin color is related to earnings and occupational prestige, even when
other factors are controlled (Espino and Franz 2002; Telles and Murguía
1990, 1992).

This new thinking on assimilation theory offers a much more involved
and variegated set of potential outcomes for immigrants and their descendants. The role of ethnic relations in the host society is also key, specifically
the history of race relations in the United States. Even in an America that has
inaugurated its first African American president, barriers still exist. National
origin indicators, skin color, and related ethnic markers serve to condition
or bind the paths that ethnic minorities may take.

We find the term *conditional assimilation*, which Ross Stolzenberg advanced
in 1990, helpful. Writing about trajectory from the viewpoint of occupational attainment for U.S. Hispanics, Stolzenberg argued that the upward
trajectories can be conditioned on a set of initial traits. Hispanics with a high
school education and suitable language skills can achieve what whites
achieve; those with less human capital do less well (Stolzenberg 1990). In

this way, Stolzenberg's model can be seen as analogous to bumpy-line or segmented assimilation, but it more precisely specifies how ethnicity, net of other characteristics, predicts success in the labor market. The historical and contemporary fact that race and ethnicity have played a key—some would go so far as to say decisive—role in shaping socioeconomic outcomes translates into a strong predictive place for race and ethnic background in any model of immigrant and second generation achievement.

Richard Alba and Victor Nee, in their synoptic treatment of assimilation, *Remaking the American Mainstream*, clearly agreed that the old Eurocentric and asymmetric (only the immigrants and their children change) view of assimilation is outdated and offered a more critical eye to some recent treatments of assimilation (2003). They extended ethnic pluralism to include recent discussions of transnationalism. They acknowledged as well the recent framework of segmented assimilation and focused on the potential downward route of disadvantaged ethnic minorities, a negative trajectory launched by racial hierarchy and associated discrimination their ethnic forebears experienced. At the same time, these authors were cautious about relying too much on this alternative framework. They pointed out, first, the variety of cultural models exhibited in the African American community as a reference point in the discussion. They concluded that "thus, segmented assimilation, which has a value in calling attention to an emergent social problem facing Afro Caribbeans and arguably Mexicans and other Latinos, may predict an excessively pessimistic future for central city minority youths" (8). Alba and Nee went on to argue that, even where alternative and segmented paths are allowed, assimilation into the mainstream is well within the realm of possibility. Indeed, Alba and Nee envisaged a continuing place for assimilation.

These various theoretical presentations on assimilation theory offer important advancements over previous thinking about the immigrant and second generation experience. Most notably for our purposes, they indicate that

- race and ethnicity influence in critical ways the trajectories of immigrants and their children;
- socioeconomic background is key, buttressed further (for some) by family involvement and social capital;
- no single teleology can be identified for assimilation; and
- assimilation may persist overall, even in a pluralistic world.

At the same time, these discussions leave us with the view that matters of theory, let alone empirical manifestation, are anything but resolved in the subject of assimilation. Although the age-old conventional view—the canonical view, in the words of Alba and Nee—no longer has many adherents, it has yet to be replaced with a new consensus. We are left with everything from straight-line assimilation, offered as a likely upward path for some fortunate immigrants, to segmented assimilation (more limited or ethnically differentiated), for others. Some commentators raise concerns about outright downward mobility of immigrants and their immediate descendants. Taken together with the variability introduced by ethnic pluralism and socioeconomic conditions, the range of possible outcomes is large.

There is more. This formulation cannot yet completely guide one's analysis. These theories concentrate on the outcomes of large groups classified by generation and ethnicity. We should see all these changes manifest in the aggregate characteristics of the group and in aggregate statistics about them. The next step is to consider how these theories translate into testable propositions about the experience of immigrants and the second generation when we observe them individually over time. We offer a model for examining and testing for assimilation with individual longitudinal data.

The recent expositions rightly articulate the diversity of outcomes for immigrants and their ethnic descendants. These characterizations of outcomes are useful and appropriate ex-post—after we have observed the path that Mexican Americans or Korean Americans have traced. It is another matter to formulate the theory in such a way that it offers a priori expectations that are testable with the data we have at hand. In our case, we examine the structural outcomes (schooling, labor market, residence) of immigrants and their ethnic descendants. In those cases where we have access to individual longitudinal data, we can better trace the temporal evolution of a person's structural assimilation and better assess how generation and national origin (ethnicity) influence the path toward mainstream or downward assimilation.

STRUCTURAL ASSIMILATION: SCHOOL AND THE LABOR MARKET

Our approach recognizes and incorporates the important, if not overriding, role of context of reception in determining the outcomes of immigrants and their descendants. Conditions set by social policies—refugee assistance, language support, income transfer, labor market regulation, schools—all bear on how well immigrants will do. Taken together, the considerations of segmented assimilation and some parallel theories suggest that racial-ethnic differences will be sharply manifest in the experience of immigrants and their children. At the same time, both assimilation theory and the voluminous work on status attainment and differential outcomes argue that family background factors matter heavily in the life cycle. Our effort now is directed toward laying out a model of socioeconomic assimilation, a model that incorporates some of the key theoretical features described above. We also seek a model that is appropriate for examining with longitudinal data, something we do in chapters 4 and 5.

The *starting point* and *trajectory distinction* is crucial in longitudinal analysis in that our analysis follows individuals over time through school and into the labor force. What is more, the residential patterns we examine are both a result of societal context and a determinant of access to spatially distributed resources, such as schools and safe neighborhoods.

It is not news that, on average, immigrants start with some disadvantage relative to those who have been in the host society for many generations. Thus, it becomes important to separate initial conditions, those of both the immigrant generation and the second generation, from the path traced by the individual over time. As youths' lives unfold in our analysis, these initial conditions will often be family background, marked by family structure and socioeconomic status.

Consider figures 3.1 through 3.3. Here we describe simplified and stylized hypothetical trajectories of immigrants, the second generation, and the natives of higher-order generation. Each line (or more generally, curve) is characterized by a starting point and a trajectory or slope. It is a useful exercise to consider how the broad verbal formulations in the discussion of assimilation might translate into more specific predictions about starting point and trajectory across generations.

The archetypical model is one characterized by lower socioeconomic status of immigrants upon arrival (starting point). Figure 3.1 depicts one realization of straight-line assimilation. (We recognize the lines are not literally straight, but we keep with the conventional wording, noting that the distance between trajectories is about the same.) Straight-line assimilation incorporates the notion of continuous relative improvement and eventual catch-up across generations, or at least that is our interpretation of the meaning of those using the phrase. The most optimistic scenario is a path in which the line traced by the first generation catches up to that line traced by the reference group third-and-higher-order generation[5] within the lifetime of the first generation. (This is a steeper slope than figure 3.1 shows.) Indeed, Barry Chiswick's original results seemed to indicate that immigrants exceeded the native born within the first generation (1978). Still optimistic, but slightly less dramatic, is a relative gain of the first generation: immigrants approach parity with the native reference population, but may not achieve equal outcomes, depending on the relative starting point for the two groups.

The path traced by the second generation is also of keen interest. In fact, there is considerable discussion of the experience of the second generation, with models of superior and inferior achievement both suggested (Farley and Alba 2002; Gans 1992). Figure 3.1 again displays a useful comparison. Single generation adaptation would imply that—net of family background

Figure 3.1   Alternative Assimilation Trajectories, Straight-Line
                Assimilation

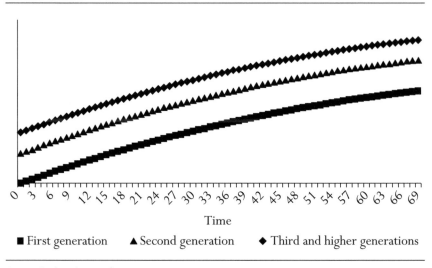

Time

■ First generation   ▲ Second generation   ◆ Third and higher generations

Source: Authors' compilation.

and other traits—the second generation's curves overlay the curve for the natives of the three-plus generation.

Alternatively, still presumably within the straight-line rubric, a pattern of declining deficit would indicate that adaptation cannot be achieved in a single generation. Rather, the second generation's membership would trace a curve that remained below the reference three-plus-generation curve, perhaps including some within-generation gains relative to the reference stock. In this model, each successive generation would exhibit a diminishing gap with the reference population until the deficit became infinitesimal, presumably within just a few generations. This pattern of incremental assimilation would rest on within-generation relative improvements in trajectory and cross-generation improvements (versus the first generation) in starting point. Still other trajectories are possible. Second-generation overachievement, or superachievement, is a scenario of particular interest. In this case, the first generation performs much as we described, but the second generation gains more rapidly in their trajectory. This we depict in figure 3.2.

Empirical evidence for second-generation overachievement has been found from time to time. It was found, notably, in work for earlier cohorts of immigrants and their descendants (Neidert and Farley 1985). In more recent work, Reynolds Farley and others have continued to find that the edu-

Figure 3.2   Alternative Assimilation Trajectories, Second-Generation Super Achievement

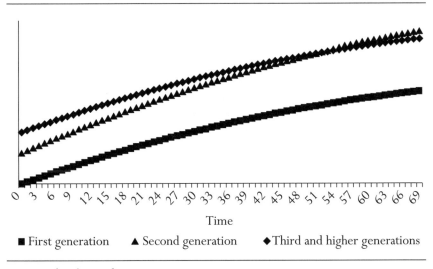

Time

■ First generation   ▲ Second generation   ◆ Third and higher generations

Source: Authors' compilation.

cational attainment of the second generation exceeded that of the third and higher-order generation (Farley and Alba 2002). The implication of second-generation superachievement is that at the same point in time (life cycle, labor market experience, U.S. residential experience) the second generation stands above both the first and the third. Although many mechanisms have been suggested for such superachievement, the combination of strong achievement orientation on the part of the immigrant (parental) generation tied to the acculturated advantage of the second generation, all of whose experience is in the host society, leads to a socioeconomic outcome superior to what would otherwise be expected (Kao and Tienda 1995). One does not need to adopt a mode of full incorporation or claim the absence of discrimination; one must merely assert that the countervailing forces of family achievement expectations are enough to overcome some of these obstacles.

Segmented assimilation theory gives us another very different model for the second generation experience. As discussed earlier, the clash of initial disadvantage and the less-than-welcome context of reception may make for an inferior trajectory in the second generation. Discussion of segmented assimilation seems to offer less explicit prediction of the overall second-generation path compared to the first, but one might consider that even the curve traced by the second generation may not reach parity with that of the

Figure 3.3   Alternative Assimilation Trajectories, Segmented
             Assimilation

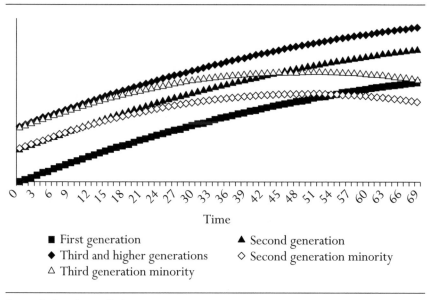

Time

■ First generation   ▲ Second generation
◆ Third and higher generations ◇ Second generation minority
△ Third generation minority

Source: Authors' compilation.

first. Most important, the segmented assimilation approach would argue for
a variety of curves, trajectories that would differ markedly by the circumstances—especially ethnically based discrimination—that minority and national origin groups face.

Figure 3.3 offers a stylized depiction of segmented assimilation. Here descendants of immigrants who are members of minority groups trace trajectories that do not keep pace with the majority reference group (here labeled
three-plus generation). By contrast, members of the majority group trace
the expected line, akin to that in figure 3.1. Segmented assimilation theory
is not clear on the relative starting position of the second (and even third)
generation, but it does generally argue that the trajectory is one of falling
behind or, perhaps, absolute decline. In most of the writing regarding segmented assimilation the focus is on the second-generation experience.

What is missing from this simple generational model is the heterogeneity
within the first generation, in terms of entry point to the receiving context.
Consequently, immigrants who arrive as children are often termed the 1.5
generation to indicate that their experiences lie somewhere between immigrants who arrive in adulthood and the second generation born in the

United States (Rumbaut 2004). Scholars have defined the 1.5 generation with various age cutoffs, but there is strong theoretical motivation to use early or middle childhood as the cut point. Children's age at arrival in the United States has important implications for the development of language skills, years of completed schooling, or even whether individuals "drop in" to U.S. schools at all (Gonzalez 2003; Allensworth 1997). Defined during childhood, 1.5-generation individuals share the experience of moving to the United States from another country with other members of the first generation. They also share several important socialization experiences with the second generation. For example, 1.5- and second-generation individuals likely live with immigrant parents but receive most their schooling and their first labor-market experiences in the United States alongside third-generation peers. Thus, differences in subsequent educational attainment and earnings may be smaller for immigrants arriving in childhood and their second-generation peers than among immigrants who arrive later when schooling is well under way (Bleakley and Chin 2004). From a straight-line assimilation perspective, then, age at arrival and duration of residence in the receiving community yield identical expectations. From a segmented assimilation perspective, the story may not be as clear. Perhaps the 1.5 generation succumbs to similar negative forces exerting influence on the second generation. Alternatively, the 1.5 generation may still be protected by a fairly recent immigrant family context that leads to outcomes more similar to other immigrants.

Although the experiences of child migrants may be distinct from adolescent or adult arrivals, it is the experience of the second generation that appears particularly critical to the politics and policies of immigration. Rapid adaptation in the second generation would mean that policy interventions could be directed to immigrant adjustment alone. By contrast, poor adaptation of the children of immigrants leaves the nation with native-born citizens who have serious deficiencies. Some might take from this a lesson to alter admission criteria; others might argue that intervention in the first generation or the problematic second generation is in order.

Generational position and assimilation trajectory have been implicated in recent debates about social welfare provision. As we discuss in some more detail in chapter 4, partisans have debated about whether noncitizen immigrants (legal permanent residents) should be eligible for benefits. Michael Fix and Wendy Zimmerman pointed out the complexities of intergenerational coresidence. They found that 9 percent of U.S. families have at least one noncitizen parent and at least one citizen child, thus making issues of program eligibility and assimilation all the more complicated (Fix and Zimmerman 2001).

Other views of assimilation can be incorporated within this framework. The concern raised by George Borjas, among academic authors, and by a host of more general writers is that more recent arrivals to the United States possess lower levels of skills, a phenomenon of "declining cohort quality" (Borjas 1985).[6] The concern—whether raised in scholarly or policy circles—has significant implications. The view that contemporary immigrants are less skilled or less equipped to succeed in American society buttresses an argument to reduce the flow of immigrants or change immigration policy to favor the more skilled. Regardless of the policy argument, the cohort-quality discussion places in relief the issue of separating starting point from trajectory. If Emma Lazarus's "your tired, your poor" arrive with fewer resources, but find structural assimilation within a generation or two, the argument against admission is weakened. If, on the other hand, large proportions of recent arrivals spiral downward through segmented or negative assimilation, the case for restructuring or reducing immigration is strengthened. Trajectory is key.

Figures 3.1 through 3.3 give us another window on the assimilation comparison: composition. Group differences in composition (human capital, time in the United States, family structure, age) almost always are manifest. If one takes a snapshot of people of working age in the United States, one finds myriad differences between natives and immigrants. What is critical is that these differences are a combination of starting point and trajectory. Such direct but simple comparisons, frequently cited in policy arguments, may indicate a lack of parity, but they leave questions of composition and process unresolved. Differences in the age and educational composition of the two groups could drive the discrepancy in their outcomes. Suppose, for example, that immigrants have the same earnings profile over the life course as native workers; immigrants, if younger on average, would have lower earnings.

Recent debate in the social science literature (including the theory just reviewed) and in policy circles ties in directly with this concern about starting point and trajectory. The concern is most readily seen in some of the debates that have arisen about the economic success of immigrants and the second generation. On the one hand, immigrants might be superachievers, with their wages or other economic outcome rising faster with labor market experience than natives. Indeed, this was initially the finding of Chiswick (1978), using (now dated) cross-sectional data. By contrast, the phenomenon of declining cohort quality could generate the apparent superior trajectory of immigrants when examined in the same cross-sectional framework, while in fact deriving from deterioration in the starting point of successive waves of immigrants.

Although the cohort quality debate has received its own attention and subsequent modifications, we use it here simply to illustrate the point that both starting point and trajectory matter. The consensus social science view would be that immigrants arrive with less socioeconomic status than those already in the United States. The image of the Ellis Island immigrant stepping off the boat with only a few coins in his or her pocket may be a dated caricature, but it is the case that, on balance, immigrants arrive with fewer socioeconomic resources. Nevertheless, contemporary immigrant streams are heterogeneous, and some non-negligible fraction arrives with appreciable skills and status. In this respect, Waters and Jiménez warned, "generalizations about immigrants gloss over huge class, race, ethnic, gender, and legal status differences" (2005, 108). Lawrence Kahn, for instance, provided evidence that the immigrant skill distribution for the United States and other industrialized receiving countries is bimodal for both males and females (2004). However the skill mix of new U.S. arrivals differs from historical circumstances, it is valuable to take into account initial conditions. Because any cross-sectional measurement will reflect both starting point and trajectory, it is invaluable to try to disentangle these two features of the life experience of the first, second, and subsequent generations. In our case, for schooling and labor market outcomes we will take into account initial conditions (family background) of these youths while they are in school.

Schooling and employment analyses, following in chapters 4 and 5 respectively, tell us much about the socioeconomic benchmark of assimilation that Waters and Jiménez identified. They, among many authors, also see spatial patterns—who lives where—as indicative of the movement of immigrants and their descendants into the wider society (Massey 2008; Waters and Jiménez 2005). We examine this spatial feature of immigrant incorporation by drawing on a tradition of analyzing neighborhood patterns in American urban areas: residential assimilation.

STRUCTURAL ASSIMILATION: THE RESIDENTIAL ENVIRONMENT

A particularly revealing realm in which to look for this interplay between newly arriving groups and the host society is in urban residential patterns.[7] We argue that residential patterns offer a crucial window on the social relations of groups. The axiom was set out by Robert Park of the early Chicago School: physical distance reflects social distance (1924, 1950). Thus, residential patterns will reflect wide social patterns. What is more, residential patterns offer a window that differs from the view given by individual indicators of structural assimilation, such as educational attainment or labor force information. Residential patterns impact individual structural opportunities and exposures yet reflect cultural social distance and comfort across groups.

Although residential patterns provide our third window on structural assimilation, we do not, unfortunately, have access to the same sort of data as we do for schooling and labor market achievement. Our empirical analysis in chapter 6 looks mostly at census data, which is rich in terms of needed neighborhood spatial detail, but lacking the simultaneous information on starting point and trajectory. We are particularly interested in the measurement of residential segregation, and we use cross-sectional 2000 census data. Even so, we can still conceptualize the residential assimilation process in parallel dynamic terms and use small-area census data to peer into assimilation through this third window.

Residential assimilation is the process of reduction of group differences—generation or ethnic group—in urban housing. It implies the reduction of residential segregation. As residential assimilation proceeds, an individual's housing and neighborhood location is less predictable on the basis of ethnic traits or generation. The theory of residential assimilation, or equivalently residential attainment, argues that with time and assimilation on other dimensions, residential intermingling will occur. Residential assimilation is a concept of particular value because it highlights the interplay between the host society and the immigrant-ethnic group in a domain where nearness matters much.

From a sociological point of view, neighboring occupies an important position in a typology or hierarchy of social distance. It is noteworthy that *neighbor* appears midway in a sequence of social proximities in a social distance scale that asks the respondent to rate ethnic (or other) groups in terms of the degree of proximity in seven situations, ranging from marital partner to coresident of a broader territory, such as a region (Owen, Eisner, and McFaul 1981). In this way neighboring patterns can be particularly revealing. Even if immigrants and their ethnic descendants manage to succeed in several structural domains (income, occupation, education), there is no guarantee that they will intermingle with the host society in others. Because the neighborhood is so socially proximate an arena, we argue that it is particularly worthwhile to examine residential assimilation. There is an asymmetric role for the public sector here as well. Although housing laws prohibit discrimination on the basis of race or ethnicity, such statutes cannot prohibit departure from a neighborhood and very few public sector interventions actually encourage underrepresented ethnic groups to enter a specific neighborhood.

A challenge in understanding and measuring residential assimilation takes us back to some of the original theoretical debates about assimilation itself, most notably issues of comparisons across groups. One version of the model takes residential assimilation to be indicated by increasing proximity to Anglos (Massey and Mullan 1984; White, Biddlecom, and Guo 1993). We here use the term *Anglo* in its more recent sociological meaning of non-Hispanic whites, as characterized by U.S. Census data. This usage does not imply a return to notions of Anglo-conformity, as described earlier. Rather, if non-Hispanic whites are the advantaged group in society, residential proximity indicates acceptance or, probably more significantly, access to the spatially distributed resources of Anglos. On the other hand, residential assimilation may be taken to be, more generally, the decline in predictability of ethnic group location. In such circumstances, ethnics come to be less isolated residentially, perhaps intermingling with others. In a perfectly (residentially) integrated society, ethnicity would not predict residential patterns.

Conventional applications of the residential assimilation paradigm generally take proximity to non-Hispanic whites (Anglos) as the outcome of interest. In part, this is a carryover from considering Anglos to be the markers or possessors of the dominant culture. This can certainly be critiqued for its rejection of a more pluralistic approach, but it has some utility. More important for us here, intermingling with non-Hispanic whites is still a useful indicator in that the intermingling presages access to advantaged spatially allocated resources. Non-Hispanic whites often have access to better schools, city services, and the like, and the reality of residential segregation relegates minorities, and here perhaps immigrants, to neighborhoods with fewer amenities and lower levels of resources (Alba and Logan 1993; Charles 2003; Massey, Condran, and Denton 1987). Counterarguments on the consequences of segregation do exist. For instance, clustering of an immigrant or ethnic group might support entrepreneurship. Mary Fischer and Douglas Massey review potential mechanisms that might link segregation to entrepreneurship. After conducting their own empirical analysis they find mostly negative effects of residential segregation on entrepreneurship (2000).

The conventional residential assimilation paradigm thus draws on the Anglo reference group. One can look further when possible and think of general intermingling (lack of isolation) as the outcome of interest. Such an outcome would imply relative decline in segregation from all groups. Equivalently, generalized intermingling would mean less ability to predict neighborhood location from an individual's ethnic group identity. A more sophisticated version of this residential assimilation paradigm, often beyond the purview of contemporary spatial census data availability, would hold that net of purely compositional aspects, ethnic group would not predict neighborhood location at all.[8] One exception to the lack of longitudinal studies is provided by the work of Scott South and colleagues. They examine the pattern of residential movement among U.S. Latinos, and do find, on balance, that socioeconomic achievement translates into residential proximity with Anglos (South, Crowder, and Chavez 2005a, 2005b).

Some analysts would argue that the prevailing American ethnic social construction is imbued with an ethnic hierarchy. Thus, proximity to the groups found at the top of that hierarchy and distance from those nearer the bottom is what ethnic individuals (and hence groups) would seek in the housing market. Although this is not our guiding orientation, we acknowledge that this line of thinking and the behavior it implies would generate the same expectations. To be sure, we recognize that social science research (much of it through the Multi-City Study of Urban Inequality project) on neighborhoods has identified a clear ethnic hierarchy in preference for proximity to certain groups as neighbors (Charles 2006).

Trajectory is important in residential assimilation as well. If individuals intermingle residentially over time, then residential segregation among the first generation will decline with duration. Both individual starting point (socioeconomic resources and language ability upon arrival) and individual socioeconomic trajectory would be expected to matter in predicting residential assimilation. While enough data are difficult to come by for contemporary immigrants and impossible to find for historical waves, contemporary cross-sectional evidence does show that both socioeconomic status and individual duration predict residential intermingling (White, Biddlecom, and Guo 1993; White and Sassler 2000).

At the group level, we expect residential assimilation, both from the aggregation of individual residential assimilation and from collective experience. Time does wear away at residential segregation by ethnicity. An ethnic group's vintage (length of time in the United States) is associated with lower levels of segregation.[9] A group entering the United States on average around 1900 would be predicted to be segregated at 31 points (on a 0 to 100 scale) less than a group that entered on average around 1980 (White and Glick 1999). Although data do not exist for a formal statistical test, the vintage analysis suggests that some national origin groups integrated residentially at more rapid rates than others. A more extensive analysis of fifty Canadian groups and their mutual segregation reveals significant clustering by original world region and language group, regardless of vintage, but still with measurable ethnic separation within world region, such as Europe (White, Kim, and Glick 2005).

Precisely because context of reception can differ, and because a disjuncture between socioeconomic outcomes and full social integration is possible, looking through the window of residential assimilation offers added value. Segregation may persist for several reasons. First, the group may differ on its socioeconomic outcomes. Simply, a group with a lower average household income would not be expected to be intermingled evenly with the majority population. Second, discrimination operates. Language, cultural, and racial minority group members can be excluded from neighborhoods. Both subtle and blatant forms of prejudice and discrimination can bring this about. Third, groups may self-segregate. Indeed, a strict interpretation of the pluralism model would suggest precisely this outcome—that is, socioeconomic incorporation without acculturation or residential intermingling. Further, this residential distinction may derive from a variety of factors, ranging from access to resources specific to a cultural heritage to unwillingness to face the pressure of integrating a majority neighborhood, to the possibility of more instrumental benefits of residing with coethnics. The residential ethnic enclave, a parallel to the economic enclave, could provide social capital and resources uniquely available in the ethnic neighborhood.

It is likely a mix of all these mechanisms that yields residential distinctiveness. The crux is that the accumulation of factors still indicates lack of assimilation. Of interest to us is the net intermingling itself. Residential outcomes are most assuredly the result of a combination of social process (such as networks, discrimination, and status-seeking) and the housing market decisions based on household size, composition, and income. A wealth of studies has now shown that, at least in the case of black-white segregation, significant residential separation persists even when socioeconomic composition is controlled. While it may be difficult to adjust for composition in all studies, such accumulated findings lend backbone to the notion that residential patterns themselves—the presence or absence of residential assimilation—is remarkably indicative of the assimilation of immigrant groups, the second generation, and others in American assimilation overall.

CONCLUSION: FRAMING STRUCTURAL ASSIMILATION

Assimilation theory, such as it is, needs continuous rethinking. The once-dominant paradigm has been challenged in social science, yet it is not exactly clear what is to take its place. Simple Anglo conformity was long ago challenged by a melting pot notion that allowed for some give-and-take by the host society and the newcomers. More recent work on adaptation and identity has emphasized the role of the host society and the interplay of various groups. Waldinger emphasized the way in which ethnicity intersects with the occupational division of labor in major cities, as groups by choice or not become identified with certain niches (1995). The notion of segmented assimilation builds on the contention that immigrants—soon to be ethnic groups—experience different paths in the host society (Portes 1995).

We suggest that an empirical test of these theories consider the importance of the starting point—that is, the relative position at one time of immigrants, the second generation, and higher-generation individuals—and trace their individual paths to educational and labor market achievements. This way we can evaluate the multiple paths and the factors that help determine the relative improvement or decline over time. Surely, one path may parallel the conventional assimilation route with a lower starting point, but still lead to ultimate convergence with higher generation peers. This path would imply a decrease in the predictive power of generation status over time. Another path may lead to the underclass, and still another to economic success by establishing and maintaining ethnically distinct patterns (including residential separation). Recent empirical evidence does suggest the importance of ethnic niches (concentration in certain occupation and industries) associated with immigration (Wilson 2003). The effect of such concentration on economic opportunity beyond individual skills is open to question, although some studies suggest that occupational concentration may push natives up the occupational ladder (Rosenfeld and Tienda 1999).

As immigrants arrive and settle in their host country, they begin to form the set of identities that will translate in part to ethnic group membership in current and future generations. To be sure, migrants follow many routes to becoming ethnic groups. Some new arrivals are voluntary migrants, others are forced through enslavement or refugee movement, and indigenous populations who have not migrated become identified as ethnic minority groups as well. As we have argued, the characterization and treatment by the host population and the interplay between physiognomic and behavioral traits further articulate the self-and-societal classification of ethnic groups. Events on the communal, national, and international stages help determine which ethnic identities are most salient at a given time.

Much sociological ink has been spilt on analyzing and debating the social meaning of ethnic groupings and attachments. The large amount of literature on the mutability and even the arbitrariness of these labels notwithstanding, ethnic group membership forms a set of categories within which Americans operate (Waters 1990). Despite the problems of defining ethnicity and finding a model for immigrant adaptation, it is useful to invoke a "stylized assimilation model" (White, Dymowski, and Wang 1994), building on the claim that such a model has provided an organizing framework for much of the twentieth century's immigrant and ethnicity studies (Hirschman 1983). In discussions of policy, this stylized model is every bit in evidence. As new arrivals succeed within and across generations, they climb the ladder and either adapt or approach parity with the host society. The question we address throughout this volume is: What characteristics help determine the extent to which immigrants and their descendants successfully climb this ladder of structural assimilation in the contemporary era?

Regardless of which theory of assimilation one finds most compelling, all imply some process that takes place with the passage of time. Yet differences observed among immigrants and the descendants of immigrants past do not capture this movement. Only by observing both the characteristics individuals possess at one point in time and the effect of these characteristics on their progress over time can we really gain purchase on this process.

Chapter 4

Immigration and Immigrant Policy

IMMIGRATION IS one of the few areas of population change where governments can actively intervene to control or direct population. High-income societies—western Europe, Canada, Australia, Japan, and the United States—make rules about who gets in. Equally important, rules about admission also determine the composition of the immigrant flow. In this chapter we discuss policy regarding immigration, setting the backdrop for our understanding of the scale and origin of contemporary immigration flows, the assimilation of new arrivals and their offspring, and current debates about policy. We briefly outline complex (even convoluted) arguments that have, on and off, occupied policy debate for many decades. Our objective here is twofold. First, we wish to call attention to the continuing recurrence of the tension among stakeholders regarding how many and who gets in. Typically, though not exclusively, employers have favored access to the deep pool of labor that immigrants represent. Others remain concerned about employment for those already here or raise concerns about the ability of the new arrivals to fit into U.S. society—sometimes both. Second, we call attention to the way in which immigration policy has been augmented by immigrant policy, making more important a contemporary understanding of immigrant assimilation in a reshaped context of immigration.

This distinction is related to the framework we invoked in the previous chapter and used throughout this book: that of starting point versus trajectory. Decisions about who gets in (composition) play a substantial role in deciding the starting point for the immigrants. Skills, network ties, geographic locations, national origin (ethnicity), are all explicitly determined by immigration policy. Decisions about what happens to immigrants once in the host country may play a major role in trajectory. Such decisions are part of the context of reception discussed by immigration theorists. The public policy aspect of this context includes rules about employment conditions, access to schooling, eligibility for health and welfare benefits, and so on. The rules and how these resources are used may help determine the rate of immigrant adjustment, and in turn, the path of structural assimilation traced by immigrants and their descendants.

Although the current controversy over immigration is often most heated regarding illegal immigration—both unauthorized entry to the United States and what to do about illegal aliens within the U.S. borders—we would argue that not far beneath the surface of this debate, in Congress and in the media, is concern about assimilation as well. The relative success of immigrants influences the policy circuit. Perhaps equally significant, perceptions about assimilation feed powerfully and directly into the policy circuit through public opinion and the views of legislators and other stakeholders. Consider the portent of the words offered on the Senate floor by Alan Simpson more than a decade ago: "Curbing, even stopping, illegal immigration is not enough. It is time to slow down, to reassess, to make certain we are assimilating well the extraordinary level of immigration the country has been experiencing in recent years" (William Branigin, "Sen. Simpson Offers Overhaul of Legal, Illegal Immigration," *Washington Post*, November 4, 1995, A8).

Clearly the new round of debate has many echoes with the past. Contentious debate erupted periodically in the nineteenth and throughout the twentieth century. The aftermath was often a shift in policy. The individual stakeholders have changed, but the sharp contests remain between those who think the door should be opened more widely and those who think the door is already too far ajar. These stakeholders are often organized around several diverse issues, including the provision of industrial and agricultural labor and the assimilability of new arrivals (Alba and Nee 2003, chap. 5; Cornelius and Rosenblum 2005). This can be traced in legislation at least as far back as 1864, when the U.S. Immigration Bureau was established to encourage immigration to meet requirements for industrial production (Calavita 1994). Even the more restrictive measures of the late nineteenth and then early twentieth centuries were compromises that included efforts to improve access to labor (Calavita 1994). The United States, not unlike many other industrialized societies at other times, has alternately opened and closed the door to various contract and temporary labor routes.[1]

These partisan debates about immigration—who gets in, legally or illegally, and what happens to them—place in relief basic questions of citizenship and the privileges, rights, and obligations of members of a society. These sorts of issues trace even to basic constitutional interpretations (Neumann 1996).[2]

THE IMMIGRATION POLICY CIRCUIT

The perception of how immigrants adapt to U.S. society feeds into policies regarding how many immigrants will be admitted and what criteria for admission will be employed. Wayne Cornelius and Marc Rosenblum concluded along these lines: "Even if the actual effects of immigration on receiving countries are typically modest, many citizens of migrant-receiving states perceive negative consequences—economic and noneconomic—that lead them to prefer more restrictive immigration policies" (2005, 104). The reality of immigrant absorption and assimilation may—or may not—match the perception.

As surely as the night follows day, a sharp upswing in the influx of immigrants to the United States brings about increased public debate about the value and assimilability of these new arrivals. As this book is being written, the United States is passing through another phase of such public wrangling about immigration. The debate in turn spurs efforts to develop legislation and revise regulations that govern the flow of immigrants into the receiving society. The economic downturn of 2008 to 2009 may sharpen the debate. Figure 4.1 presents one view of the process. Several aspects are noteworthy. First is the interplay between the flow of new residents and public sector action. Pivotal in this are the perception of the public about how well immigrants do and the impact of immigrants on the host society. Perceptions—of who the immigrants are, what route they used to get to the United States, how well they are faring—are important because they help drive the making of policy. Second is that tinkering with admissions criteria necessarily influences the composition of the flow of immigrants. This, in turn, has implications for the adaptation of immigrants, the competition they may represent to native labor (more contentious in a weaker economy), and, perhaps less well understood, the politics of future revisions to immigration legislation. For instance, the well-known decision to revise immigration law in the 1960s to favor family reunification as the entry route to the United States set up linked migration, often called the immigration multiplier (Jasso and Rosenzweig 1990), in which new permanent residents and citizens can bring other relatives. Such a policy revision created a substantial pool of citizens who have an interest in maintaining these admission criteria.

IMMIGRATION POLICY AND IMMIGRANT POLICY: A QUICK TOUR

We make a distinction between immigration policy and immigrant policy. Both are part of the rules of the game:

Figure 4.1   The Immigration Policy Circuit

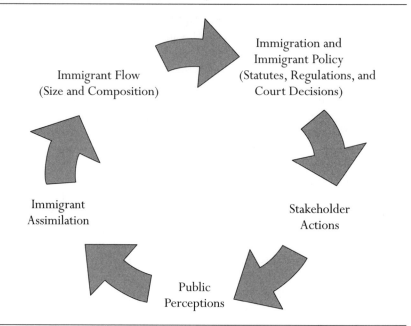

Immigrant Flow
(Size and Composition)

Immigration and
Immigrant Policy
(Statutes, Regulations, and
Court Decisions)

Immigrant
Assimilation

Stakeholder
Actions

Public
Perceptions

Source: Authors' compilation.

Immigration policy regulates who gets in. Under the immigration statutes and the enforcement of those statutes the United States regulates entry within its borders. Immigration policy, simply stated, determines the overall size and composition of the flow of foreign-born persons into the United States. Immigration policy thus sets the starting point for adaptation in the receiving society.

Immigrant policy, by contrast, regulates treatment of foreign-born residents in the United States. It is immigrant policy, actually in combination with a host of other policies in the United States, that determines rules for naturalization, assistance in learning English, eligibility for social programs, and the like. Immigrant policies are widespread, and many operate in an indirect way rather than directly on immigrants themselves. So, immigrant policies, along with other conditions inside the receiving country, set the context for the trajectory of adaptation.

Historically, most of the activity of the U.S. and other governments has concentrated on immigration policy. Only with the growth of the social welfare state in the twentieth century has commensurate concern arisen about the comprehensive (or cumulative) aspects of immigrant policy. A few key aspects of the legislative history are particularly relevant to set the context for understanding immigration (and then immigrant policy) today. We touch only the surface, whereas others have written in more detail. Aristide Zolberg provided an extensive account of how immigration policy has been tailored to the express purpose of United States' nation-building (2006). The historian David Reimers reviewed legislative acts and a myriad of other efforts to exclude or restrain immigrants during the great waves of immigration from the late nineteenth century through much of the twentieth century (1985). Guillermina Jasso and Mark Rosenzweig provided a succinct chronicle of major U.S. immigration legislation through the 1980s and some of its demographic antecedents and consequences (1990).

In the eighteenth century, very little was done about immigration regulation, except to make (and change) rules about the minimum length of residence required for naturalization. Jasso and Rosenzweig labeled this period the prerestriction era. Most of the nineteenth century passed with little activity on immigration legislation, but by the end of the century, following on the sharp upturn in new arrivals (more than 5 million for the 1880s), various acts were passed. Almost all these pieces of legislation were restrictive in some way. Several emphasized composition of the immigrant flow—one, for instance, prohibiting the entry of certain classes of individuals based on behavior (prostitutes, convicts). More consequential were the barriers erected on the basis of national origin. The best known is the Chinese Exclusion Act of 1882, which prohibited Chinese immigration. Relatedly, the Alien Contract Law of 1885 barred the recruitment and importation of contract labor. Immigrants deemed likely to become public charges were also restricted, a policy not exactly in line with the mythology of "give me . . . your poor," an irony that Zolberg has pointed out (2006). The concern regarding the risk of becoming a public charge, never rescinded, continues to echo in the recent era in discussions surrounding the rate of welfare receipt—assimilability—among the foreign born (Lofstrom and Bean 2002).

As Carl Wittke has detailed, literacy figured prominently in the late nineteenth century and early twentieth century (1949). Wittke described the contentiousness regarding a literacy test for immigrants, with Congress initially passing such a requirement in 1891, successive presidents vetoing the bill, and then passage and signature at the time of World War I. Here then, couched in terms of literacy, was a contentious discussion of skills-based criteria for admission.

As is well known to students of U.S. immigration history and policy, the 1920s were noteworthy for the introduction of the two most restrictive acts up to that time. These actions followed on the heels of two decades of then-extraordinary immigration flow. The 1921 act introduced national origin quotas and the 1924 legislation refined the system. These quotas reoriented the immigrant flow, favoring those nationalities whose distribution was already represented in the United States and basing allotments on earlier decennial census values for ethnic groups.[3] This ethnically based regulation of immigration remained in force for several decades. These restrictions, the Great Depression, and World War II sharply curtailed immigration in the 1930s and somewhat in the 1940s.

Public opinion polls are not available from these early twentieth century decades, but as Edward Hutchinson wrote, looking back from mid-century, "As the tide of immigration rose higher and higher through the nineteenth century and up to World War I, restrictionist sentiment also rose" (1949, 15). Reimers's account succinctly connects the relative opening and closing of the door linked to both ethnocentrist tendencies and the rise and fall of labor demand in the U.S. economy (1985). The shift is again illustrated in the World War II era with the creation of the Bracero Program. Putatively a guest-worker program, the Bracero Program was initiated in 1942 and was renewed successively through 1964 (Reimers 1985).[4] It too had controversy, and indeed some of the rhetoric surrounding the Bracero Program pointed to doubts about desirability of new conventional permanent immigrants, predominantly from Mexico, amid the growing demand for agricultural labor (Tienda and Mitchell 2006, 27).

Two things are relevant for us from this portion of the twentieth century. First, assimilability—that is, the quality of new immigrants and prospective ability to adapt in the new society—was assumed to be predicted by national origin, with a companion part played by skills. The quality of new immigrants was presumed to be bound up with origin, and thus, the national origin quotas instituted and maintained that view.[5] Second, the narrowing of the doorway into the United States in this period reveals some role for public opinion in the policy circuit.

The next major shift in immigration policy did not come again until the 1965 Immigration and Nationality Act, also known as the Hart-Celler Act. This act occupies a signature place in scholarly and policy-oriented discussion of U.S. immigration, even today. Hart-Celler is widely regarded as a watershed event in U.S. immigration history, though more influence may be attributed to it than warranted. It essentially removed the national origin quotas, then and now seen as ethnically biased. In doing so, it helped expedite (though probably not inaugurate) the shift in origin of U.S. immigration from Europe to Latin America and especially Asia. The act set into place the well-known family preference system (although the 1952 McCarran-Walter Act did introduce some family reunification features), now an intrinsic part of U.S. immigration policy. This preference system exempts the most immediate family members from quotas, and introduced a seven-tier preference system for remaining relatives and nonrelative admissions. These revisions to immigration law are associated with sizable changes in immigrant flow and composition. In the first full fiscal year of the act's operation (July 1966 to June 1967), 362,000 people immigrated to the United States. In the following year the figure was 454,000, up by more than 50 percent from the figure recorded in 1964. By the 1990s, the annual number of immigrants approached 1 million in some years, about one-third of whom were immediate relatives of U.S. citizens; another quarter arrived under other forms of family reunification. The regional shift—away from European origins and toward Latin American and Asian origins—is well known and a common part of any policy discussion.

The attempt to grapple with undocumented immigration goes back for decades now as well. Although the size of the flow of undocumented migration increased in the post-1965 era, the first major piece of legislation to tackle the issue came into being in 1986. The Immigration Reform and Control Act (IRCA) introduced several provisions, most notably increased border enforcement and, for the first time, legal sanctions on employers for hiring undocumented workers. IRCA also contained a major provision to allow undocumented migrants (under certain eligibility criteria, such as minimum length of residence) to apply for permanent residency. This so-called amnesty program eventually led to the legalization of hundreds of thousands of individuals. IRCA, at least in its initial design, was also envisioned to provide federal government financial transfers to those states and localities most heavily impacted by the adjustment of these new legalizing residents. Suffice to say, the 1986 IRCA reform did not resolve the undocumented migration issues. Some migrants still come without authorization (as many as 200,000 annually in recent estimates), and the debates over the advisability of amnesty, increased border enforcement, and employment of undocumented workers are all part of the current debate.[6]

In the 1990s we see some growth of debate over immigrant policy. Issues of immigrant eligibility for public benefits became ever more sharply contested in the last two decades as the pace of immigration has picked up, as those immigrants have continued to come from new origins, and as concern has grown about social provision, such as apparently higher rates of public assistance and lower coverage by health insurance (Borjas 2003). In various legislative items debated or introduced, it has been proposed to make undocumented aliens ineligible for some services. Still other proposals challenged the schooling of the children of undocumented aliens, even those children who are citizens by birth under U.S. law.

Explicit immigrant policy intervention is seen most acutely in the exclusion of legal immigrants from certain social services. As such, several of these controversial cases revolve around immigrant policy pertaining to noncitizens. These debates invoke claims of who has access to what kinds of social welfare state provisions. Although these restrictions may be targeted solely at noncitizens, immigrant policies necessarily have spillover effects on the subsequent outcomes for the second generation as well, even though these offspring of immigrants are U.S.-born citizens with all the rights that citizenship implies. These issues become all the more complicated when, as Michael Fix and Wendy Zimmerman noted, a substantial fraction of U.S. families have mixed citizenry in their households (2001).

Such tension came into high relief in the mid-1990s with the California Proposition 187 ballot initiative, and has resurfaced repeatedly with other legislation and court cases since. Proposition 187 sought to prohibit access of undocumented migrants to several social services. Although the proposition was passed readily by California voters, almost all of its provisions were struck down after court challenges (Massey and Capoferro 2008).[7] Provisions in the landmark welfare reform legislation of 1996, the Personal Responsibility and Work Opportunity Reconciliation Act (PROWORA) significantly cut back on the eligibility of immigrants, including legally resident aliens, for certain public benefits (Zimmerman and Tumlin 1999), a retraction of policy and practice that had been in place since the mid-1960s (Martin and Midgely 2006). The act and those who supported it were roundly criticized for these cutbacks (Edelman 1997). Congress later restored access to benefits for legal aliens, though criticism for the patchwork of eligibility criteria remains (Martin and Midgely 2006; Singer 2002).[8]

After a historical review of immigration policy initiatives, Fix and Passel wrote of this period: "The pace of immigration policy reform has accelerated. Before 1980 major reform of immigration policy took place every quarter century. Now less than four years after enactment of the 1990 Immigration Act, immigration policy and its reform are again a central focus of congressional attention" (1994, 12). Our own accounting would agree that the pace of immigration—and immigrant—policy activity has increased in recent years. The policy circuit remains quite active and contentious.

POPULAR ATTITUDES AND GOVERNMENT COMMISSIONS

Ambivalence might be the most appropriate word to characterize the American public's view toward immigration. The arrival of newcomers is at once seen as a source of strength and identity and a threat to that strength and identity. A recent *New York Times*/CBS news poll is illustrative. Although the majority (57 percent) of those surveyed agreed with the sentiment that immigrants "contribute to this country," about a third also agreed with the view that immigrants take jobs from citizens. Still another 59 percent agreed that immigrants "mostly take jobs that Americans do not want." The same poll indicated concerns that the United States was on a path to increase illegal immigration (Julia Preston and Marjorie Connelly, "Immigration Bill Provisions Gain Wide Support in Poll," *New York Times*, 25 May 2007, 1).

Over the past few decades, public opinion has shifted on immigration. Figure 4.2 presents various Gallup Poll results from 1965 through 2007. A nationally representative sample of adult Americans was asked to respond to the question, "In your view, should immigration be kept at the present level, increased, or decreased?" From the 1960s through the mid-1990s, we see a rise in the fraction of respondents who would prefer to decrease U.S. immigration. This more restrictionist view falls in the late 1990s and jumps to a temporary peak in June 2002. Since that time, interestingly, the proportion advocating decreased immigration has trended downward, to a point where by June 2006, the value stood at about 40 percent. One year later, perhaps in response to the more heated 2006 and 2007 controversy about immigration, the decrease figure increased several percentage points. Throughout this time, the proportion of Gallup respondents who preferred to maintain immigration at the present level fluctuated to complement the movement of the *decrease* proportion, and those expressing the view that the U.S. should increase immigration crept up slowly from single digits in the 1970s and 1980s to between 15 and 17 percent by the end of the series.

This opinion trend is not the whole story, however. Although the opinion about immigration may fluctuate in response to national debate and major incidents, other factors are also at work. Several analysts call attention to labor market competition—and perceptions of that competition and the role of skill mix—as a key element of public opinion trends (Espenshade and Hempstead 1996; Mayda 2006; Scheve and Slaughter 2001). It is likely that such worries continue to drive opinion. Of course, during this time the proportion of immigrants in the U.S. population (and thus represented in the Gallup Poll) has gradually increased. But this would not appear to be driving the sentiment we see in figure 4.2. If we limit the analysis to non-Hispanic whites (less likely to be immigrants themselves), something we can do for 2001 through 2007 (tabulations not shown), we still see the modest upward trend in pro-immigration sentiment, with the vast majority of respondents favoring *same* or *decrease*, and some fluctuations between those two categories. In focus group discussions, which probe views more deeply but less representatively, it is not unusual for respondents to express more favorable views about some (personally known) recent immigrants yet offer resentful and stereotyped comments about immigrants more broadly (Fennelly 2008).

This ambivalence about immigration is seen in other contemporary receiving societies. Cross-national opinions gathered by the Pew Global Attitudes Project point to significant majorities, from 66 to 87 percent, in Italy, Spain, Canada, France, and Germany agreeing with sentiment to further restrict and control immigration (Pew Research Center 2007). Respondents in the last three countries plus Sweden, at 53 percent, express less restric-

Figure 4.2   Attitudes Toward Immigration, Gallup Poll 1965 to 2007

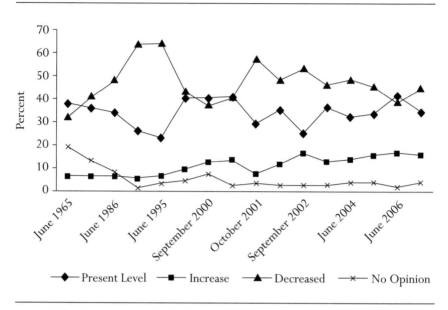

Source: Authors' compilation from Gallup Organization 2008.
Note: Gallup question asked: "In your view should immigration be kept at the present level, increased, or decreased?" X-axis not to time scale.

tionist sentiment than Americans in this poll. The Pew report authors state, however, that "although Western publics remain concerned about immigration, they generally are less likely to back tighter controls today than they were five years ago, despite heated controversies over this issue in both Europe and the United States over the last few years" (3). The link between public policy debate and general sentiment toward immigration may be less obvious than it seems. What also emerges from the Pew study is that the United States, as a historical country of immigration, falls in the middle of this group in terms of restrictionist sentiment.

Public opinion polls are both provocative and problematic. Generally such questions do not probe too deeply into preferences about composition of the immigrant stream by country of origin and skill level. This may be particularly problematic for U.S.–Europe comparisons in that now significant migration across international boundaries may be relatively free movement within high-income European Union member states. For instance, in 2006 Luxembourg's resident population was nearly 40 percent foreign born, yet 85 percent of these were from other European Union countries (Kollwelter 2007). To the degree that receptivity to immigration is expansive or restrictive with regard to countries of origin is difficult to discern for most conventional public opinion polls, whether American or European.

Concern over illegal or undocumented migration is again a prominent feature of U.S. public opinion, as it was before and after the IRCA debate. Such concerns are echoed in the current policy discussion about immigration, and are now amplified with worries about security and terrorism. Widely varying estimates of the number of illegal aliens in the United States have also played into the debate. In the 1980s, numbers with as much as a fivefold variation were in circulation, serving to further ignite debate (Bos 1984; Bean, Edmonston, and Passel 1990). Probably the most authoritative estimates at the time put the figure at about three million (Woodrow and Passel 1990). More recent estimates, as of March 2004, place the number of unauthorized residents of the United States at 10.3 million (Passel 2005). Critics then and now have argued that the United States has lost control of its borders, and organizations have called for measures to redress varying degrees of stricture and penalty. Bean and Stevens pointed out the somewhat stereotyped media and policy attention given to unauthorized migration from Mexico, even though the flow from Mexico is quite heterogeneous (2003). Moreover, the unauthorized from any country include a substantial number of visa-overstayers as well as illegal border-crossers.

Difficult to discern is the degree to which sentiment against illegal immigration covers a more general negative sentiment against further immigration itself. The highly contentious debate in 2006 and 2007 over immigration reform pivoted on the provisions related to undocumented migration. To what degree anti-illegal-immigrant sentiment reflected broader reservations about the scale and composition of the immigrant stream is difficult to tell. The identity of America as a country of immigration combined with deep reservations about the consequences for jobs, security, and the rule of law of illegal immigration make it difficult to disentangle.

Traveling back a decade to the U.S. Commission on Immigration Reform is instructive.[9] The commission was created as part of the 1990 Immigration Act, with a mandate to review the impact of immigration policy. The 1990 act had again altered policy, raising the cap on numerical restrictions, increasing the number of skills-based immigrants, and introducing a diversity provision (by way of lottery) to allow migration from countries with a small number of immigrants in the United States (USCIR 1994). In 1994 and 1995 the commission issued two reports, the first concentrating on the issue of illegal immigration and the second devoted more to an evaluation and recommendations regarding legal immigration. Even in the title of this second report, we see the dual policy channels: *Becoming an American: Immigration and Immigrant Policy* (USCIR 1997).

The commission also posed a general question about immigrant adaptation and assimilation, one that is implicit in almost all initiatives to modify

American immigration policy: "How do we maintain a civic culture based on shared values while accommodating the large and diverse population admitted through immigration policy?" (USCIR 1994, iii).

Notably, the report included a section on Americanization and the integration of immigrants. The commission endorsed "a properly regulated system of legal immigration," but cautioned in its discussion of the national interest that "legal immigration, however, has its costs as well as benefits. Immigrants with relatively low education and skills may compete for jobs and public services with the most vulnerable of Americans. . . . Concentrated and/or rapid entry of immigrants into a locality may impose immediate net costs. . . . Concentration of new immigrants can exacerbate tensions among ethnic groups" (USCIR 1995, 1).

The text, in its carefully modulated prose, reflects the abiding concerns of the American public and those charged with making policy. In many respects, the commission mirrors the ambivalence visible in public opinion and public debate. On the one hand, immigration has been a positive force for the United States; on the other, it raises difficult questions of access, competition, public costs, and accommodation. As with its illegal immigration report, the commission made an extensive review of circumstances and trends in legal immigration, offering recommendations ranging from the size of the immigration stream to criteria for admission to refugee policy.

This commission actually recommended a reduction in annual immigrant admissions from the overall flow of the time, bringing admissions down to 550,000 annually. The subsequent reality has been anything but that reduction. The commission advocated for restructuring family reunification priorities, generally in the direction of more evidence of financial support, and it recommended the elimination of some family-based categories. The commission favored a labor market test for most skills-based immigrants, thus favoring skilled workers and leading to the elimination of the admission of unskilled workers as a distinct category.

This commission saw several of its recommendations make their way into law. The Immigration Act of 1996 and the 1996 welfare reform legislation both cut back on the eligibility of immigrants for certain public benefits and instituted the requirement of an affidavit of support for the sponsor of a new immigrant.

What does one take away from the experience of the efforts of the Commission on Immigration Reform and its aftermath? We certainly see policy pressure to reduce the flow of new arrivals and shift admission criteria toward skills-based criteria. Although such recommendations—even from high-profile groups—have not found their way wholly into law, they do reveal the undercurrents of contemporary immigration policy debate.

POLICY AVENUES AND ASSIMILATION PATHS

In its strictest form, features of immigration policy are chosen precisely to determine the relative starting point (advantaged or disadvantaged) of new arrivals. In the Ellis Island era, the archetypical immigrant arrived with little and entered a place in the American scene somewhere near the bottom of the ladder. More recent immigrant waves have diversified, not only by nationality but also by skill. Some describe current immigrant flows as bimodal or hour-glass shaped with many low-skilled arrivals and a substantial flow of high-skilled arrivals as well (Kahn 2004; Cornelius and Rosenblum 2005).

From the beginning, immigration policy debates have been about the starting point. Attempts to change the composition of immigrant streams through these policies are aimed at improving the quality of skills of those admitted and improving the life chances of their descendants. And the evidence suggests that some of the policy tweaking that has taken place has, in fact, measurably altered the skill mix (Jasso, Rosenzweig, and Smith 2000). These debates turn on the question of whether immigrants will ultimately benefit the receiving society. Recent debate on immigrant policy turns on this issue as well, as some advocate for expanding visas for individuals with high levels of skills (or reducing immigration types that less clearly rest on skill, such as family-based visas), and even talk of mimicking point systems used elsewhere, in which points are given for skills desired in the host country. In Canada and Australia, skills-based admissions account for up to half of immigrant admissions, several-fold the U.S. fraction (Antecol, Cobb-Clark, and Trejo 2001).

Throughout much of American history the focus has been on immigration policy, that is, who gets in. It is understandable that a country would turn its attention first to the gatekeeping role, a task intrinsically bound up with the notion of the sovereign nation-state. In this regard the United States is very similar to other countries that receive immigrants. To some degree, immigrant policy is a luxury; it requires a social welfare infrastructure of some sort, if the attention of that infrastructure is to be rechanneled to immigrants.

Immigration and immigrant policy are, however, interwoven. Immigrant performance in the host country—and, more important, perceptions about that performance—will inform and influence decisions about who will be allowed to enter in the future. This link is featured prominently in figure 4.1. Thus, perceptions that undocumented migration consists mostly of entries across the southern U.S. border (rather than less than half) fuels legislation that ultimately results in increased border enforcement. Efforts to control undocumented migration through the mechanism of visa-overstay are much less in evidence, and this piece of the issue garners far less attention. In the wake of the events of 9/11 and the subsequent enactment of the Patriot Act, immigration policy was revised yet again to step up border enforcement. The underlying assumption is that undocumented immigrants are less desirable or, at the very least, have not been appropriately vetted.

Much immigrant policy is implicit, a happenstance of the programs in place at a point in time and the eligibility rules that govern them. Restrictions of employment in sensitive government jobs to native-born citizens and the preference given to citizens over (legal) aliens, as written into law in 1986, are simple examples. Similarly, eligibility of citizens, legal immigrants, and illegal immigrants and their children for public assistance, public education, and health care are all central to current debate about immigration policy, as we suggested can be seen in actions by voters, legislatures, and the courts during the 1990s. Of course, the effort to restrict access of undocumented immigrants or legally resident noncitizens to social services can also be seen as an effort to reduce the incentives to migrate. Thus, immigrant policy may be perceived to be a tool in immigration policy.

More explicit immigrant policies do exist, of course, and these policies are more clearly targeted at assimilation. Training in English as a second language (ESL) is the best example. Although ESL is available and used by some native born with limited English proficiency, the central concept of ESL is compatible with assisting immigrants in adapting to their new setting. Among the many specific recommendations of the U.S. Commission on Immigration Reform were interventions and resources to enhance English-language acquisition (for all) and adult education for literacy and basic skills. The immigration reform debated by Congress and the nation in 2006 and 2007 included features that might shift the path to admission or subsequent citizenship based on English language ability. Although legislative outcomes change over time and shift with political winds, language ability—including requirements for admission and subsequent hurdles and resources for aiding the acquisition of English language skills—is an element of immigrant policy that figures prominently in such debates. Implicit in all these policies is a hierarchy of those deserving of assistance. In popular discourse, immigrants are expected to be independent strivers who are a net gain to the receiving society. If immigrants are expected to assimilate into the United States by the majority population, they are expected to do so at minimal cost.

A scan of the history of U.S. legislation on immigration and its accompanying discussion reveals that the early activity was all immigration policy—restrictions were placed on persons with certain characteristics or from certain national origins. The ethnically based quota systems of the past have been discredited and have been replaced by humanitarian (family reunification, refugee) concerns or meritocratic (skills-based) criteria. Only a residual limit on the absolute number of admissions from individual countries remains.

We now turn to understanding some broad contemporary forces that impinge on the current debate and the increasing salience of immigrant policy in that debate.

THE TWENTY-FIRST CENTURY CONTEXT FOR POLICY

The United States has been absorbing immigrants—and debating about policy regarding how many and whom to admit—since the nation's birth, and quite vocally for much of the last century. What, if anything, is new about today's immigration and its attendant debate? What is different about the policy setting facing the United States in the twenty-first century? We suggest that three broad trends will affect the starting points and potential trajectories for new immigrants in the twenty-first century: the growth of the welfare state, repositioning affirmative action, and globalization.

THE GROWTH OF THE WELFARE STATE

The growth of the social welfare state is probably the most consequential feature of the landscape that differentiates the present from the period of great American immigration a century ago. It is arguably one of the greatest changes in twentieth century political economy. Although the United States is seen as far less generous a welfare state than its European cousins, social provision is still substantial and has grown over the twentieth century. Scholars have debunked the notion that there was no public provision before the watershed decade of the 1930s, but it is true that when waves of immigrants arrived between 1900 and 1915, the United States offered no Social Security system, no Medicare, no Medicaid, and only limited public assistance.[10] As a consequence, detailed eligibility rules did not need to be written into legislation regarding immigration. Not-for-profit organizations (churches, philanthropic organizations, and settlement houses) provided many more of the social services consumed by the less fortunate of American society. The settlement house system so much a part of the immigrant history of New York, Chicago, and other large cities played a central and nongovernmental role. Historical immigration policy, despite the compelling Ellis Island story, did attempt to exclude, among others, those who might become a public charge.

The new immigration has raised exceedingly difficult issues of eligibility for the benefits conferred by contemporary social welfare programs.[11] As we have described, these issues have been manifest in several settings from the ballot box through the courts. In the current context the debate has focused on access for legal permanent (noncitizen) residents and for undocumented migrants. Lack of any access or longer waiting times for access would discourage migration, but it is not clear how much they would. Most observers see contemporary U.S. immigration driven predominantly by economic opportunity (Bean and Stevens 2003). Summarizing extensive review and analysis of costs and benefits of immigrants and natives in public program participation, a National Academy of Sciences expert panel wrote that "combining the costs and benefits from all programs, there is little difference between immigrants and the native-born" (Smith and Edmonston 1997, 11).

Still, perceptions matter for the policy circuit. To the extent that stakeholders perceive that immigrants move to the United States to receive public benefits, to have access to them, or to disproportionately consume them, there will be pressure to alter eligibility rules (immigrant policy) or admission criteria (immigration policy). The growing pool of potential immigrants to the United States and the continuing presence of a complex array of public provisions ensures that this will be part of the contested terrain (whether at or below the surface) of immigration and immigrant policy in years to come.

REPOSITIONING AFFIRMATIVE ACTION

A product of the civil rights revolution of the 1960s, affirmative action was a recourse not available for turn-of-the-century immigrants. Now, quite to the contrary, immigration has muddied the waters. Who has standing? Do new arrivals who are members of ethnic categories, technically protected under civil rights law, and the offspring of those arrivals have as much claim as others whose ancestry in the Americas traces to pre-colonial or colonial times? Even in a world of affirmative action, debate exists on its net impact as well. Mary Waters put it this way: "Where will the color line be drawn in the twenty-first century? Are some new groups 'becoming white,' as older groups of immigrants did? If so, what does that mean for black Americans and for immigration and poverty policy in the United States?" (2000b, 46).

Besides whatever reconsideration might have taken place in the 1990s to a system of affirmative action (and any attendant preferences), the arrival of new residents and their ethnic diversity challenges the standard operating procedure of a dichotomous, black-white society. The debate about the apparently unbounded success of some minorities (notably Asian) in university admissions and some sectors of the labor market has encouraged some to doubt the wisdom of affirmative action and has led to new terminology such as "underrepresented minorities."

Previous waves of immigrants faced discrimination, to be sure. They may have benefited from certain patterns of ethnic group enclave economies and from sectoral economic development, but in the nineteenth and early twentieth century no codified affirmative action program of the present form existed. The apparent success of these earlier waves of immigrants and of some members of more recent waves has provided some grist for those who would argue that contemporary affirmative action should be dismantled.

In chapter 3, we discussed the concept of segmented assimilation, in which immigrants from certain racial and ethnic minority groups are segmented into an inferior achievement path from those in other groups. This segmentation takes place because of the pattern of racial and ethnic relations in the host society. Here, then, is a particularly problematic scenario. What if immigrant from such groups do, it turns out, trace lower trajectories? This may justify renewed attention to racial and ethnic disparities, the potential of discrimination visited on newcomers. On the one hand, the apparent success of immigrants from an increasingly diverse pool of national (and ethnic) origins can be cited as impetus to withdraw from affirmative action interventions. On the other, a finding of segmentation of new immigrants' diverse origins might justify renewed vigilance regarding ethnic discrimination and perhaps further intervention in the mold of affirmative action.

GLOBALIZATION

Technology has linked the world in a way that has enormous implications for economic development and international migration.[12] Writing under the aegis of the International Labor Organization, Peter Stalker observed that "globalization is more realistically viewed as the latest phase in a long historical process" (2000, 10). He sketched the picture more fully, arguing that globalization involves a complex set of processes. Most significantly, perhaps, Stalker and others have noted that governments seem quite willing to accept international flows of trade and finance, but are much less willing to accept flows of labor (Freeman 2004; Stalker 2000). Douglas Massey and his coauthors went so far as to suggest that international migration "is a natural outgrowth of the disruptions and dislocations that occur in this process of market expansion and penetration" (Massey, Durand, and Malone 2002, 13).

The UN estimates that, as of 2004, 191 million people live outside their country of birth. This is about 3 percent of the world's population, but it is a figure that is likely to grow over the twenty-first century (United Nations 2006). We need not repeat the many arguments about how the world economy has become increasingly integrated, but a few observations from the vantage point of international migration are warranted.

First, global economic activity and interdependence is asymmetric. Capital moves more freely than labor across international boundaries. As Stalker pointed out, capital now moves fairly freely across international boundaries, following comparative advantages of proximity to raw materials, productive factors, and consumer markets. Now agricultural products can be grown throughout the world and shipped to global markets. Paper and data processing for U.S. companies can be moved to offshore locations. And, of course, low-skilled manufacturing can be moved to developing economies. Even as countries limit human resettlement across their borders, global production and markets create additional opportunities and gaps that would otherwise encourage labor migration. Where allowed, these differentials generate significant flows of legal migrants, generally to the high-income economies of North America and Europe. Where not allowed, the gaps spur unauthorized migration—Albania to Italy, Mexico to the United States—with appreciable social stress and political wrangling in its wake.

Global communication exacerbates the pressure for international migration. Not only is information available about potential destinations and the condition of their economies, it is available quickly and with modest cost. Awareness of gaps and different opportunities provides additional incentive to migrate. Although technological advances do somewhat alter the speed and manner of information flow, plenty of room remains for contract labor recruitment, not unlike low-wage labor recruitment in decades past (Parrado and Kandel 2008). Interpersonal networks also continue to matter (Hagan 1998; Sanders, Nee, and Sernau 2002). As Hirschman and Massey wrote, summarizing a collection of studies focusing on recent immigration and settlement patterns, "social mechanisms allow immigrant workers to respond to changes in economic demand. Just as social networks and institutions of mutual support have led to the concentration of immigrants in traditional gateway cities, immigrant entrepreneurs recruit family friends and co-ethnics to new destination areas" (2008, 10). Thus, these social networks and the intermediaries along them can provide alternative paths for information flow.

The global technological transformation can influence international migration indirectly. The ability to communicate with the home county regularly and at low cost (relative to historical standard of dollars and time) lowers the psychological and social barriers to migration. Mexican, British, or Senegalese migrants to the United States can more easily stay in touch with home than before. Even for immigrants from low-income, low-technology countries, inventiveness of getting messages through can overcome the hardship of distance. This technological revolution is implicated in transnationalism, with migrants maintaining social ties in both origin and destination. The phenomenon has grown among U.S. immigrants, and research is beginning to uncover how the ties are maintained (or attenuate) and the struggles that transnationals endure as they participate economically and socially in more than one society (Levitt and Waters 2002).

Just as this technological evolution changes the costs for the potential migrant and family members, so too does it change costs for producers of goods and services. Not only does all this interconnection raise the awareness of those who would migrate to industrialized countries, it also creates downward pressure on the wages of those who work in industries where global pressure is particularly keen. Thus, in apparel and basic fabrication, the fact that manufacturers can outsource portions of the production process may have much to do with wages for those with less education and skill in the U.S. economy. The rub is that the perception of the competition may be attributed disproportionately to immigrants, and so, too, might policy initiatives.

These perceptions are important to the policy circuit. Individuals with more pessimistic views of the U.S. economy are more likely to oppose further immigration (Espenshade and Hempstead 1996). Even at the macro level, Espenshade and Hempstead point to trends in U.S. unemployment rates that appear to track with this opinion index. Although econometric studies might question the link at the level of the economy, there is no question about the association between these attitudes at the level of the individual. Perceptions can feed into a call for legislation or other public sector intervention.

However one interprets the transformation of the American economy, several aspects of change are clear. First, a global economy has emerged, providing international pressures on wages and job growth (in certain industries) in the United States. Second, substantial sectoral shifts have occurred in the American economy, which now relies less on low-skilled and semi-skilled physical labor, and in which employment growth in services far eclipses that in manufacturing. Third, per capita income continued to rise between 1965 and 2005, but in recent years income inequality has also risen.[13] Arthur Alderson and Francois Nielsen observed this potential link in their analysis of cross country income inequality and wrote that "migration has come under serious suspicion as a factor in the inequality upswing (2002, 1256). Few question the shifts in the American economy, but the degree to which the pace of the American economic transformation has been exacerbated by immigration remains subject to debate. In their own empirical work, Alderson and Nielsen found some evidence in support of the immigration-inequality link, though the relationship depends on model specification (2002).

Some might add the events of the September 11 terrorist attack to the list of globalization's influence on immigration. To be sure, there is some connection. The U.S. presence as the remaining superpower, and the extent of its economic and military power and visibility, make it a potential target. The overlapping of these features with those of deep cultural differences only increases such potential conflict. The effect of 9/11 on immigration is most directly seen in the Patriot Act of 2001. The act dramatically changed some parts of the immigration landscape, extending the government's authority to detain and deport aliens, and especially to increase resources for patrolling (and reducing unauthorized movement across) the U.S. border. As Susan Martin argued, this shift may have been under way before 2001, spurred by trends and events—such as the 1993 World Trade Center bombing, growing illegal immigration, and the perceived welfare costs of immigrants—that found their way into some immigration law provisions in 1996 (2003). She argued further that attention shifted after September 11 from concern about numbers of new arrivals to tracking those who were allowed to enter. Others have questioned how much really changed in the wake of that event (Dobson 2006; Greenblatt 2008). All in all, in the wake of 9/11, excepting a significant downturn in 2003, the United States has continued to receive new residents on a par with the pre-9/11 era, and public opinion, as we have seen, has shifted only modestly.

CONCLUSION

Immigration and immigrant policy have much to say about immigrant assimilation, the experience and relative structural integration of America's new faces. Policy helps determine both starting point and trajectory. Although immigration in the United States is closely allied with national identity, recent experience shows that immigration issues offer a warren of difficult policy choices about who gets in and what happens afterward. The simple yet persistently powerful notion of "give me your tired, your poor"—even when acknowledged as a mythological construction within contested territory regarding labor force needs, social openness, and ethnocentrism—has been augmented by a thicket of regulations. Immigration policy evolves and contemporary policy stakeholders jostle for their particular provision in the policy circuit. Globalization, the growth of the welfare state, and affirmative action—to name just three key arenas—have shifted the context of the twenty-first century debate. Outcomes for immigrants, however they arrived, help determine the path in the policy circuit.

Categories of admission are now far different for immigrants to the United States than they were in 1900 or 1910. This is due, of course, to the substantial revisions in the Immigration and Nationality Act that have taken place over time. In fiscal year 2004, two-thirds of authorized U.S immigrants arrived through family channels (U.S. Department of Homeland Security 2005). Despite the both quiet and vocal calls for the revision of immigration policy in favor of skills-based and labor market immigration, the proportion of new arrivals coming through family channels has actually increased over time. In 1994, the figure stood at 57 percent. These persons come as spouses, children, parents, or siblings of an American citizen or legally resident immigrant.

At the turn of the century, the family preference system did not exist. If anything, decisions on admissibility (once an individual had made the voyage) were based on ethnic background and various other mental and physical criteria. Without a doubt, family networks operated powerfully on the pathway to the United States. We lack, however, solid, comparable, empirical evidence on the extent of family reunification and family connection at this earlier time. The upshot is that an unattached individual, who has heard vaguely about American opportunity, had a better shot at getting into the United States in the first half of the twentieth century than in the latter half. Moreover, the family preference provisions of contemporary immigration law suggest that recent arrivals may have put in place a social (and perhaps economic) support system unavailable to earlier waves.

Despite significant reservations about the volume of immigration and intermittent policy interventions, the actual flow of documented immigrants to the United States was at nearly 1 million annually in the 1990s. It has fluctuated in the first decade of the twenty-first century but appears to keep pace with the 1990s. At the same time, the family-linked component of those flows (at least those that are documented) continues to grow. Policy analysts and advocates will continue to debate—often quite vocally and stridently, as the 2006 to 2008 legislative struggles made clear—many actions about immigration and immigrant policy.

The policy circuit sets the backdrop for our analysis. In the three chapters that follow we concentrate on what we term structural aspects of immigrant assimilation: schooling, labor market, and housing. These are three stages on which the drama of assimilation, regardless of origin or route, plays. They also vary in the degree of social proximity of the host society and the newcomers. Additionally, they connect to the policy circuit in different ways from one another and from other realms of assimilation investigated by social scientists and policy analysts.

In the case of schools, immigrant and second-generation children encounter a universal institutional environment with broad public policy input. Decisions about whether immigrant children are eligible for public education, and for which educational resources they are eligible, bear directly on outcomes. Because so much of school resources depend on the public sector, any shifts in resources, whether explicitly directed to or from immigrant and second-generation pupils, are likely to bear directly on outcomes. If schools fail to provide some key skill or produce a disparate pedagogical environment, they may widen differences among the generations and across ethnic groups.

The economic stage features prominently in the immigration policy circuit. As we indicate, and as others have pursued in more detail, the dynamic tension between the desire for more labor and that to restrict new arrivals to the labor market is a core feature of the controversy in immigration policy debates. To be sure, these tensions have alongside them philosophical debates about who should be admitted through the golden door of American immigration. The policy sector—mostly from the federal level—does intervene, determining the number of new entrants, how vigilant to be about undocumented workers, and penalties applied to employers (and indirectly in-centives for unauthorized migration). All of this determines, in part, the skill mix of the U.S. labor force and the competitive environment all work-ers face. Moreover, when the specters of discrimination and its redress are added to the mix, room for policy intervention widens. Although the role the public sector plays in a relatively laissez-faire economy such as the United States is limited, interest in the outcomes—across natives and immi-grants and across ethnic groups—is keen.

Our third stage on which to view structural assimilation is the housing market. We argue that housing, or more specifically residential integration, is particularly instructive. This is the stage on which we observe the social intermingling of immigrants and their ethnic descendants. Policy is designed to intervene to prohibit housing discrimination along several traits, includ-ing national origin, yet does little to affirmatively promote intermingling across ethnic groups or between immigrants and natives. The degree to which contemporary immigrants and their ethnic descendants are residen-tially integrated may say much about assimilation. Neighboring patterns will help illuminate the twenty-first century immigration picture as one of a melting pot or one more characterized by ethnic pluralism (Lieberson and Waters 1988). In turn, neighboring patterns may have important implica-tions for the schooling and labor market opportunities for the second gen-eration and their descendants, taking us full circle across the domains of structural assimilation.

All three dimensions bring to light important features about structural assimilation. They are all amenable to policy intervention. Other dimen-sions of assimilation, such as intermarriage or religious affiliation, can pro-vide quite powerful indicators of assimilation (and host-newcomer dynam-ics) and have been seen as such by social scientists (Levitt 2007; Qian and Lichter 2001). They are, however, less indicative of structural assimilation and are less likely to intersect directly with contemporary policy. Rapid and successful structural assimilation, along the lines of the straight-line model, might argue for keeping open the door at least as wide as it is now. More problematic or segmented assimilation paths might suggest the need to re-visit admission criteria. By contrast, others might take differential outcomes to signal the need for further investment in building human capital through schooling or revisiting policies such as affirmative action in the workplace or housing antidiscrimination efforts. Our argument is not that there is a sim-ple and straightforward policy prescription attached to any empirical result. Indeed, different observers will be inclined in different directions. Rather, our hope is that a better understanding of structural assimilation can better inform any policy direction that is placed on the table.

In our view, these many debates, especially those concerning skills versus family-based criteria and other admissions requirements, speak directly to the immigration versus immigrant policy duality and the associated starting point and trajectory framework we use here. Immigration policy can directly shift composition of immigrants and, in turn, the starting point for the foreign born and their children. The continuing debate counsels us to better understand trajectory: How well immigrants and their children do. Our following chapters look exactly at how well immigrants do, first in the educational realm, then in the labor market, and then in neighborhood residential integration.

Chapter 5

School: Educational Attainment of Immigrants and the Second Generation

FOR THE individual, educational attainment is a key determinant of future economic mobility in the United States (Becker and Tomes 1986; Blau and Duncan 1967). Certainly, our conventional American dream is predicated, in part, on the notion that universal access to education is a hallmark of opportunity. In the case of minority groups, education, often in combination with subsequent geographic mobility, has been shown to be critical to reducing disparities (Smith and Welch 1986; Montero and Tsukashima 1977). Schools provide the key sites in which a society provides human capital, the resources for achievement and income later in life. A wealth of social science evidence has accumulated to demonstrate the important intermediary position of schooling between family background and subsequent success in the labor force (Sewell, Hauser, and Featherman 1976; Jencks et al. 1979; Hogan 1981).

This centrality of schooling to the status attainment process carries over with even more force for immigrants and the second generation. Educational attainment is a marker for socioeconomic assimilation and mobility across immigrant groups and a measure of the degree to which descendants of immigrants are progressing (Gordon 1964; Alba and Nee 2003). In this chapter we turn to schooling and focus on the relative progress of immigrant youth and their peers over time. Our examination sets the stage, in turn, for our analysis of labor force outcomes, which follows in chapter 6.

We draw on our theoretical model of chapter 3 and ask whether the trajectory of educational attainment for the first- and second-generation youths differs from that of their classmates, controlling for the starting point. We know that on average, immigrant children and second-generation children have somewhat disadvantaged socioeconomic origins. We examine whether once adjusting for socioeconomic and family origin in a nationally representative sample, generation status carries additional predictive power. Immigrants and the second generation do not have some of the advantages of others. Once this starting point is taken into account, we find that differences traced though high school in the trajectories of immigrants, the second generation, and higher-order generations are modest. Issues of time—especially those across generations—are critical precisely because they translate into long-term, intergenerational differences.

We also ask whether these trajectories differ for two cohorts of youth in the United States to test expectations of theoretical views of immigrant youth adaptation. We note that assimilation theory posits a universal process that adheres in the migration process and thus should be applicable to generation status groups across time. On the other hand, concern about the composition of the immigrant stream—specifically, concern about decline in skill levels among recent immigrants—has given rise to predictions that the more recent arrivals and their children will somehow not follow the straight-line assimilation path of previous cohorts.

Research on the children of the new immigrants presents somewhat conflicting images of their educational trajectories. Some researchers point to a decline among second-generation youth. Others suggest that immigrant youth have access to familial resources that lead to remarkably high levels of educational attainment. From a conventional straight-line assimilation perspective, we would expect the greatest differences, from a comparison group of students in the third and higher-order generation, among recent immigrants. We would expect the gap from the third and higher generations to decrease for immigrants with more time in the United States, and we would expect an even smaller gap for second-generation students. Further, this view anticipates gains in achievement among immigrants over time that pulls them closer to the next generation. In other words, we should see a decrease in the difference among the generations over time, net of family background characteristics. Finally, such a series of declining differences is attributed to the migration-adaptation process and therefore is not expected to be different for cohorts of immigrants, regardless of changes in the conditions in the receiving society.

The segmented assimilation framework, presented in chapter 3, offers a variation on intergenerational assimilation. Segmented assimilation sees different trajectories emerging over time. This orientation suggests that adaptation in the host society varies such that there is a net disadvantage for some immigrants or a net advantage for others not accounted for by compositional characteristics. In this perspective, the host society fails to produce assimilation for some, especially for immigrants from historically disadvantaged ethnic subgroups, a failure that continues to the second generation (Zhou 1997). Thus, we might expect some immigrants to progress less well than their native counterparts, possibly falling further behind over time. This divergence of trajectories would be especially likely if immigrant youth encounter less favorable structural conditions within the United States (Portes and Rumbaut 2001).

Empirical results regarding educational achievement feed directly into public-policy decisions facing the United States. Myers refers to an assimilation bonus arising from the benefit of U.S. schooling that would accrue to those who are more settled within and across generations (Myers 2007). Results from a longitudinal view can be particularly informative for policy, as discussed in chapter 4, for both the admission of immigrants (immigration policy) and the treatment of U.S. residents of foreign birth (immigrant policy). For instance, finding relatively rapid social and economic assimilation of immigrants will buttress arguments for raising the ceiling on the number of immigrants. Conversely, a finding that foreign birth and English-language deficiency are severe impediments to achievement will feed arguments that the composition of the immigrant stream be altered, say by using English-speaking ability as a criterion for admission. In examining the trajectories of adolescents, we will be able to identify even more focused implications. If the language effect only appears during school and not later (although weak school performance may have long term consequences), policy could be directed more aggressively to English language training soon after immigrant arrival, particularly in the case of young children. All these policy options have, in fact, been debated.

Our analyses are based on cross-sectional data available for the entire U.S. population and two cohort surveys that allow us to trace progress from adolescence into young adulthood. These surveys provide information about the family background of students, factors important for predicting later life outcomes. We also have access to standardized test scores in school and can control for this trait in looking at subsequent educational attainment. The unique contribution of the work presented in this chapter is the simultaneous examination of the relative strength of ethnicity, immigrant status, and language in the presence of controls for other background characteristics. Debate persists about the importance of each of these factors on their own. Studying them as a group, however, enables us to differentiate effects and determine which, if any, is most important to school completion and socioeconomic achievement in adulthood.

We turn next to an examination of cross-sectional results for educational differences by generation. Such numbers are often cited in reviews of immigrant achievement. They help set the stage for our cohort analysis. As those results will show, the picture is not always the same. After these cross-sectional results from the 1994 and 2004 Current Population Survey (CPS), we present our empirical results for the two longitudinal surveys, first at the starting point 1980 or 1990 sophomore year standardized test score, then test score growth over the next two years. We then examine educational attainment by looking at high school graduation and then categories of postsecondary education.

THE VIEW FROM THE CROSS-SECTION

If one compares the foreign-born to the U.S.-born population generally at a given time, one finds substantial differences in educational attainment, but these differences are not always simple and uniform. Comparing educational attainment by generation status over time may yield different conclusions as well. To demonstrate this, figure 5.1, taken from the nationally representative CPS in 1994 and 2004, presents some relevant information on school attainment by nativity and age. The first two panels (A and B) clearly demonstrate that first-generation adults are much less likely to have achieved a high school diploma than their second-generation or third-generation counterparts in both 1994 and 2004. Such data may at first glance lend support to the notion that immigrants do not fare as well in the educational system as natives. When we compare the second panels (C and D) for the upper end of the educational distribution, the gaps between first, second, and third generations are much smaller at all ages. What is striking, in fact, is that in the 2004 data, we observe a higher proportion of the second generation achieving at least a baccalaureate degree.

These are cross-sectional figures that include in the first generation new arrivals at each age interval along with those who have been in the United States longer. Thus we cannot tell whether generation status differences in education would be even smaller if we confined the analyses to those who enter the United States during or before formal schooling. These tabulations also give some support to the notion of an hourglass-shaped distribution of education among immigrants. Clearly a substantial number of immigrants have very limited education (panels A and B). At the same time, the proportion with a baccalaureate degree does not fall below the second and third generation.

Such apparent contradictions in immigrant educational attainment presented by figure 5.1 have been observed before. The most likely explanation comes from the routes though which immigrants of different backgrounds find their way to the United States. Many immigrants—for instance, rural immigrants from Latin America—have minimal schooling. Others arrive by way of skill preference visas or remain in the United States after obtaining higher education and thus are represented in the more highly educated population. Such findings also indicate that individuals who respond in a survey or census are from all arrival periods; they also immigrated at different ages. These effects underscore the importance of examining individual cohorts

Figure 5.1   Educational Distribution by Generation Status and Age, United States, 1994 and 2004

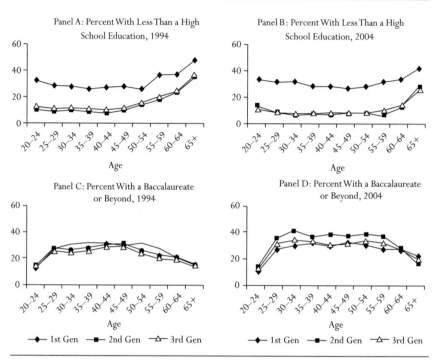

Panel A: Percent With Less Than a High School Education, 1994

Panel B: Percent With Less Than a High School Education, 2004

Panel C: Percent With a Baccalaureate or Beyond, 1994

Panel D: Percent With a Baccalaureate or Beyond, 2004

—◆— 1st Gen   —■— 2nd Gen   —△— 3rd Gen

Source: Authors' compilation from U.S. Bureau of the Census 1994, 2004, Current Population Survey (March).

using longitudinal data to make proper inferences about immigrant educational attainment compared to natives.[1]

PROGRESS OVER TIME: A VIEW FROM TWO COHORTS

We now turn to longitudinal analysis. Drawing on the framework of starting point and trajectory introduced earlier, we examine the educational outcomes with a multivariate model that takes into account the youth's earlier educational performance and socioeconomic origins. Thus, achievement (here academic performance within high school and high school graduation) is taken to be the result of the comparative influence of generation status, family structure and socioeconomic status, language background, and access to familial social capital. This will give us a window on the straight-line assimilation, superachievement, and segmented assimilation frameworks.

It is worth considering how these frameworks intersect with the statistical models we estimate in this chapter. Most notably, many sweeping depictions of immigrant and second-generation assimilation (or lack thereof) lack specificity on the modeling dimension. Our main concern is identifying the effects of immigration status after other factors have been controlled. We suggest that the conventional straight-line assimilation approach expects to find differences in educational achievement across immigrant status, but would also anticipate that these would be attenuated once family background and socioeconomic characteristics of origin are controlled.

The superachievement perspective would expect to find that a variable measuring immigrant status would be positive in sign, pointing to superior test scores or greater probability of high school completion than one would expect on the basis of family background alone. Some recent immigrants may have greater faith in the use of education to achieve upward mobility than established racial-ethnic minorities in the United States (Gibson and Ogbu 1991). Recent Hispanic and Asian migrants may be particularly motivated and emphasize the importance of success—in school and at work—to their children because these parents are a select group with high motivation that led to their emigration (Kao and Tienda 1998). Thus, some youth, particularly those in immigrant families, may achieve higher levels of education than their U.S.-born peers with similar available economic resources because immigrant families maintain an environment that strongly encourages academic achievement by its high expectations, greater involvement with schools, and close communication with children regarding school-related issues (Stanton-Salazar 1997). Such a finding would be consistent with the superachievement perspective.

The segmented assimilation perspective would anticipate large effects for race and ethnicity, and in some cases, negative effects for immigrant status itself. Besides expectations produced by these assimilation frameworks, models of discrimination in the labor market would suggest that foreign birth itself, particularly when associated with an identifiable physiognomic appearance, distinct language, or membership in an ethnic minority group, might lead to disadvantaged socioeconomic outcomes. The last of these would overlap with segmented assimilation. Frank Bean and Gillian Stevens raised the specter of economic incorporation amid the maintenance of ethnic identification. In such a case, socioeconomic factors would be predictive in a multivariate model, but ethnic effects would be muted; ethnicity would matter for identity, but not as much for socioeconomic attainment, our focus here (2003).

Language and ethnicity are assuredly intertwined with immigration, but there are competing ideas about how language ability and bilingualism influence achievement in school. Analysts may differ on how these traits and their performance in statistical models align with the precepts of various frameworks. For pragmatic policy as well as for overarching theory, the differential effects of language background are of critical interest. From considerable research, we know that language proficiency does improve markedly over time, especially for immigrants under age forty (Myers 1995). English-language proficiency itself is associated strongly with time in the United States and age on arrival (Espenshade and Fu 1997; Bean and Stevens 2003). Work with 2000 census data (thus cross-sectional) indicates that years in the United States, years of education, attending school in the United States, and younger age at immigration are all strongly associated with English-language proficiency (Bean and Stevens 2003). In a more subtle way, language background may also present a unique structural barrier for the children of immigrants. Parents who are not confident speaking English may be less willing to engage in contact with schools and thus less able to help their children navigate through school. Disadvantages associated with the child's limited English skills may be associated with lower academic achievement (Kao and Tienda 1995). Students with poor English-language skills may be placed in lower grades than they otherwise would be (Suarez-Orozco 1991; Zsembik and Llanes 1996). We do know that, overall, foreign-born students are more likely to be held back a grade than their U.S.-born counterparts (Bean and Tienda 1987). However, it is not clear whether these students recover or fall further behind their U.S.-born peers who are also held back.

Despite the apparent disadvantages of a non-English background, other research suggests that there is a positive, if temporary, effect of coming from a bilingual background. Bilingualism may allow immigrant and second-generation children to tap into the resources available in their parents' communities as well as participate in regular school activities (Lindholm and Aclan 1991; Mouw and Xie 1999; Rumbaut 1996; Zhou and Bankston 1994). In effect, a bilingual home may provide access to greater social capital (Zhou 1997). Parents who speak both English and their native language are better able to help their children by maintaining ties with the immigrant community as they interact with other social institutions such as schools (Bankston and Zhou 1995; Hao and Bonstead-Bruns 1998). Thus, that immigrant children appear to acquire English-language skills relatively quickly does not negate the potential benefits of their having some fluency in their parents' mother tongue (Portes and Schauffler 1994).

Determining the role of language skills on enhancing educational and subsequent labor market outcomes is not a simple task. That, on average, immigrants perform less well in school may be due more to language background and proficiency in English than to being new to the United States. An analysis of grade point average (GPA) scores for San Diego high school students found that immigrants from non-English backgrounds received higher GPA scores than Anglos and others of similar ethnicity from English-only backgrounds (Rumbaut 1995). Because these results did not control for other factors, questions about the unique influence of ethnicity persist. We need to be able to disentangle statistically the effects of language background from those of foreign birth. Further, we need to understand the role that schooling plays in mediating between the non-English environment and the wider English-speaking culture. If language barriers are the problem, differences by nativity and length of residence in the United States should disappear when language is controlled.

An enormous amount of literature has focused on the varying achievement of major American ethnic groups, especially on the disparities between blacks and whites. To be sure, ethnic group performance has been one key aspect of the original High School and Beyond study (Coleman, Hoffer, and Kilgore 1982; Coleman and Hoffer 1987). It is a challenge to separate the effects of ethnic origin and language proficiency (Nielsen and Lerner 1986). After all, international migration generates ethnic diversity. In a statistical regression analysis, a measure of ethnicity may reflect discrimination or, more generally, context of reception. It may signify a distinct cultural background that has a unique effect in the school setting (Trueba 1988), or it may reflect social capital available for the student. Historical studies frequently point to ethnic differences in schooling even in the presence of statistical controls (Glenn 1990; Sassler 1995). Alejandro Portes and Rubén Rumbaut argued that context of reception matters greatly (2001). They noted, first, the substantial variation in occupational skill level and propensity for self-employment of the foreign born by national origin. They argued further that the context of reception, in terms of national government admission policy and subsequent labor market discrimination, also helps determine outcomes. They advanced the notion that the ethnic enclave serves as an important conduit to success in the host country (Portes and Rumbaut 1990, 2001). Because ethnicity may exert independent effects on achievement from those of generation status and language, our models control for all three.

Two important temporal dimensions emerge in the discourse on immigrant adaptation. First is the question of generational progression implied by the assimilation perspectives. Second are the patterns of assimilation, which, some argue, have been changing across arrival cohorts so that the immigrants of today are less well-suited to socioeconomic incorporation in the United States than those arriving at some previous point. For some, the comparison is to the European immigrants at the turn of the twentieth century (Alba and Nee 2003). For others, the appropriate cohort comparison is one that has arrived more recently (Borjas 1999). We choose two contemporary cohorts of youth to compare: one from the 1980s (High School and Beyond, or HSB) and a second from the 1990s (National Education Longitudinal Study, or NELS). These will shed light on the contemporary cohort quality debate. Necessarily, inference about changes over several decades will involve comparisons beyond the scope of our sample. But we can look at the differences across generations within these cohorts as we follow these cohorts over time.

We first analyze the factors that predict achievement in the sophomore year for each cohort of adolescents and then turn our attention to the dynamics of school performance, as measured by change in achievement tests from sophomore to senior year and at graduation.

The Data

We use multiple waves of the High School and Beyond survey and the National Education Longitudinal Study.[2] These school-based surveys share several important characteristics, making them ideal for comparing two cohorts of adolescents in the United States. Because both surveys made special efforts to follow high school dropouts, we are able to follow youth with very different educational trajectories. Further, both surveys oversample some minority groups, providing ethnically diverse samples with considerable numbers of both immigrant youth and children of immigrants. The data also contain many measures not available in other sources, including information on personal attitudes, performance on standardized tests, parental background, and school context. Finally, both surveys repeatedly interview the respondents, allowing us to follow their progress into their mid-twenties. Our samples from HSB and NELS are representative of sophomores in high school in 1980 and 1990, respectively, and both include a large number of immigrant children and children of immigrants.

Data of this sort allow us to address several of the lingering criticisms of research on immigrant adaptation. Most of the previous inferences about immigrant adaptation and achievement in American society come from comparisons of cross-sectional data, or, sometimes, successive cross-sections of data. In fact, the data we use here were collected not for the express purpose of studying immigrants, but rather to understand the contemporary high school achievement process. The researchers purposefully oversampled certain kinds of schools, and, with proper sample weights, the data are still representative of students in the United States. This does limit our longitudinal analyses to those children who attend school in the United States and thus may miss some immigrant youth who arrive at older ages and never enroll. However, the advantages of the school-based studies in the form of detailed measures of academic achievement, educational attainment, and subsequent earnings bolster support for relying on these studies.

Because these samples are followed from wave to wave, the sample size is limited by the number of individuals re-interviewed in the follow-up surveys. Despite attrition, sample sizes for this study are on the order of several thousand persons. These large samples provide enough numbers of immigrants and children of immigrants to measure the effects of birthplace and language background on achievement and to test these effects with statistical precision. We make use of the sophomore cohorts, which were followed from 1980 to 1992 in the HSB cohort and from 1990 to 2000 in the NELS cohort.[3]

We begin observing our first cohort as high school sophomores in 1980. The High School and Beyond Survey then follows these youth into young adulthood. To create a parallel analysis, we rely on the 1990 wave of the National Education Longitudinal Study for a comparable cohort of high school sophomores. Most background traits (age, immigrant status, home language, ethnicity, sex, and parental involvement) are obtained from the 1980 base year survey from the High School and Beyond survey and the 1990 first follow-up from the National Education Longitudinal Study, at which time the respondents were sophomores in high school. We identify respondents as recent immigrants if they arrived roughly six years before their sophomore year. We distinguish these from the 1.5-generation respondents, who arrived as young children and therefore obtained most of their schooling in the United States. These are compared to the second generation, who are identified as respondents born in the United States with at least one foreign-born parent, and to those in the third and higher generation, who are identified as U.S. born with U.S.-born parents.

For our analyses, socioeconomic status is a composite measure constructed from information on mother's education, father's education, family income, father's occupation, and household possessions. Our measure of the home language background of the respondent includes four categories: English is the sole language used in the home, more than one language is spoken but English predominates, more than one language is spoken but a non-English language predominates, and a home in which a non-English language is the sole or virtually only language. Ethnicity is determined by the student's self-report on two survey variables: race and ethnic origin. Following previous work (White and Kaufman 1997), we recode these into a set of dummy variables: black, Mexican, Cuban, Puerto Rican, other Hispanic, Asian, and other. Non-Hispanic whites are the reference category. Although there is considerable linguistic, religious, and cultural heterogeneity across Asian subgroups, the small size of the Asian sample precludes further disaggregation in the overall analysis. Table 5.1 provides the descriptive characteristics of the cohorts broken down by generation status. Of course, we cannot observe the characteristics of those who have dropped out of high school by tenth grade or have never enrolled in the United States.

There are considerable similarities in the background traits by generation status across the two cohorts. First, recent immigrant high school sophomores are more likely to be older than seventeen in their sophomore

Table 5.1   Sample Characteristics of High School Sophomores

High School and Beyond Cohort

	Recent Arrivals	1.5 Generation	Second Generation	Third+ Generation
Over age seventeen	19.1	7.4	5.4	4.9
Sex				
Male	55.2	53.2	49.3	47.6
Female	44.8	46.8	50.7	52.4
SES	−0.41	0.04	−0.01	0.05
Family structure				
Two married parents	65.3	68.1	65.2	70.6
Parent and partner	4.7	8.4	9.8	8.6
Single mother	20.8	14.3	16.7	13.9
Single father	2.7	3.1	3.0	2.9
Neither parent	6.4	6.1	5.4	4.0
Family size				
No siblings	2.2	3.9	5.9	4.5
One or two siblings	47.5	54.1	49.0	49.6
Three or more siblings	50.4	42.0	45.2	45.9
Race-ethnicity				
Non-Hispanic white	28.6	55.4	65.3	81.7
Non-Hispanic black	15.7	14.7	16.7	12.4
Mexican	10.8	8.0	7.4	3.0
Puerto Rican	3.6	4.7	3.2	0.4
Other Hispanic	9.0	9.5	3.3	1.8
Asian	32.3	7.8	4.0	0.8
Language				
Non-English	21.9	7.3	4.6	0.4
Bilingual, non-English dominant	29.7	18.0	7.1	0.8
Bilingual, English dominant	9.0	21.1	21.2	7.0
English only	39.4	53.6	67.1	91.8

National Education Longitudinal Cohort

	Recent Arrivals	1.5 Generation	Second Generation	Third+ Generation
Over age seventeen	29.1	14.3	5.6	7.6
Sex				
Male	59.0	50.2	46.4	49.7
Female	41.0	49.8	53.6	50.3

National Education Longitudinal Cohort (*Continued*)

	Recent Arrivals	1.5 Generation	Second Generation	Third+ Generation
SES	−0.54	−0.30	−0.22	−0.03
Family structure				
Two married parents	60.0	69.4	70.5	62.0
Parent and partner	13.2	15.7	12.2	17.5
Single mother	9.5	9.4	12.8	13.9
Single father	3.3	2.6	2.1	2.9
Neither parent	13.9	2.9	2.4	3.7
Family size				
No siblings	21.4	10.7	14.5	10.0
One or two siblings	35.9	43.8	49.9	53.4
Three or more siblings	42.7	45.5	35.7	36.6
Race-ethnicity				
Non-Hispanic white	17.5	26.1	38.8	82.5
Non-Hispanic black	8.6	3.9	6.1	12.4
Mexican	15.2	21.6	24.9	2.9
Puerto Rican	0.7	3.2	7.0	0.2
Other Hispanic	20.3	9.7	10.6	1.2
Asian	37.7	35.4	12.6	0.9
Language				
Non-English	19.4	15.2	13.2	1.1
Bilingual, non-English dominant	54.5	40.1	30.6	1.3
Bilingual, English dominant	9.4	20.4	25.5	5.0
English only	16.8	24.4	30.7	92.7

Source: Authors' compilation from High School and Beyond data (weighted) N = 12,807; National Educational Longitudinal Study data (weighted) N = 16,376.
Note: Sample excludes Native Americans.

year. This likely reflects both students placed in a lower grade than their age mates on entering school in the United States as well as some previous grade retention. We also note that recent arrivals in both cohorts come from lower socioeconomic status backgrounds than their higher-order generation peers. Recent arrivals are also more likely to come from homes in which non-English languages predominate than their higher order generation peers. These characteristics suggest that the first generation in both cohorts is starting from a disadvantaged position in their sophomore year of high school relative to their third- and higher-order generation peers. Our regression analyses will control for these traits to determine if they help account for subsequent differences in educational achievement and attainment.

The racial and ethnic composition of the first and higher-order generations does vary across the cohorts reflecting differences in sampling strategies.[4] The third and higher generations in HSB and NELS are quite similar in racial and ethnic composition. The recent arrivals, 1.5 generations, and second generations include proportionately more Asian-origin and Mexican-origin youth in the NELS cohort than the HSB cohort. This is also reflected in the language backgrounds of the recent arrivals, 1.5 generations, and second generations in both cohorts.

The analysis examined several alternative statistical models, sometimes altering the set of variables included and sometimes altering the statistical technique. Most of these approaches were cross-validating and are not reported here. Details are available elsewhere (Glick and White 2003, 2004; White 1997; White and Glick 2000).

Achievement Within High School

We now turn to a comparison of academic achievement by generation status across the two cohorts. There are, of course, many ways to conceptualize and measure success in school. We rely on achievement tests, a common feature of high school life, as our indicators of academic performance for several reasons. First, standardized test scores are often used for placing students in special education or accelerated school environments as well as assessing the progress of students in school over time (Gonzalez, Brusca-Vega, and Yawkey 1997). Second, the use of standardized tests administered across schools allows for academic achievement of students from diverse social and educational settings to be compared (Bankston and Caldas 1996). Grades or other teacher assessments are less likely to be comparable across these settings or comparable across the two cohorts. Finally, mathematics and reading ability should translate into labor market outcomes (Farkas 1996). Despite the continuing debate about the utility and validity of such tests, these several reasons substantiate their value to us here.

The HSB and NELS studies administered standardized tests to 1980 sophomores and repeated the test in 1982, when most of them had become seniors. Such a standardized test can give us useful insight into achievement over the period and the reasons for it. More specifically, this information allows us to test whether immigrants trace different achievement paths from other students. That this is a true cohort should not be lost: we can look at the same students two years after the first test, see how their scores improve (or not), and use characteristics at the starting point to help explain differentials in achievement.

The test administered as part of the NELS study contains different items from that contained in the HSB survey, though both tests were designed to tap similar skills. Besides differences in the items contained in the cognitive tests, there were different rates of nonresponse to the surveys in general and to the cognitive tests in particular. Our multivariate models are therefore separate for each cohort, and we take steps to account for nonrandom missing test data (Glick and White 2003).

We first examine test performance on the standardized math and reading tests at the outset when students were sophomores in high school. We can take this first test to be, within the context of the overall model, a statement of initial conditions. We might expect immigrants to differ in achievement for a variety of reasons. A more telling test of immigrant versus native achievement and the influence of language and other related traits can be found in the gain in test score over the period from sophomore to senior year. We separate reading and math tests because reading skills may be more closely linked to language skills (facility in English), and math tests may reflect academic abilities somewhat independently of language background.

The Achievement Tests

Figure 5.2 gives an overview of the initial situation. It shows how the initial scores for each cohort differ by generation status without adjusting for any differences in family background, ethnicity, or other characteristics. The bars for each generation status group represent the average point difference from the mean score for third- and higher-generation youth. Reading scores for the 1980 and 1990 cohort are presented first, followed by the math scores for each cohort. Looking first at the reading scores for 1980, we observe a pattern consistent with expectations from a classic straight-line assimilation model. Students in the recent immigrant group (arriving within the last six years, most likely while schooling was already under way), scored about 6 points (about 9 percent) below those of the third—and higher—generation. Immigrants arriving over six years before the survey (and most likely before first grade) scored about 1.5 points below the reference group, and second-generation students scored less than a point below.[5] The lack of symmetry suggests that recent immigrant students are more heterogeneous than the other three groups—1.5-generation immigrants, the second generation, and the higher-order natives—to which they are being compared.

When we examine reading scores in 1990, the pattern by generation status is less monotonic, though recent immigrant youth still lag behind the most. For math scores, recent immigrants look more similar to their U.S.-born counterparts, and 1.5-generation and second-generation youth actually outscore their third- and higher-generation counterparts in the 1990 cohort. These simple unadjusted comparisons lead to the next question: how

Figure 5.2   Differences in Test Scores from Third and Higher Generation

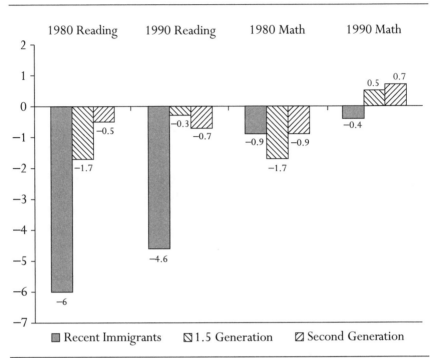

Source: Authors' compilation from High School and Beyond Survey, 1980; National Educational Longitudinal Study, 1990.
Note: Graph represents distance from third and higher generation in the unadjusted average test scores for each generation group.

much of any deficit is attributable to traits associated with generational status, and how much is to being in the first or second generation itself? We do know that differences in ethnic background, SES, and other traits that sort out across the generations are notable, for example. Recent immigrant students come from family backgrounds with considerably lower SES than those of the third- or higher-order generations in both cohorts. Inspection of the data reveals that both recent immigrant and 1.5-generation students have more heterogeneous family SES than the higher-order natives.

Our examination of descriptive data indicates that home language background strongly differentiates outcomes in the standardized test. Students who come from a home in which English predominates or in which English and another language are spoken (bilingual homes) score almost five points higher on the composite test than those from non-English backgrounds. Socioeconomic background differs markedly and significantly also for these students. Those from non-English homes come from family backgrounds that are about one-half standard deviation below those whose language is English. Compared to these two measures of initial conditions in the sophomore year, the 1980 to 1982 gain in test score is less differentiated. Those from non-English speaking home environments gained about four-tenths of a point more than English speakers, but a statistical test indicates that this is not a significant difference.[6]

In sum, these descriptive results point to major differences in initial conditions. Immigrant students and those from homes where English does not predominate (two heavily overlapping groups) have lower socioeconomic resources and score several points lower initially on the standardized test.[7] Yet, in the subsequent two years, differences in achievement growth between immigrant and native students are more difficult to detect. To shed more light on the determinants of growth over the two years, we now turn to multivariate models.

Predicting Achievement Levels

Immigrants and U.S.-born youth come from different language, ethnic, and socioeconomic groups, and these compositional differences could help explain any divergence in academic performance. To address this possibility, we estimate models that adjust for the relative impact of these other characteristics closely tied to generation status. The measures included in our analyses represent the student's demographic characteristics, access to human capital, family environment, ethnicity, and language background.

We include measures of ethnicity in our models to control for the possibility that ethnic identification and not migration status, per se, results in differential academic achievement. Although we recognize that panethnic categories combine many distinct national origin groups, we must identify respondents as members of one of several racial-ethnic groups common to both surveys. These include non-Hispanic white (reference group), non-Hispanic black, Mexican, Puerto Rican, other Hispanic, and Asian.

Table 5.2 presents a statistical model predicting the 1982 or 1992 math test results. We present similar models in table 5.3 predicting the 1982 or 1992 reading test results. All the models correct for selectivity of test-taking itself using a two-step Heckman selection approach. The Heckman model allows us to estimate the outcome of interest (test result) and account for the fact that a selection process may operate in determining who takes the test, given that it is unlikely that the test-takers are a random sample of all students. The first three models in each table demonstrate the effects of the baseline characteristics on the subsequent test scores. The

Table 5.2   Regression Models Predicting 1982 and 1992 Math Test Scores

High School and Beyond Cohort

	1	2	3	4
Generation status (third-plus as ref.)				
Recent arrivals	0.00	0.11	0.01	0.04
1.5 generation	−0.12	−0.09	−0.07	0.00
Second generation	−0.10**	−0.06	−0.04	−0.01
Over age seventeen (under seventeen as ref.)		−0.46***	−0.46***	−0.15***
Male (female as ref.)		0.11***	0.08***	0.07***
SES		0.36***	0.28***	0.09***
Family structure (both parents as ref.)				
Parent and partner		−0.09*	−0.04	−0.05*
Single mother		−0.10**	0.01	0.00
Single father		−0.12	−0.13*	0.02
Neither parent		−0.45***	−0.37***	−0.07
Family size (one or two siblings as ref.)				
No siblings		0.06	0.04	0.04
Three or more siblings		0.00	0.01	0.01
Race-ethnicity (white as ref.)				
Non-Hispanic black			−0.47***	−0.07***
Mexican			−0.36***	−0.07*
Puerto Rican			−0.39***	−0.08
Other Hispanic			−0.34***	−0.04
Asian			0.12	0.06
Language (English only as ref.)				
Non-English			0.00	0.11*
Bilingual, non-English dominant			0.09	0.04
Bilingual, English dominant			0.20***	0.01
1980 math test score				0.79***
Constant	0.18***	0.10***	−0.05***	−0.02***
Log pseudolikelihood	−20120.85	−18727.52	−18337.44	−13108.37
rho	−0.91	−0.31	0.93	0.04
lambda	−1.02	−0.27	0.90	0.02

Table 5.2   (Continued)

National Education Longitudinal Cohort

	1	2	3	4
Generation status (third-plus as ref.)				
Recent arrivals	0.09	0.22*	0.25*	0.02
1.5 generation	0.21***	0.29***	0.36***	0.07*
Second generation	0.06	0.10*	0.20***	−0.01
Over age seventeen (under seventeen as ref.)		−0.32***	−0.29***	−0.05
Male (female as ref.)		0.12***	0.12***	0.06***
SES		0.34***	0.29***	0.04***
Family structure (both parents as ref.)				
Parent and partner		−0.09**	−0.08**	−0.01
Single mother		−0.08**	−0.02	−0.03
Single father		−0.31***	−0.31***	0.04
Neither parent		−0.19*	−0.14	0.04
Family size (one or two siblings as ref.)				
No siblings		−0.19***	−0.14***	−0.04*
Three or more siblings		−0.06**	−0.03	0.01
Race-ethnicity (white as ref.)				
Non-Hispanic black			−0.45***	−0.02
Mexican			−0.49***	−0.09***
Puerto Rican			−0.48***	0.01
Other Hispanic			−0.30***	−0.05
Asian			0.02	0.03
Language (English only as ref.)				
Non-English			−0.03	0.04
Bilingual, non-English dominant			−0.01	0.06*
Bilingual, English dominant			0.07	0.01
1990 math test score				0.89***
Constant	0.42***	0.36***	0.41***	0.06***
Log pseudolikelihood	−25441.88	−24068.58	−23806.04	−15377.79
rho	−0.94	−0.73	−0.78	−0.71
lambda	−1.17	−0.71	−0.76	−0.34

Source: Authors' compilation from High School and Beyond data (weighted) N = 12,807; National Educational Longitudinal Study data (weighted) N = 16,376.

Notes: Family structure and SES variables refer to conditions in sophomore year. Sample excludes Native Americans. Heckman selection models used to predict missing test score data.

* $p < .05$, ** $p < .01$, *** $p < .001$

fourth model in the tables demonstrates the effect of these baseline characteristics on the 1982 or 1992 tests while also controlling for performance
on the 1980 or 1990 tests. We interpret these final models as demonstrating the cumulative impact of baseline characteristics on students' achievement trajectories.

We first examine the role of generation status on test scores without
other controls. The first models suggest some differences in the effects of
generation status. Second-generation youth in the 1980 High School and Beyond cohort do not perform as well as those in the third and higher generation on the math test. The 1990 National Education Longitudinal cohort, on
the other hand, consists of 1.5-generation youth who outperform their third
and higher generation counterparts. In table 5.3, immigrant youth from the
1980 High School and Beyond cohort lag behind their peers on the 1982
reading test, and 1.5-generation youth outperform their peers on the 1992
reading tests for the 1990 National Education Longitudinal cohort.

Model 2 then adds controls, and the importance of family background
becomes clear. For the 1980 High School and Beyond cohort, scores on the
1982 math test are no longer differentiated by generation status but are instead predicted by age, gender, family socioeconomic status, and family
structure in 1980. For the 1990 National Education Longitudinal cohort, an
advantage among first- and second-generation status students emerges once
these background traits are included. There is a very similar role for these
background traits in model 2 in table 5.3 predicting reading scores.

Model 3 includes the variables for race-ethnicity and language background when predicting the 1982 and 1992 math test scores (table 5.2) and
reading test scores (table 5.3). The coefficients for generation status remain
quite dissimilar for the 1980 and 1990 cohorts in model 3. Sample design or
the testing instruments themselves conceivably could create differences in
the effects of generation status, but this seems less likely in the face of the
overwhelming consistency of the other controls in the models (see Glick
and White 2003). Overall then, it appears that the effect of being an immigrant adolescent or child of immigrants in 1980 had a different implication
than in 1990.

These results are all the more striking when we examine the very consistent effects of other characteristics across cohorts. For example, the socioeconomic background of the students operates as a critical predictor of initial
test scores whether we are predicting math or reading scores in 1982 or
1992. Differences across ethnic background are also quite pronounced in
this model in the same manner for both cohorts. Net of SES and the other
controls in the model, black students and those of Mexican, Puerto Rican,
and other Hispanic origin score below non-Hispanic whites on both the
math and reading tests in the 1980 cohort and the 1990 cohort. In other
words, those minority groups who lag behind in the 1980 cohort are the

Table 5.3   Regression Models Predicting 1982 and 1992 Reading Test Scores

High School and Beyond Cohort

	1	2	3	4
Generation status (third-plus as ref.)				
Recent arrivals	−0.32*	−0.33***	−0.27**	−0.02
1.5 generation	−0.12*	−0.10	−0.06	0.01
Second generation	−0.03	−0.01	0.01	0.01
Male (female as ref.)		0.04	0.02	0.03*
Over age seventeen (under seventeen as ref.)		−0.37***	−0.37***	−0.11**
SES		0.31***	0.24***	0.09***
Family structure (both parents as ref.)				
Parent and partner		−0.05	−0.02	−0.01
Single mother		−0.05	0.05	0.03
Single father		−0.08	−0.06	0.03
Neither parent		−0.43***	−0.34***	−0.16***
Family size (one or two siblings as ref.)				
No siblings		0.07	0.01	−0.01
Three or more siblings		−0.03	−0.01	0.00
Race-ethnicity (white as ref.)				
Non-Hispanic black			−0.45***	−0.19***
Mexican			−0.32***	−0.11*
Puerto Rican			−0.31***	−0.09
Other Hispanic			−0.32***	−0.10
Asian			−0.11	−0.04
Language (English only as ref.)				
Non-English			−0.04	0.03
Bilingual, non-English dominant			0.02	0.04
Bilingual, English dominant			0.19***	0.04
1980 reading test score				0.68***
Constant	0.17***	0.10***	−0.04***	0.08***
Log pseudolikelihood	−20051.54	−19100.56	−18783.71	−15431.78
rho	−0.96	−0.24	0.91	−0.52
lambda	−1.09	−0.21	0.91	−0.35

Table 5.3   (*Continued*)

National Education Longitudinal Cohort

	1	2	3	4
Generation status (third-plus as ref.)				
Recent arrivals	0.04	0.00	0.12	0.04
1.5 generation	0.14**	0.19***	0.31***	0.05
Second generation	0.04	0.05	0.18***	0.06
Male (female as ref.)		−0.16***	−0.15***	−0.06***
Over age seventeen (under seventeen as ref.)		−0.23***	−0.20**	−0.02
SES		0.25***	0.21***	0.05***
Family structure (both parents as ref.)				
Parent and partner		−0.01	−0.01	0.01
Single mother		−0.04	0.02	0.02
Single father		−0.29**	−0.29**	−0.04
Neither parent		−0.08	−0.04	0.05
Family size (one or two siblings as ref.)				
No siblings		−0.14***	−0.10**	−0.03
Three or more siblings		−0.07**	−0.04	0.00
Race-ethnicity (white as ref.)				
Non-Hispanic black			−0.41***	−0.15***
Mexican			−0.40***	−0.13***
Puerto Rican			−0.41***	−0.10
Other Hispanic			−0.26**	−0.10
Asian			−0.13*	0.16
Language (English only as ref.)				
Non-English			−0.12	0.06
Bilingual, non-English dominant			−0.10	0.04
Bilingual, English dominant			0.02	0.02
1990 reading test score				0.75***
Constant	0.49***	0.61***	0.65***	0.22***
Log pseudolikelihood	−25241.63	−24491.03	−24287.16	−19520.49
rho	−0.99	−0.93	−0.93	−0.79
lambda	−1.29	−1.06	−1.05	−0.55

Source: Authors' compilation from High School and Beyond data (weighted) N = 12,807; National Educational Longitudinal Study data (weighted) N = 16,376.

Notes: Family structure and SES variables refer to conditions in sophomore year. Sample excludes Native Americans. Heckman selection models used to predict missing test score data.

* $p < .05$, ** $p < .01$, *** $p < .001$

same groups with a disadvantage in the 1990 cohort. Asian-origin students are not as easily categorized. We speculate that the mixed results come, in part, from the differential oversampling techniques in each survey. Other variables are also important influences on test scores for both cohorts. Students who are old for their grade do significantly less well on the examination than those who are at age-for-grade parity, as do those students who were held back at least one year in school before their sophomore year. Students who live with both parents score higher than those from other family structures.

Some alternative models (not shown) tell about the importance of family socioeconomic status and ethnic background for both cohorts. When SES is not controlled, the negative effect of recent immigrant status is augmented, and the effect of non-English language background grows by more than 50 percent. Removing the indicators for ethnic group is associated with a further drop in explanatory power. In this model, the magnitude of coefficients for immigrant status fall, and those for non-English language background rise. Thus, the lower gross achievement of some immigrants is also attributable in part to the fact that immigrants, especially recent immigrants, have lower socioeconomic status than those to whom they are compared. Furthermore, the ethnic composition of the immigrant stream matters somewhat. That the effect of being a recent immigrant is more muted when ethnic characteristics are removed indicates that immigrant stream is not composed overwhelmingly of ethnic groups who perform less well on the standardized test. Models run separately for the largest ethnic groups suggest some modest differences in the initial test scores for first- and second-generation youth from different ethnic backgrounds. For example, Asian immigrants and second-generation youth outperform their third- and higher-generation counterparts. Likewise, Mexican immigrant and second-generation youth appear to outperform their third-generation counterparts, but only on the initial math tests, not on the reading tests. Overall, we find no evidence that any one group of first-generation youth perform dramatically lower than their coethnic U.S. born counterparts.

Sophomore-Senior Trajectory

The final models presented in tables 5.2 and 5.3 demonstrate which characteristics have a cumulative effect on the 1982 or 1992 math and reading scores once we adjust for previous test scores. Recall that even for students who dropped out of high school, the HSB and NELS survey staff still attempted to locate the individuals. Successful administration of the standardized test was possible for most of the sample (for more details on test availability, see White 1997; Glick and White 2003). We also estimated models predicting whether students drop out of high school in these two years for each sample. There are some modest differences in the likelihood of dropout between the two cohorts, but generation status does not exert an independent effect on the likelihood of being enrolled in school by the follow-up survey two years after the sophomore year of high school for either cohort (for detailed results, see Glick and White 2003).

The fourth models in table 5.2 and 5.3 address whether the trajectory of the student is predicted to shift on the basis of generational status and language background. Positive values on coefficients in these models indicate catching up for those who were behind in 1980 (or pulling away for those who were ahead), and negative values indicate falling behind the relative position established by the sophomore year score. In other words, models predicting performance on a second test and controlling for it on the first test provide insight into which characteristics have a cumulative effect on academic performance beyond the effect on the first test. If we find, for example, while controlling for 1980 tests that the coefficient for recent immigrants is positive in a model predicting 1982 tests, we might conclude that these youth are gaining on their third- and higher-generation peers with increased experience in the United States.

The results indicate that previous test score is strongly predictive of performance on the follow-up test. This is no surprise. Besides providing strong evidence for the continuing importance of cognitive ability over the period, the high correlation may also be seen as evidence of the reliability of the test. Whatever the standardized test measures, it does capture the same skills when repeatedly administered. The other variable that carries consistent and fairly large significance in the model is previous grade retention. It is not surprising to find that students who were retained in school are not performing apace with those who remained on time or are age-for-grade in school.

The fourth models suggest no cumulative impact of generation status on test score performance over time. Only the 1.5 generation in the 1990 National Education Longitudinal Study cohort shows a larger growth in math test scores when compared to their third- and higher-generation peers. Overall, the two subgroups of immigrants and the second generation do not have an appreciably different trajectory in achievement, when family background, ethnicity, and previous test score are taken into account. Once again these results are striking considering the consistent effect of some other characteristics. Socioeconomic status, for example, continues to exert an effect on both reading and math test scores for both cohorts even beyond the effect it had on initial test score and the probability of dropping out of school. Although this is not a new finding, it does reaffirm the long-term importance of family socioeconomic background in later outcomes.

Black and Mexican-origin youth from both cohorts also continue to see their scores decline relative to the scores of non-Hispanic whites, particularly on the math tests. We examined the possibility that black or Mexican immigrant or second-generation youth are particularly disadvantaged in this regard and have differential trajectories than their counterparts from other racial or ethnic groups (see Glick and White 2003). The only evidence we observe for a possible second-generation decline occurs in the HSB cohort for blacks and Mexicans (reading only). We actually observe improvement in reading scores among second-generation Mexicans and Asians in NELS. Note that this failure to find a second-generation deficit has some parallel with the Current Population Survey results presented at the outset of the chapter.

That immigrant status does not emerge as an important predictor of the achievement trajectories over time is noteworthy. A better view of this result is evident in figure 5.3 with the predicted math test score trajectories by generation status. Here the initial gaps in test scores are apparent with the second and third generation outpacing the first in the 1980 cohort, and the first and second generation outperforming the third in the 1990 cohort. However, although the gaps remain, just as the simple statistical test found no significant difference in test gain across the four immigrant status categories, these regression results reveal that the immigrant and the second generation differ little in their overall trajectories, even with the addition of controls. Although unmeasured compositional differences may contribute to the differences we observe at the outset, we find little evidence that generation status continues to exert an independent effect on academic performance over time.

Graduation from High School

Test scores may be meaningful for future educational and labor market opportunities, but education credentials are more directly observable by individuals, and a high school diploma is the key initial credential for labor force advancement and further study (Heckman, Krueger, and Friedman 2003; Jaeger and Page 1996). Further, educational attainment carries both ability and behavioral components and therefore may be a better indicator of effort to participate in the formal status attainment process in the United States than test scores or even grades.

Children of immigrant parents—both immigrant or second-generation youth—may be particularly encouraged to remain in school in spite of encountering structural barriers (Kao and Tienda 1995). One view of immigrants, then, is that they persevere in the face of constraints, such as socioeconomic disadvantage, thanks to familial support (Stanton-Salazar 1997). We test whether that image is correct, particularly after we control for family background, ethnicity, and the like, as we did earlier. The approach is similar to the above examination of in-school performance and again makes use

Figure 5.3   Predicted Math Test Scores from Sophomore Year and Two Years Later, by Generation Status

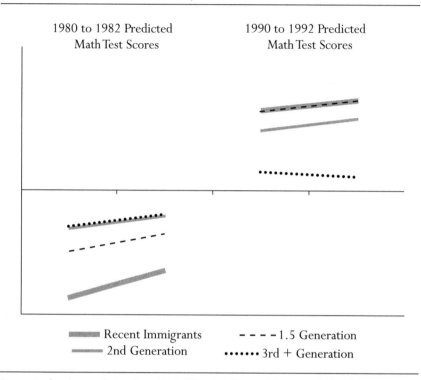

Source: Authors' compilation from High School and Beyond Survey, 1980 and 1982; National Educational Longitudinal Study, 1990 and 1992.
Note: Some proximate lines appear to overlap.

of a regression model. Once again the High School and Beyond data and the National Education Longitudinal Study data enable us to conduct a cohort-specific analysis. We predict high school completion six years after the sophomore year, that is, 1986 and 1996. We then turn to models predicting final educational attainment, when these individuals are in their late twenties, which is 1992 for HSB respondents and 2000 for NELS respondents.

Overall, most adolescents in both cohorts complete high school or earn its equivalent. We observe more variation in completion by race and ethnicity, however, than by generation status. As illustrated in figure 5.4, when we compare by generation status, we see differences in the pattern exhibited in each cohort. For the HSB cohort, the third and higher generations have the highest completion rates (92.4 percent), and the recent immigrants and the second generation the lowest (both approximately 90 percent). For the

NELS cohort, variation is greater, such that the recent immigrants exhibit the highest completion rates (95 percent) and the other generation status groups exhibit similar percentages completing high school (approximately 90 percent). There are some variations by race and ethnicity. Asian youth in both cohorts have the highest completion rates (92 percent in HSB and an even higher 97 percent in NELS) and Mexican-origin youth lag in both cohorts (approximately 83 percent in both). Once again, there is much consistency across the cohorts. The largest difference appears for Cuban youth who have lower high school completion in the HSB cohort (82.5 percent) than in the NELS cohort (92 percent). These slightly differing rates, however, may be just the effect of cross-cutting influences (including age, parental background, and the like) that mostly cancel in the sample we examine. Thus, it is valuable to see what effect, if any, nativity and duration have when one introduces controls for age, family socioeconomic status, ethnic group, and the like.

The multivariate logistic regression models predict high school completion by 1986 or 1996. In other words, we estimate a relatively conservative model such that the student does not need to make an on-time graduation, simply to graduate six years after sophomore year. The vast majority of high school graduates obtain their degree with their cohort or in the following year or so. The results of the models are presented in table 5.4 with one panel for the High School and Beyond cohort predicting graduation by 1986 and a second panel predicting graduation by 1996 for the National Education Longitudinal cohort. The models demonstrate that the little variation in high school completion by generation status is no longer significant once we adjust for the differences in background traits.

Several characteristics in the models are important when predicting high school completion. First, we note that family background, SES, and the like from the sophomore year on continue to exert an impact on educational outcomes even several years later. For both cohorts, higher family SES is associated with a greater likelihood of completing high school. Although this is not surprising, it is worth noting that the strong, predictive effect of SES persists, even controlling for test score (itself partly a function of SES) and parental presence, which is correlated with SES. All told, these results recapitulate many of the results obtained by earlier studies of student achievement. Students with both parents present are also more likely to complete their schooling.

For both cohorts, previous school experiences also continue to impact educational trajectories. Older students, that is, those who are above-age for sophomores, are much less likely to graduate. This most likely reflects earlier poor achievement (or behavioral or family problems) that retard normative movement through school. This is further supported by the significant direct effect of previous grade retention and performance on the standardized tests.

Figure 5.4   High School Completion Six Years After Sophomore
            Year, by Generation Status

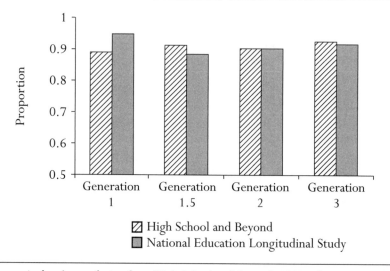

Source: Authors' compilation from High School and Beyond, 1980 cohort; National
Educational Longitudinal Study, 1990 cohort.

In model 3 we include race-ethnicity and language background. We note
some significant differences in the patterns by ethnicity across the cohorts.
African American students in the HSB cohort from backgrounds comparable to the reference group of native non-Hispanic whites have a higher likelihood of completing high school. Although we no longer observe statistically significant coefficients for African Americans in the NELS cohort, the
coefficients are positive, suggesting the lower test score performance for
these students observed earlier is not carried over to high school graduation. We also observe a greater likelihood of school completion among
Asian-origin youth with backgrounds comparable to the reference group of
native non-Hispanic whites for the National Education Longitudinal cohort.
The sample size for Asian-origin youth is larger in this cohort than in the
High School and Beyond cohort, suggesting greater power to detect differences here. The effect of language background is also somewhat different in
the two cohorts, as those from bilingual and non-English homes are more
likely to graduate than those from English-only backgrounds in the High
School and Beyond cohort.

The final models (model 4) include measures for previous school experiences, and the coefficients for them are consistent in both cohorts. The ef-

Table 5.4   Logistic Regression Models Predicting High School Completion Six Years After Sophomore Year

High School and Beyond Cohort

	1	2	3	4
Generation status (third-plus as ref.)				
Recent arrivals	−0.41	0.11	−0.03	0.10
1.5 generation	−0.15	−0.02	−0.08	0.05
Second generation	−0.28*	−0.21	−0.24	−0.13
Male (female as ref.)		−0.19*	−0.19*	−0.17*
Over age seventeen (under seventeen as ref.)		−1.35***	−1.34***	−0.82***
SES		0.49***	0.48***	0.26***
Family structure (both parents as ref.)				
Parent and partner		−0.73***	−0.73***	−0.75***
Single mother		−0.64***	−0.65***	−0.72***
Single father		−0.74***	−0.76***	−0.67***
Neither parent		−1.21***	−1.21***	−1.03***
Family size (one or two siblings as ref.)				
No siblings		−0.03	−0.02	−0.04
Three or more siblings		−0.21*	−0.21**	−0.23**
Race-ethnicity (white as ref.)				
Non-Hispanic black			0.12***	0.57***
Mexican			−0.58***	−0.25
Puerto Rican			−0.60*	−0.26
Other Hispanic			0.03	0.36
Asian			0.04	0.03
Language (English only as ref.)				
Non-English			0.52*	0.46*
Bilingual, non-English dominant			0.40*	0.16
Bilingual, English dominant			0.32*	0.16
Previous grade retention				−0.35***
1980 math test score				0.76***
1980 reading test score				0.19**
Constant	2.50***	3.20***	3.19***	3.44***
F statistic	12.27***	46.46***	29.74***	31.69***

Table 5.4   (Continued)

National Education Longitudinal Cohort

	1	2	3	4
Generation status (third-plus as ref.)				
Recent arrivals	0.48	1.21*	0.84	0.67
1.5 generation	−0.35	0.04	−0.18	−0.30
Second generation	−0.21	0.04	0.06	−0.06
Male (female as ref.)		0.08	0.08	0.04
Over age seventeen (under seventeen as ref.)		−0.82***	−0.83***	−0.27
SES		0.91***	0.94***	0.65***
Family structure (both parents as ref.)				
Parent and partner		−0.58**	−0.60**	−0.60**
Single mother		−0.18	−0.22	−0.28
Single father		−0.11	−0.20	0.32
Neither parent		−0.22	−0.32	−0.12
Family size (one or two siblings as ref.)				
No siblings		−1.56***	−1.56***	−1.37***
Three or more siblings		−0.44*	−0.46*	−0.39
Race-ethnicity (white as ref.)				
Non-Hispanic black			0.26	0.61
Mexican			0.22	0.38
Puerto Rican			−0.39	−0.10
Other Hispanic			0.32	−0.10
Asian			1.45**	1.12*
Language (English only as ref.)				
Non-English			0.01	−0.05
Bilingual, non-English dominant			0.08	0.23
Bilingual, English dominant			−0.72	−0.76
Previous grade retention				−0.54**
1990 math test score				0.93***
1990 reading test score				0.08
Constant	2.42***	3.79***	3.84***	4.07***
F statistic	3.51**	17.15***	15.98***	17.70***

Source: Authors' compilation from High School and Beyond data (weighted) N = 12,697; National Educational Longitudinal Study data (weighted) N = 11,077.
Notes: Family structure and SES variables refer to conditions in sophomore year. Sample excludes Native Americans. Heckman selection models used to predict sophomore test score data.
* $p < .05$, ** $p < .01$, *** $p < .001$

fects for race-ethnicity and language background change with the presence of these variables. The results show, for example, that controlling for lower test scores and higher levels of grade retention among African Americans in the High School and Beyond cohort yields an even greater likelihood of high school completion when compared to the non-Hispanic white reference group.

The final models also show no statistically significant difference in the likelihood of graduating from high school across youth of different generations in either cohort. It is worth remembering that immigrants who arrive as adults are much less likely to already have a high school degree. They thus remain counted as such in statistical sources such as the Current Population Survey. This pooling of immigrants who arrive at all ages into one static comparison is difficult to interpret if one wishes to tell an assimilation story that necessarily expects change as part of the process. Rather, the regression analysis of longitudinal data here tells us that two similarly situated fifteen-year-old sophomores, one an immigrant and one not, both stand a very good chance of graduating from high school.

Educational Attainment in Early Adulthood

Completing high school is an important step toward economic stability and independence. Increasingly in the United States, however, higher education is necessary to secure stable employment with earnings enough for a middle-class lifestyle. Whether because of an increasing demand for consumption or actual increases in living costs, achieving this American Dream is less possible with only a high school diploma in hand. Earnings growth for those with more education has continued to rise but it has leveled off for those with less education (Day and Newberger 2002). Therefore, it is important to look beyond high school at postsecondary education. We last observe our cohorts when they are in their mid-twenties. To the extent that most people have completed their education or are well on their way to completing professional training at this point, we can get some insight into the extent to which immigrant and second-generation youth vary from third- and higher generation peers.

We estimate multinomial logistic regression models of highest education completed by 1992 for the High School and Beyond sophomores and by 2000 for their National Education Longitudinal Study counterparts. This means that we examine completion twelve years after the sophomore year of high school for the HSB cohort and ten years after the NELS cohort. Table 5.5 presents these results comparing four categories: less than high school, high school graduation (reference group), some college, and four-year degree or more. The models continue to control for the background traits in the sophomore year (1980 and 1990), just as our previous models have done.

Table 5.5 Multinomial Logistic Regression Models Predicting Educational Attainment in Young Adulthood

	High School and Beyond Cohort (1992)[a]			National Education Longitudinal Cohort (2000)[a]		
	Less Than High School	Some College	Four-Year Degree or above	Less Than High School	Some College	Four-Year Degree or above
Generation status (third-plus as ref.)						
Recent arrivals	−0.52	0.04	0.71*	−0.33	−0.71	0.45
1.5 generation	−0.27	−0.06	−0.24	0.92	0.30	0.62**
Second generation	0.03	−0.15	−0.11	0.57	0.15	0.52**
Male (female as ref.)	0.19	−0.43***	−0.33***	−0.10	−0.30**	−0.60***
Over age seventeen (under seventeen as ref.)	0.39*	−0.28	−1.33***	0.48	0.08	0.00
SES	−0.21**	0.12**	0.79***	−0.64***	0.02	0.85***
Family structure (both parents as ref.)						
Parent and partner	0.11	−0.29*	−0.53***	0.59*	−0.20	−0.82***
Single mother	0.53***	−0.03	0.01	0.19	−0.17	−0.39**
Single father	0.48	−0.05	0.16	−0.35	−0.28	−0.58*
Neither parent	0.84***	0.06	−0.64*	0.05	0.21	−0.79***
Family size (one or two siblings as ref.)						
No siblings	0.09	−0.23	−0.02	1.39***	0.15	−0.19
Three or more	0.08	−0.23***	−0.25***	0.15	−0.10	−0.30***

Race-ethnicity (white as ref.)						
Black	-0.63***	0.13	0.48***	-0.43	-0.06	0.43*
Mexican	0.36	-0.11	-0.18	-0.51	-0.46	-0.40
Puerto Rican	0.03	-0.33	-0.37	-0.16	-0.68	-0.82*
Other Hispanic	-0.34	0.01	-0.16	-0.57	-0.45	-0.09
Asian	0.65	-0.11	0.31	-1.08	-0.64*	-0.11
Language (English only as ref.)						
Non English	-0.56	0.65**	1.20***	0.02	0.64*	0.25
Bilingual; non-English dominant	0.24	0.41*	0.60**	-0.33	0.36	0.29
Bilingual; English dominant	0.14	0.10	0.07	0.37	0.48*	0.00
Previous grade retention	0.47***	-0.01***	-0.04	0.40	-0.36*	-0.87***
Sophomore math test scores[b]	-0.85***	0.15**	0.90***	-0.87***	-0.07	0.81***
Sophomore reading test scores	-0.30**	0.03	0.36***	-0.05	0.01	0.22***
Constant	-3.79***	-0.60***	-0.86***	-3.99***	-0.91***	-0.16
F	22.06***			20.07***		

Source: Authors' compilation from High School and Beyond Survey data, sophomore cohort (n = 10,985); and National Educational Longitudinal Study, sophomore cohort (n = 11,077).

[a] High school completion is reference group.

[b] Actual test score in 1980 or 1990 for those with available data. Predicted 1980 or 1990 test score for those missing test score.

* $p < .05$; ** $p < .01$; *** $p < .001$

There is little difference in the educational achievement of immigrants, second-generation, and third- and higher generation young adults for the HSB cohort. The positive coefficient for recent arrivals completing a four-year degree or more is based on a rather small number of cases, but the pattern by language background reinforces the sense that these youth may indeed be outperforming peers from English-only homes. For this cohort, non-English and bilingual homes are associated with a lower likelihood of stopping with a high school education net of family background. For the NELS cohort, young adults from the 1.5 and second generation are more likely to complete college than their third- and higher-generation counterparts. Here, too, language background reinforces the message such that those from non-English backgrounds are more likely to have some college education than to stop at a high school education than their peers from English-only homes.

Few racial and ethnic differences remain with background characteristics and school performance in the models. We observe some greater likelihood of college completion for African Americans in both cohorts. What is most striking, however, is the consistent cumulative effect of family background in adolescence on subsequent educational attainment. Family socioeconomic status and structure remain strong independent predictors for both cohorts when they are in their mid-twenties. Results for SES indicate that students who are from more advantaged backgrounds, regardless of immigrant status and background characteristics, are much more likely to attend college in both the HSB and the NELS cohorts, even when we control for previous academic performance, here measured with academic tests and grade retention before tenth grade. The effects of previous school experiences are also consistent across cohorts. Clearly, academically successful high school sophomores are those who are the most likely to complete a four-year degree.

CONCLUSION

Many school systems are wrestling with providing education for recent arrivals, leading perhaps to a perception that immigrants are not doing well in school. Simple descriptive tabulations indicate lower educational attainment on the part of immigrants compared to the native-born. Schools undoubtedly face challenges associated with a rapid influx of children from immigrant backgrounds, including teaching children from many linguistic origins and abilities. Yet such broad-brush comparisons tell only part of the story. Immigrant students (both those who arrived before schooling commenced and those who arrived while it was under way) and second-generation students differ in family background, test score, and ethnicity. These differences may exert independent influences on school completion. Once these other factors—themselves acknowledged to be related to the process of immigration—are controlled, the picture of the difference between immigrants and natives begins to change, and maybe inevitably, it also grows more complicated.

Even when we follow these cohorts well beyond their high school years, it is clear that they carry the effects of their family environment with them. Adolescents from lower SES backgrounds continue to lag behind their more advantaged peers. Even when we control for academic performance in high school, youths from economically disadvantaged backgrounds are much less likely to achieve higher education. This cumulative effect is not a new finding, but, coupled with the results for the declining importance of generation status and race (which mattered significantly for test trajectories but has a much reduced effect beyond high school), it suggests that family resources are key to overcoming structural barriers to educational attainment.

This status attainment process appears to operate similarly across generation status groups. In other words, those youth with higher stores of family and human capital behind them tend to go further in school than those who do not, regardless of whether their parents are foreign born or U.S. born. We do not explain away ethnicity to the same degree, however. So, new arrivals may not do as well as non-Hispanic white natives not because they are immigrants or children of immigrants per se, but because they are members of ethnic minority groups whose trajectories are less positive overall regardless of generation. Although immigrants and those in the second generation are not separate from their racial or ethnic identity, a focus on disparities in attainment by race or ethnicity is applicable to all who contend with the U.S. racial-ethnic system.

Educational achievement is an important ingredient to success in the labor market. More and more analyses point to the dual labor market that has economic rewards for those who attain a college degree and disadvantages for those who do not. We turn in the next chapter to an analysis of labor market outcomes by generation status.

Chapter 6

Work: Labor Market Achievement

THE QUESTION of how well immigrants do is often answered with an evaluation of the labor force experience and earnings of the foreign born. Of all the areas of immigrant adaptation that generate concern in the policy realm, labor market performance has received perhaps the most attention and research.[1] Much of the economic focus has been on the relative performance of new immigrants. Controversy about the economic success or poor performance of immigrants probably accompanies all waves of immigration. The most recent came in the 1980s and 1990s with the claim that previous cohorts of immigrants started out less disadvantaged and experienced more rapid progress to join the ranks of the middle class than more recent cohorts. Although research has certainly gone beyond relying on simplistic assumptions, the debate over declining cohort quality or slowed generational progress has hardly been settled. Early work suggested substantial immigrant socioeconomic assimilation, subsequent work challenged this viewpoint (Borjas 1999), and still more recent work has begun to revisit the question yet again. David Card, in a recent review wrote, "my conclusion is that the revisionist view of recent U.S. immigration is overly pessimistic" (2005, F300). Even one of the key participants in the discussion has examined the seemingly favorable turnaround in immigrant earnings in the 1990s, though seeing some of the apparent upturn in U.S. policy to attract higher skilled immigrants (Borjas and Friedberg 2007). Still, concern persists that recent cohorts are not experiencing the same economic mobility as previous immigrants (Chiswick and Miller 2008).

Often missing from discussions of immigrant success or failure—entering the middle class or forming a new underclass—is attention to the life cycle model and the need to distinguish starting point and trajectory. In this chapter we first set the stage with a few simple descriptive comparisons of immigrant and native outcomes with the Current Population Survey (CPS). Although cross-sectional in design, the CPS has the advantage over other data sources in sample size and focus on economic indicators. Further, the CPS allows us to gain purchase on the debate over changing immigrant cohort quality by examining patterns for immigrants with different periods of entry to the United States. Taking advantage of the fact that the CPS resumed ascertaining detailed immigration information in 1994, we make a number of comparisons of changes for immigrants by period of entry over the 1994 to 2004 decade. We also make cross-sectional comparisons by generation status to illustrate the relative position of the second generation to the first and third or higher. To compare the socioeconomic assimilation picture by immigrant cohort and then by generation, we use CPS data to examine several domains: occupation, poverty, and income.

The CPS data, however, limit our ability to tell the whole story. To gain an even more refined look at the immigrant economic assimilation experience, we turn to truly longitudinal data. Although the framework of chapter 4 (starting point and trajectory) is particularly useful for our understanding of the labor force adaptation of immigrants, information available in the past rarely allowed the researcher to construct a true cohort trajectory. Statements made about immigrant achievement therefore had to be limited to cross-sectional snapshots or inferred indirectly from data on synthetic cohorts drawn from repeated cross-sectional data (Borjas 1985; Chiswick 1978). This difficulty—the lack of nationally representative longitudinal data—and the challenges of modeling and interpreting socioeconomic outcomes led to confusion and debate. (Even the most recent analyses use repeated cross-sections of census and CPS data.) The advantage of looking at younger cohorts and tracing their relative success over time is that we can observe their path from schooling, shared in the United States, through their transition to the labor force (Regets 2001; Zeng and Xie 2004). Here we can again exploit the panel data from the two school-based surveys. We examine the lifecycle experiences of the High School and Beyond (HSB) and National Educational Longitudinal Study (NELS) cohorts as they enter the labor market. Consistent with a life-cycle approach, we can assess early labor market outcomes (at about age twenty-five) as a function of family origins and a variety of other personal characteristics. We can determine how those in the first or second generations differ, if at all, in their trajectory from their starting point.

If the achievement process is the same for natives and immigrants, they will trace identical or parallel paths over time. Chapter 5 suggests this may be the case when we examine paths through schooling, particularly when one considers adjusting for family background and other factors at the starting point. But success is harder to discern if one group, say immigrants, begins at a lower starting point, and traces its trajectory from there. This is particularly true for economic status. Much work of this sort has been conducted, by Borjas and others, where extensive analysis is made of detailed census or cross-sectional survey data. Recent advances in linking Social Security earnings data with census or CPS data can contribute as well, but these approaches still offer a limited view of cross-generation trajectories (Lubotsky 2007). This kind of concern immediately places the question of immigrant attainment in a lifecycle framework, and it calls for the kind of approach we use. Outcomes could differ because only one part of the process differs for immigrants and natives; other aspects do not.

A SNAPSHOT OF DIFFERENCES

We start where most national economic analyses of immigrant progress have started. This has the advantage of capturing the largest groups of immigrants and their earnings at one point in time. Such aggregate snapshots from the census (see Schmidley 2001) or representative cross-sectional surveys almost invariably indicate that immigrants have lower household income, lower annual earnings, and higher poverty rates than natives, but the picture is actually somewhat more diverse. We first make some comparisons of immigrants with their U.S.-born counterparts using the Current Population Survey, a key source of information on the U.S. labor force.[2]

Table 6.1 presents several basic statistics for the immigrant and native population, using the 2004 Current Population Survey as a benchmark. Immigrants and natives are both heavily committed to the labor force, but there are some differences, especially by gender. Immigrant males are more likely to be in the labor force than native males, a difference of roughly 9 percentage points. Table 6.1 also shows that foreign-born males record about a 1 percentage point lower incidence of unemployment than native men. The pattern is reversed among females. Immigrant females are noticeably less likely to be found in the labor force (53.3 percent) than native females (60 percent), and immigrant women are more likely to be unemployed. These patterns have varied somewhat across time. Tabulations from the 1994 CPS indicated that both male and female immigrants had higher rates of unemployment at that time. In addition, table 6.1 shows that the 2004 immigrant poverty rate is nearly half again as high as the native rate.

Another way to compare immigrants' and natives' labor market success is on the basis of earnings and income. Income and earnings data in table 6.2 (also from 2004 Current Population Survey data) indicate that about nearly 27 percent of immigrant male workers make less than $20,000 per year, whereas only about 12 percent of native workers do. Conversely, four in ten

Table 6.1   Labor Force Traits by Nativity, United States 2004

	Native	Foreign Born
Labor force participation - male	70.8%	79.5%
Labor force participation - female	60.0	53.3
Unemployment rate - male	6.7	5.8
Unemployment rate - female	5.4	6.8
Poverty status	11.8	17.2

Source: Authors' compilation from Current Population Survey, March 2004; U.S. Bureau of the Census 2004, Table 1–7; detailed tables PPL-176, available at: http://www.census .gov/population/www/socdemo/foreign/ppl-176.html.

native male workers earn more than $50,000, but only about one in four immigrant workers does. Among female earners the differences are less pronounced, though the earnings differentials clearly favor native women. An examination of data for earlier periods indicates that average native income and earnings have remained significantly higher than income and earnings of immigrants for some time.

On average immigrants are less well-off than natives, but this aggregate fact merely raises questions about the internal diversity of the two groups. It has become common to refer to immigrant socioeconomic outcomes as hourglass shaped, with relatively larger proportions of the immigrant population at both the less and more well-off ends of the spectrum. The idea here is that many immigrants enter at lower levels of education and skill and thus are constrained to the lower wage sector of the market. Conversely, a substantial minority of immigrants enter as highly skilled and sought after and thus earn quite high salaries. Far fewer immigrants, therefore, would be represented in the middle of the income distribution. But this story is only partly reflected in the data. Additional scrutiny of the recent CPS data on income and educational attainment is informative on this point.

As chapter 5 showed, a snapshot of immigrant-native educational differentials shows a complex picture. Current Population Survey data (figure 5.1) clearly indicate that significantly more of the foreign born are without a high school diploma. Further, the immigrant-native differential in 2004 roughly matches that in 1994, especially in the prime labor force years. As we saw for higher education, the immigrant deficit mostly disappears. (In fact, it is the second generation in 2004 that shows highest achievement levels.) Thus, among those in the greater population with at least a high school degree, a larger proportion of immigrants than natives hold baccalaureate or more advanced degrees, 40.6 percent to 33.5 percent (Larsen 2004). This phenomenon is explained by immigrants whose primary and secondary

Table 6.2   Earnings Distribution by Nativity, United States, 2004

Earnings	Male		Female	
	Native	Foreign Born	Native	Foreign Born
$1 to $9,999 or less	2.1%	3.2%	3.7%	5.6%
$10,000 to $14,999	3.6	9.2	6.8	13.7
$15,000 to $19,999	6.2	14.4	9.9	16.0
$20,000 to $24,999	7.9	13.1	12.9	14.8
$25,000 to $34,999	17.5	17.8	23.9	17.9
$35,000 to $49,999	22.3	16.5	22.4	14.9
$50,000 to $74,000	21.6	13.1	13.6	10.9
$75,000 and over	18.6	12.7	6.8	6.4

Source: Authors' compilation from Current Population Survey, March 2004; U.S. Bureau of the Census 2004, table 1–10.
Note: Data for the foreign-born population refer to full-time, year-round workers age sixteen years and older. Data for native workers refer to full-time, year-round workers age fifteen and over. Income in 2003.

schooling has been in the United States pursuing higher degrees and by foreign nationals coming to the United States expressly to do so.

Furthermore, the income distribution statistics indicate something less obvious. Consider the relative proportion of immigrant and native workers within income distributions in table 6.2. The bottom end (among full-time, year-round workers) differs for immigrants and natives. Among males earning less than $20,000 in 2004, 17.6 percent of natives and about 12 percent of immigrants fall in the lowest category (less than $10,000). For native women, the share is about the same as men; for immigrant women the share is higher than for immigrant men, but is still lower than that of native women. Although the overall immigrant earnings distribution is shifted downward, the suggestion is that there are somewhat fewer immigrants in the highly disadvantaged tail of the earnings distribution. The idea that immigrants are forming an underclass of disproportionate size relative to natives gets no support from these tabulations.

At the upper end of the earnings distribution, among males we find that the very highest category ($75,000 and up) is 46.3 percent of those over $50,000; among the foreign born the corresponding share is 49.2 percent, suggesting a slightly more pronounced upper tail for immigrants. A differential in the same direction holds for women's earnings by nativity. All this is to say that these admittedly descriptive tabulations suggest that a closer look is in order. Although immigrants appear to be disadvantaged with respect to natives, this aggregation merely raises questions about the internal diversity of the two groups.

Economic Outcomes by Period of Entry

To this point, our analyses have followed the snapshot approach, comparing all foreign born to all natives in one moment in time. We have not considered the length of time people have lived in the United States or the period of entry to the United States. Certainly much of the debate over immigrant socioeconomic attainment (or lack thereof) has centered on the question of declining cohort quality, suggesting more recent cohorts of immigrants fail to keep pace economically. We take up this comparison relying on the 1994 and 2004 rounds of the Current Population Survey. This gives us a good sense of a decade of cohort progression using synthetic cohorts, that is, a broad comparison of arrival cohorts even though the same individuals may not be reinterviewed.[3] We can then take stock of the occupational distribution, income, and poverty rates for these cohorts. Later we return to analyzing our longitudinal data for cohorts of youth and examine their individual earnings.

Occupation

Of course, some of the inequality observed between immigrants and natives is attributable to their different occupational distributions. If immigrants disproportionately occupy some niches relative to natives, the earnings differentials between immigrants and natives will reflect the imbalance. In addition, if some arrival cohorts are differentially located within occupational niches, cohort differentials in earnings will also be apparent. The CPS offers a broad classification of ten occupations for workers. Even these relatively unrefined categories tell us much, not only about the overall match between immigrant-native occupations, but also about the places of over- and underrepresentation. To illustrate this unequal distribution, we use a well-worked indicator, the dissimilarity index, to summarize the degree of match between natives and immigrants (naturalized and not) across these ten occupations.[4] Values of dissimilarity, D, have a simple interpretation: they indicate the fraction of one of the two groups which would have to change occupation to produce a parallel distribution across the two groups. Values near zero indicate a near match in the occupational pattern; increasing values to a maximum of 100 percent point to increasing disparity.

Figure 6.1 displays the occupational dissimilarity of immigrants (versus natives) by period of entry, for males and females respectively. These graphs represent both the 1994 and the 2004 survey. Clearly, those immigrants who arrived in the few years just before the 1994 or 2004 survey, that is,

Figure 6.1   Occupational Dissimilarity by Arrival Cohort, 1994 and 2004

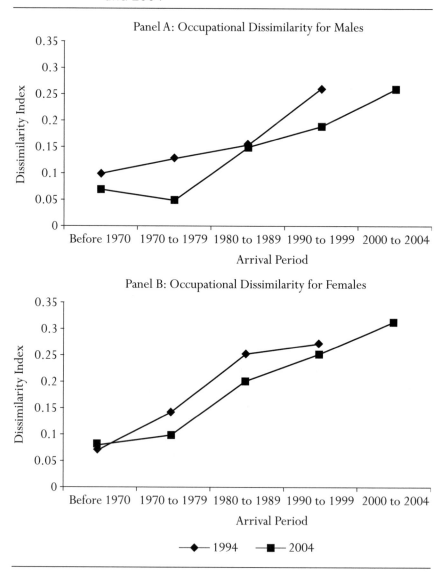

Source: Authors' compilation of U.S. Bureau of the Census, Current Population Survey datafiles, March 1994 and March 2004.

those who are most recently arrived in the United States, display an occupational distribution further removed from that of natives. In the 2004 CPS, males who arrived after 2000 show a dissimilarity of 26 percent, whereas those who arrived before 1970 are at 6 percent. More telling, however, is the cohort progression, that is, the relative position of those who entered in a given decade. For instance, consider men who arrived during the 1970s. Whereas the 1994 survey found their dissimilarity at 12 percent, the 2004 survey showed it at 5 percent. The additional decade in the United States is associated with decreasing differentiation from native workers. The same general pattern holds for women; except the earliest arrivals, the additional decade of U.S. time by 2004 is associated with lower occupational dissimilarity.

This picture is consistent with a view that immigrants do indeed assimilate into the U.S. labor force with time. The strict declining cohort quality picture is less in evidence. It is true that recent male immigrants in the 1990s (evaluated at 2004) are more differentiated from natives than their counterparts in the 1980s (evaluated at 1994); such comparisons, where possible, indicate only a modest shift for both male and female workers, however.

Although the shift in these curves does support the notion of workplace assimilation to natives, other factors could be at work. We compare here only aggregated cohorts, not individual workers. The entry and exit of workers from the labor force (linked to variation in age structure, commitments to the labor force, and even emigration) could all influence these numbers. Of course, these ten categories are crude indicators of occupational niches in a large complex economy. If one wishes to uncover greater occupational sorting among immigrant groups in the United States, it would have to come from more detailed occupational data than one can examine in a labor force survey such as the CPS used here. The promise of such knowledge exists in the New Immigrant Survey (NIS), results from which are just beginning to be seen. Early results from the NIS pilot data do point to appreciable variability in occupation status in the United States compared to the origin country, and a strong association of U.S.-based education with upward occupational mobility (Akresh 2006). Still, the CPS categories in our analysis capture a range of job skills and activities. The balance of evidence supports the view that immigrant workers become more like native workers, both male and female, with time in the American economy.

Our analysis concentrates on the national picture. Our work is also consistent with analysis of occupational distributions in southern California, one of the areas of the country most deeply affected by the arrival of immigrants. More than 25 percent of the population in 1990 was foreign born (Myers 1995). It is a common destination for both less skilled and rural-origin immigrants from Mexico and Central America, for refugees from

Southeast Asia, and for highly skilled immigrants who have received advanced training in either their home countries or the United States.

Myers (1995) examined how immigrants have fared with respect to occupational advancement in this region of the country. He assigned a standard set of occupational prestige scores to the jobs that persons reported in the census.[5] In most cases immigrants who arrived in the 1970s (and thus were tracked between the 1980 and the 1990 census) moved up the occupational prestige ladder in southern California. Young white and Asian immigrant males advanced the most; young Asian and white females also recorded appreciable gains. Latino males exhibited modest gains in occupational prestige at almost every age. Only older white female immigrants showed declines in occupational prestige, while some other groups, particularly workers over the age of forty-five (in 1980), changed little. Perhaps most telling is that all groups of workers who were age twenty-five to forty-four in 1980 (established in the labor force, but still within the first half of their career), experienced increments in occupational prestige. The gain was much more pronounced for white and Asian workers than for southern California Latinos, however. Subsequent analysis of women of Spanish origin confirms the upward mobility within cohort from 1980 to 1990 (Myers and Cranford 1998).

Poverty

Persistent concerns about immigrant failure, even to the point of forming an underclass in American society, argue for an examination of poverty rates over time within these arrival cohorts. Indeed, an examination of poverty may be especially warranted, since those occupying the very bottom rungs of the socioeconomic ladder are of particular concern to policy. A further value to looking at poverty is that poverty statistics are calculated for most persons in the CPS. Thus, unlike earnings and occupations, which provide key portals on economic conditions but are derived from data on those in the labor force, poverty covers everyone.

Figure 6.2 examines poverty status by period of entry. As with occupation, we use the 1994 and the 2004 CPS to provide comparative snapshots and trace the broad experience of the arrival cohort. Because poverty rates fluctuate for all groups according to the health of the economy, we take the ratio of the immigrant poverty rate in each entry-period group to the overall U.S.-born poverty rate. Figure 6.2 provides insight about the economic progress of immigrants—or at least the chance to escape the most disadvantaged economic circumstances. A value of 1.0 in figure 6.2 indicates immigrant-native parity in the incidence of poverty. Values over 1.0 identify higher poverty rates for immigrants than natives in the respective year.

Earlier cohorts, those arriving before 1970, exhibit appreciably lower

Figure 6.2   Poverty by Arrival Cohort, 1994 and 2004

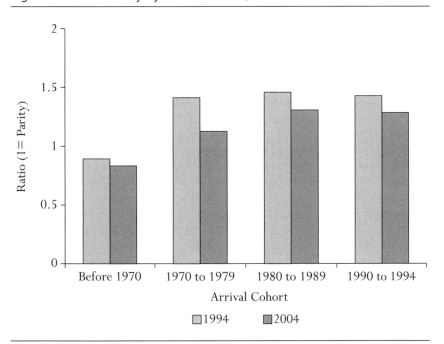

Source: Authors' compilation of U.S. Bureau of the Census, Current Population Survey datafiles, March 1994 and March 2004.
Note: Population below poverty line, ratio of foreign born to natives.

poverty rates than natives, on the order of 10 to 15 percentage points lower. In the 1994 to 2004 decade, the ratio decreased, indicating that the incidence of poverty declined for older vintage immigrants relative to natives. All immigrants who arrived after 1970 show a poverty rate that is higher (ratio > 1.0) than natives. Indeed the immigrant-native ratio reached as high as 1.4:1.0 in the 1994 Current Population Survey. This is of course consistent with much of what is available at any time from a snapshot of the immigrant-native poverty rate. It is also consistent with table 6.1 and has often been observed in basic comparisons of immigrant-native well being.

When we trace the decadal progress of the arrival cohort, we gain further insight and obtain a more dynamic reading of the socioeconomic experience. We see that for all three of the arrival cohorts (1970s, 1980s, and 1990s) the relative incidence of poverty declined over the decade. This does not mean, of course, that the poverty rates were lower for all these immigrants (quite the contrary) but rather, that the poverty gap narrowed. Immigrants who arrived in the 1970s, who had roughly thirty years of U.S. experience by the time of the 2004 CPS, narrowed the gap considerably. The narrowing of the gap for the two more recent cohorts was visible but not as pronounced.

Taken together, these results for poverty status by arrival year also point to progress among immigrants in escaping poverty in the American setting.[6] Many of the same caveats, about shifting population composition, particularly, that we discussed in the occupational case apply as well here. (All non-institutionalized residents of the United States are classified by poverty status, and they are contained in these 1994 and 2004 tabulations. The occupation dissimilarity tabulations include only those in the labor force.) That the pre-1970 immigrant cohort poverty ratio is below 1.0 (and moves downward) lends weight to the argument about declining skill levels among more recent arrivals. Although the pre-1970 comparison involves a somewhat more heterogeneous mix of ages and arrival times, extending back to the beginning of the century, it does suggest that those who came into the United States under the pre-1965 immigration policy regime exhibited traits that favored economic success. Still, post-1965 immigrants, though poorer than natives, are showing relative growth in economic position over time.[7]

Earnings

The next comparison we make is for the earnings of immigrants by arrival cohort compared to natives. Table 6.3 presents all age detail for males; results for women (not shown) are similar.[8] The ratios of immigrant to native earnings in 1994 and 2004 are presented by arrival cohort within the five-year age groups and the far right column of table 6.3 presents the difference in the ratios of immigrant earnings to natives from 1994 to 2004. Some examples help elucidate the overall earnings profiles. Men age twenty-five to twenty-nine in 1994 who have just become established in the workforce are a good illustration. These workers have matured by the time of the 2004 CPS when they are age thirty-five to thirty-nine. The story for median earnings is consistent with information we have taken from the analysis of occupation and poverty. More recent arrival is associated with lower earnings relative to the native benchmark; this is true both in the 1994 survey and in 2004. At the other end are the immigrants who arrived in the pre-1970 era who do well compared to their U.S.-born counterparts. In fact, by 1994 these arrivals had exceeded parity, and had 9 percent higher median earnings than natives in their age cohort. In the following decade their situation declined only slightly, to where their median income remained 5 percent above others in their cohort. For men who arrived during the 1970s, their 1994 position was 78 percent of natives. Their relative position improved considerably—to near parity—over the decade. Those who arrived in the

Table 6.3   Immigrant Earnings Ratio to Natives by Age and Arrival Cohort, Males 1994 and 2004

Age in 1994 (1)	Age in 2004 (2)	Arrival Interval (3)	Ratio-Native 1994 (4)	Ratio-Native 2004 (5)	Change = (5)/(4) (6)
25 to 29 years	35 to 39 years	Before 1970	1.09	1.05	0.96
		1970 to 1979	0.78	0.95	1.22
		1980 to 1989	0.73	0.71	0.97
		1990 to 1999	0.47	0.66	1.40
30 to 34 years	40 to 44 years	Before 1970	1.04	1.05	1.00
		1970 to 1979	0.83	0.77	0.93
		1980 to 1989	0.63	0.69	1.10
		1990 to 1999	0.46	0.66	1.45
35 to 39 years	45 to 49 years	Before 1970	1.09	1.13	1.03
		1970 to 1979	0.79	0.75	0.95
		1980 to 1989	0.65	0.73	1.11
		1990 to 1999	0.45	0.55	1.23
40 to 44 years	50 to 54 years	Before 1970	0.97	0.75	0.78
		1970 to 1979	0.70	0.77	1.10
		1980 to 1989	0.50	0.75	1.50
		1990 to 1999	0.37	0.52	1.42
45 to 49 years	55 to 59 years	Before 1970	0.90	0.92	1.01
		1970 to 1979	0.65	0.78	1.21
		1980 to 1989	0.48	0.65	1.34
		1990 to 1999	0.31	0.56	1.79
50 to 54 years	60 to 64 years	Before 1970	0.81	1.39	1.71
		1970 to 1979	0.69	1.67	2.42
		1980 to 1989	0.47	0.93	1.99
		1990 to 1999	0.30	1.20	3.98

Source: Authors' compilation of U.S. Bureau of the Census, Current Population Survey datafiles, March 1994 and March 2004.

1980s earned about 73 percent of the earnings of natives in the cohort, a position that hardly shifted over the decade. Finally, men who arrived in the 1990s witnessed a substantial improvement in their relative earnings, from 47 percent of natives to 66 percent. Of course, not all the 1990s arrivals had yet arrived to be counted in 1994.

The immigrants who arrived in the earlier periods and who were in their mid-twenties in 1994 are not unlike the 1.5-generation immigrants we observe with our longitudinal data. Recall from our analyses of education in chapter 5 that these immigrants arriving as young children do as well, and in some cases better, than their peers. It is likely that the 1.5-generation immigrants observed here in the CPS data received much of their schooling in the United States, just as those in our longitudinal datasets did. Our subsequent analyses of earnings for our two adolescent cohorts will offer a longitudinal comparison of earnings for these early life arrivals and their higher-order generation peers. Overall, though, the CPS data shows that even the more recent arrivals who arrived in the United States as young adults still trace improvement relative to natives over time.

A look at older workers shows a simpler pattern. For example, those age forty-five to forty-nine in 1994 show a shift downward as time of arrival becomes closer to the present. Pre-1970 immigrants among these more established workers are slightly below parity, earning about 90 percent of native workers at both times. Men arriving in the 1970s, 1980s, and 1990s all exhibit significant improvement in their relative position over the decade. Particularly instructive might be men in this cohort who arrived in the 1970s. Most arrived about twenty years before the 1994 survey and were at that time in their late twenties. This would fit the classic age-migration profile. Men in this cohort, though clearly remunerated at lower levels than their U.S.-born counterparts, gained on the reference group over the period.

It is clear that immigrants with less time in the United States—in the same age cohort—begin with inferior incomes, yet their relative position improves over time. This occurs in the preponderance of comparisons we make in table 6.3, which present, respectively, the 1994 and 2004 ratios for each cohort and arrival group. Of the twenty-four comparisons we can make of change in relative position over the decade, immigrants improved in all but four.

These results—amplified by the results for poverty—suggest that the position of immigrants, when seen in a cohort perspective, has not deteriorated in recent years. On balance, the relative position of immigrants improves relative to natives of the same age group. Our results provide more evidence for immigrant progress than declining cohort quality. We can make a further comparison from table 6.3. Consider the immigrants who have had the same U.S. experience at the time of the survey—in other words, those who arrived the same number of years before the survey. Specifically, compare 1980s arrivals in 1994 with 1990s arrivals in 2004. In the aggregate, both groups have roughly the same U.S. experience. Under the declining cohort quality argument, those who arrived more recently should have inferior outcomes, linked to lower skill levels. There is no consistent pattern in table 6.3 on this issue.

Even though they involve arrival cohorts and build on the superior quality of CPS data (which measured nativity from 1994 forward), these analyses do not track the same individuals one by one over time. So, though these CPS data do not lend support to the declining cohort quality thesis, we cannot determine the extent to which these patterns may be attributable to differences in background traits by nativity or across cohorts.

Economic Outcomes by Generation Status

Although we observe little evidence of a decline in cohort quality among immigrants, the comparison to this point has not considered the second generation. Comparisons of immigrants to all natives ignore generational progression predicted by various assimilation perspectives. So here we consider three economic indicators—occupation, poverty, and income—once again but with an eye to comparing the first, second, and subsequent generations in preparation for our longitudinal analyses.

Occupation

We have already observed considerable variation in the occupational niches occupied by immigrants and natives in the United States. The assimilation framework would forecast much less differentiation across the higher-order generations. So, we compare the dissimilarity index for adults of different generation statuses across the ten occupations we earlier examined for arrival cohorts. Table 6.4 presents the occupational distribution for immigrants, the second generation, and the third and higher generations in 2004, for males and females, respectively. Our analysis from the recent CPS data indicates that about 17 percent of male immigrant workers would need to change occupations to produce an identical occupational pattern across the third and higher generations and immigrants.[9] A closer inspection points to expected occupational differentials. U.S.-born males in the third and higher generations claim larger shares of managerial positions among workers in 2004, but professional occupations are only modestly differentiated. Immigrant men are disproportionately represented in service, construction, productions, and extractive occupations relative to the third and higher generations. The last includes farming, fishing, and forestry, a grouping in which immigrants are concentrated at nearly double the rate of natives.

Immigrants are sharply underrepresented in the professional occupations

Table 6.4   Occupational Distributions and Dissimilarity, United States, 2004

Males

	First Generation (n)	Second Generation (n)	Third Generation (n)	Absolute Difference First to Third	Second to Third
Management, business, and financial occupations	0.09 (864)	0.16 (547)	0.17 (7,027)	0.07	0.01
Professional and related occupations	0.14 (1,267)	0.18 (627)	0.16 (6,866)	0.03	0.02
Service occupations	0.19 (1,755)	0.14 (472)	0.12 (5,121)	0.07	0.02
Sales and related occupations	0.08 (732)	0.13 (435)	0.11 (4,800)	0.03	0.01
Office and administrative support occupations	0.05 (476)	0.08 (288)	0.06 (2,579)	0.01	0.02
Farming, fishing, and forestry occupations	0.02 (227)	0.01 (23)	0.01 (462)	0.01	0.00
Construction and extraction occupations	0.15 (1,409)	0.09 (297)	0.11 (4,675)	0.04	0.02
Installation, maintenance, and repair occupations	0.05 (469)	0.06 (204)	0.07 (2,887)	0.02	0.01
Production occupations	0.13 (1,168)	0.07 (242)	0.08 (3,567)	0.04	0.01
Transportation and material moving occupations	0.10 (889)	0.09 (318)	0.10 (4,288)	0.00	0.01
Total employed civilian workers	1.00 (9,256)	1.00 (3,453)	1.00 (42,212)		
Dissimilarity				0.17	0.07

Females

	First Generation (n)	Second Generation (n)	Third Generation (n)	Absolute Difference First to Third	Second to Third
Management, business, and financial occupations	0.09 (602)	0.13 (430)	0.13 (5,268)	0.04	0.00
Professional and related occupations	0.18 (1,198)	0.24 (822)	0.25 (10,066)	0.07	0.00
Service occupations	0.31 (2,065)	0.18 (614)	0.20 (8,097)	0.11	0.02
Sales and related occupations	0.11 (730)	0.14 (470)	0.12 (4,987)	0.01	0.02
Office and administrative support occupations	0.16 (1,039)	0.25 (858)	0.23 (9,469)	0.08	0.02
Farming, fishing, and forestry occupations	0.01 (78)	0.00 (11)	0.00 (108)	0.01	0.00
Construction and extraction occupations	0.00 (21)	0.00 (11)	0.00 (165)	0.00	0.00
Installation, maintenance, and repair occupations	0.00 (18)	0.00 (8)	0.00 (147)	0.00	0.00
Production occupations	0.11 (715)	0.03 (85)	0.04 (1,590)	0.07	0.01
Transportation and material moving occupations	0.03 (223)	0.02 (58)	0.02 (764)	0.01	0.00
Total employed civilian workers	1.00 (6,689)	1.00 (3,367)	1.00 (40,661)		
Dissimilarity				0.20	0.04

Source: Authors' compilation of U.S. Bureau of the Census, Current Population Survey datafiles, March 1994 and March 2004.
Note: Data refer to those sixteen years old and above. Armed Forces occupations have been dropped from the analyses.

and significantly overrepresented in manual labor. Clearly then, immigrants are finding niches in the economy that differ from natives, and these slots differ somewhat by gender. But the second generation has an occupational distribution much more similar to that of the third and higher generations. Only some 7 percent of the second generation would need to shift occupations to have a distribution identical to those in the third and higher generations. In addition, evidence of a bimodal distribution is scant, as one might expect under a segmenting process for the second generation. If anything, the second generation is overrepresented in the professions and underrepresented in the extraction industries relative to those in the third and higher generations.

Female immigrant workers show even more differentiation from third and higher generation females than males do. The patterns are presented in table 6.4. Overall, the dissimilarity index for the first generation relative to the third stands at 20 percent. Immigrant female workers are much more likely than native women to be found in service, production, and transportation. The sample size is much smaller for the second generation and we find little difference within the third and higher generations. For the first-generation women, however, we find that occupational distinctiveness from natives is even higher than for men.[10]

Several factors would lead one to anticipate occupational distinctiveness, even beyond that introduced by initial socioeconomic differentials. First, of course, is the admission criteria, which differentially select from the pool of those who want to come to the United States. Family reunification, it is argued, leads to less selective flows of immigrants. So does undocumented migration. On the other hand, some authorized categories of admission—built specifically around occupation—lead to the arrival of relatively skilled immigrants. Furthermore, some of those who ultimately obtain green cards enter the United States on other grounds, particularly as students, and then if successful obtain a permanent job and residence. Stepping back from these facets of U.S. immigration policy, one can consider the occupational distribution of the countries of origin themselves. The skill mix of the United Kingdom, the Philippines, or Mexico will influence the composition of the migration stream to the United States.

Poverty

We also consider the levels of poverty among the first, second, third, and higher generations using the Current Population Surveys. We tabulate poverty by age group and generation, comparing progress of those in the working ages. We carried out this calculation for all 1994 age groups from twenty-five to twenty-nine through forty-five to forty-nine. These capture the key labor force years. Figure 6.3 presents relative poverty rates for the first and second generation (expressed as a ratio to the poverty rate of the

Figure 6.3   Relative Poverty by Generation Status

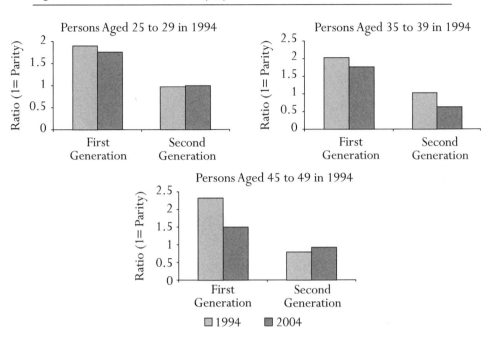

Source: Authors' compilation of U.S. Bureau of the Census, Current Population Survey datafiles, March 1994 and March 2004.

third and higher order generation) for three of these age groups: twenty-five to twenty-nine, thirty-five to thirty-nine, and forty-five to forty-nine. The figure illustrates the change in poverty for these same age cohorts ten years later (the twenty-five to twenty-nine 1994 cohort when they are thirty-five to thirty-nine in 2004, and so on). Overall, poverty levels for the first generation relative to the third decrease over the ten year intervals for all age groups. Again, the first generation is more likely to be in poverty than the third, but this difference narrows over time. Looking at these ratios for the second generation presents a slightly more mixed picture by age. Overall, however, the ratio to the third generation is very close.

Earnings

Our third indicator of economic status uses the survey data to look at median income, the best summary measure we have of the location of the aver-

Figure 6.4   Earnings Distribution, Males, 1994

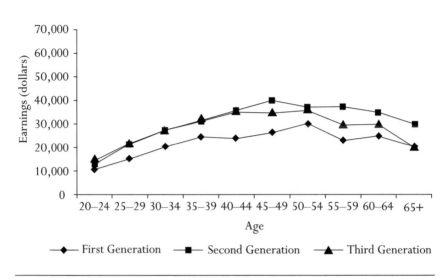

Source: Authors' compilation of U.S. Bureau of the Census, Current Population Survey datafiles, March 1994 and March 2004.

age position of immigrants and natives. Again we take data from the 1994 and 2004 CPS and compare earnings of the foreign born, the second generation, and their third- or higher-generation counterparts by age. Figures 6.4 through 6.7 present these results separately for males and females. First-generation earnings are lower than the higher generations at most age groups for both 1994 and 2004. The second generation, on the other hand, averages slightly higher earnings than the third or higher generation at several ages. This is most notable in 2004, particularly for females (figure 6.7). Overall, these results accord well with the patterns presented for education in which the second generation seemed advantaged by 2004 (see figure 5.1).

The CPS Results in Summary

These results do not suggest a decline in economic status for the second generation when compared to other natives in the U.S. labor force. The occupational distribution of the second generation hardly differs from that of the third and higher generations, and earnings are on par or even display an advantaged position among the second generation at older ages. Although these CPS results do not support the notion of a decline in economic status among the second generation relative to the third, we cannot infer the rela-

Figure 6.5 Earnings Distribution, Males, 2004

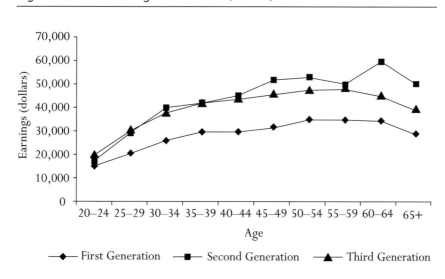

Source: Authors' compilation of U.S. Bureau of the Census, Current Population Survey datafiles, March 1994 and March 2004.

Figure 6.6 Earnings Distribution, Females, 1994

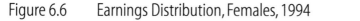

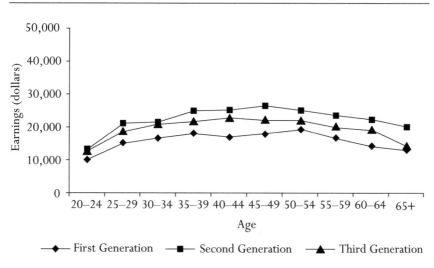

Source: Authors' compilation of U.S. Bureau of the Census, Current Population Survey datafiles, March 1994 and March 2004.

Figure 6.7   Earnings Distribution, Females, 2004

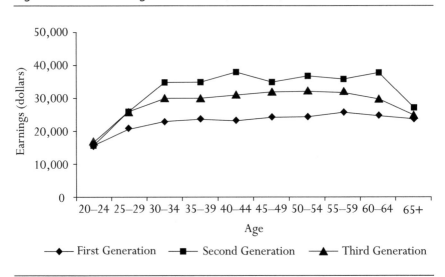

Source: Authors' compilation of U.S. Bureau of the Census, Current Population Survey datafiles, March 1994 and March 2004.

tive importance of background traits and generation in economic advancement. For this reason, we now turn to truly longitudinal (panel) data, following nationally representative cohorts of individuals who enter a survey while in their youth and tracked into their early labor force years. This restricts our focus to early labor market outcomes but gives us excellent purchase on the entrance paths of young adults.

Insights from Panel Data: Early Adult Earnings in HSB and NELS

Our earlier analyses focusing on the educational pathways of immigrant youth, the second generation, and their third- and higher-order generation counterparts suggested considerable parity in achievement once background traits are considered. Likewise, to understand how well immigrants do in the labor market, it is useful to consider the relative performance of immigrants and their peers within cohorts. The continuing debate over the relative earnings assimilation of immigrants has largely relied on comparisons by entry cohorts and has, in some cases, pointed to a negative pattern over time

(Chiswick and Miller 2008). But the story is quite complex. There are several benefits of using our longitudinal cohort data. First, we can compare immigrants and descendants of immigrants who share contexts in adolescence—that is, all going to school in the United States. This within-cohort analysis eliminates the concern about place of education as an influence on labor market returns (Zeng and Xie 2004; Clark and Jaeger 2006). Of course, the immigrant parents of our first- and second-generation respondents are selected differently, which could have an influence on outcomes at the starting point (Feliciano 2006). Our analyses for educational achievement, however, suggested family background traits have a similar influence on outcomes across generation groups. Here we go beyond the educational achievement for these cohorts and extend into the earnings of young adulthood.

We examine trajectories that stem from adolescence and continue into the early labor force years. We use the HSB data to trace the experience of high school sophomores who were about age fifteen in 1980 up through 1990, and we use the NELS to trace a comparative group from sophomore year who were near age fifteen in 1990 up through 2000. Our goal remains determining the effects of nativity and U.S. duration on socioeconomic trajectory.

Once again, the particular strength of the analysis rests on access to truly longitudinal and nationally representative data. Even the CPS data do not track the very same individuals over time. So, while we were able to make some general statements about arrival cohorts and age at arrival, this lack of panel data makes it very difficult to sort out the various influences on socioeconomic attainment. Other studies look intensely at immigrants, and perhaps the second generation, in a highly focused geographic setting, which has the advantage of limiting labor market conditions but also limits the populations under investigation.

The panel data we use here offer several advantages in the study of economic progress. HSB and NELS contain annual income information for cohort members. As we see in chapter 5, these two data sources contain information on family background and school performance (including standardized tests). The panels are nationally representative, and considerable effort was involved to follow up sample members. Thus, these panel data are well suited to help disentangle the trajectory of achievement from the influence of starting point, a task for which many other data sources are inadequate. The panels run long enough for us to observe each of the two cohorts a decade later. Thus we can measure and analyze their labor market outcomes in 1990 and 2000, with income reported for the full year prior. This period, about eight years after anticipated high school graduation for each cohort, is long enough for us to observe early labor market outcomes. And because respondents are followed up regularly and asked in detail about their work histories, wages, and sources of income, reporting of individual annual earnings should be better than from other sources.

Starting Point

That the survey tracks individuals over time means that we can examine the actual trajectories that these individuals achieve and estimate how outcomes vary as a function of immigrant status, language, and family background. We illustrated the differences in family socioeconomic status background by generation of the two samples in table 5.1. This is one way to measure the starting point for the cohorts. Immigrants and the second generation are generally somewhat disadvantaged in terms of family background compared to third- and higher-order generation natives. The difference between third-plus generation youths and recent immigrant youths in both NELS and HSB samples approaches one-half standard deviation. Differences with the 1.5 and second generation are more modest, and there is even an anomalous case that the 1.5-generation students in the HSB (1980 cohort) are more advantaged than others. Again, some of these differences are likely related to the sample structure of the earlier HSB study; our longitudinal analysis adjusts for this.

Snapshots Ten Years Out

Table 6.5 presents several basic statistics on labor force attachment for the two surveys and for both males and female, by immigrant status. Approximately 90 percent or more men (about age twenty-five) in both cohorts were working in the year before the survey. Slightly greater labor force attachment is found for the HSB (1980) cohort, which may be due to economic conditions for young workers at the time. There is very little differentiation across immigrant status in this measure of labor market outcome.

Young women exhibit lower levels of labor force participation, but the differential from men is modest, indicating the considerable labor force attachment of women in young adulthood. Women in the third-plus generation participate in the labor force at about 90 percent of the level of males from their cohort. A comparison across immigrant status points to little systematic variation: sometimes a bit lower, sometimes a bit higher. These gender-specific results do argue that the general labor force commitment (at least working in some capacity during the year) is pervasive. The consideration that young immigrant and second-generation women might withdraw significantly from the labor force and observe more traditional roles (at home, either with parents or partners) is not the picture here.

Table 6.6 presents descriptive results for the median annual earnings in the year before the most recent wave of each survey. Again, we calculate these median values for both young men and women and for both cohorts. These are earnings from all sources. Although not all of these individuals have finished schooling or other skill-building activities, the overwhelming

Table 6.5   Labor Force Participation in Young Adulthood

Worked in Previous Year	Male	Female
High School and Beyond cohort, 1989		
Generation status		
Recent arrivals	95.46	81.04
1.5 generation	94.74	87.49
Second generation	93.47	82.51
Third and higher generation	95.42	85.12
National Education Longitudinal cohort, 1999		
Generation status		
Recent arrivals	89.62	85.32
1.5 generation	91.87	74.82
Second generation	92.32	84.60
Third and higher generation	94.18	85.09

Source: Authors' compilation of High School and Beyond data and National Educational Longitudinal Study data.
Notes: HS&B sophomore cohort (weighted) N = 5,049 males; 5,368 females.
NELS sophomore cohort (weighted) N = 4,873 males; 5,460 females.

fraction has. Thus our window on the sample is well positioned to capture the relative success of individuals as a function of their background, generation, and other traits.

Some differences emerge in the table, but not always in the expected direction. Consider first the HSB sample, the 1980 cohort.[11] Men of the second and third generation earn about the same annually, and those of the 1.5 generation earn only slightly less. Men in the first generation who arrived while schooling was well under way earn more. In the younger NELS cohort we find a pattern in which the third-plus generation shows the lowest median annual earnings, and the second generation edges out both subgroups of the first generation. Members of the 1.5, second, and third generations in the younger cohort appear to have superior earnings at age twenty-five than those in the older cohort, at least given the adjustment for inflation.

Among females, there is less consistency. The likelihood of any work during the previous year and the proximity to full-time employment is more variable. In the older cohort, the 1.5 generation immigrants record the highest median income, followed by the third-plus generation. In the younger NELS cohort, the recent immigrant females show the higher income level, followed by the second generation.

This snapshot of earnings, coming after the panels had run for a decade, suggests some variability in economic outcomes for young adults by generation status. A more telling account can be presented when we consider the role of family background, ethnicity, and school progression, along with immigrant status, to help predict that outcome. In other words, we can trace a more accurate account of the opportunity structure available to young adults when we consider their diverse starting points and examine their trajectory.

Trajectory

In the years immediately following high school, young adults take an enormous variety of paths. Some go immediately into the labor force, some to the military, some to higher education, and some have difficulty finding any productive activity. Chapter 5 provided a window on schooling. Comparisons from aggregated information are especially problematic. Outcomes measured in these years cannot fully capture the heterogeneity and, more important, cannot reflect the differential returns expected to accrue to those who forgo earnings for further training. Thus the analysis of income differences as of the 1990 and 2000 survey waves, nearly a decade after the expected date of high school graduation, is able to shed considerable light into the comparative influence of family background, immigrant status, and performance in school. This span is long enough for some of those early decisions to have played out.

We now bring in our life cycle approach, akin to what we used to follow education paths in chapter 5. We analyze the earnings outcomes of the two cohorts predicted from family structure, socioeconomic status, grade completion, race and ethnicity, generation, and previous earnings. As we discussed earlier, this specification is designed to allow us to examine trajectory, as well as starting point, to better understand where immigrants, the second generation, and higher-order generations are by their mid-twenties.

These models address several theoretical concerns in our work. First, they tell us about comparative models of generational success and being left behind. A considerable literature points to the particularly successful advance of the second generation. We could see that here in the second and perhaps the 1.5 generation. Our interpretation would be that members of the second generation should super-achieve, that is, realize outcomes superior to that based on starting point and initial trajectory. Conversely, these models should help us understand and evaluate issues of declining cohort quality. Note that chapter 5 pointed out the superior education for one portion of the second generation. That chapter's longitudinal analysis also found that immigrants and the second generation do not trace inferior trajectories once we account for their starting point. Finally, this longitudinal approach can shed additional light on segmented assimilation. As we have argued, our interpretation of segmented assimilation is that achievement of immigrants and the second generation should be conditioned by their race and ethnic background. Specific measures of ethnicity can test for this in our multivariate framework.

As with our analyses for education, the analyses of earnings are presented with successively more comprehensive models. We begin with a rudimentary model that includes only generational (immigrant status) covariates. We then introduce family background measures, examining both the degree to which they are important and the degree to which their presence increases or decreases the apparent effects of immigrant status. We then add a set of race-ethnicity variables, entered as dummy variables to capture the major groups identifiable in the HSB and NELS school-based surveys. These ethnic effects also shed light on the segmented assimilation hypothesis. We next add measures of language ability, for several reasons. Non-English language origins may indicate impediments to assimilation and success in the U.S. labor market. Language also is correlated with and competes with ethnicity in determining employment and earnings. There is also some evidence in the literature that individuals from bilingual backgrounds may actually do better in their socioeconomic outcomes.

Finally, we include measures of earlier achievement—high school graduation and income two years before the survey—to get a better sense of the individual trajectory, adding these intermediate indicators of achievement. We are also interested in whether these intermediate variables shift the size and significance of other indicators in the model.

Results for Males

Table 6.7 presents earnings trajectory regression results for the 1980 (HSB) cohort and the 1990 (NELS) cohort, respectively. In all cases we regress the natural logarithm of earnings on the various covariates. Furthermore, we have estimated a selection model in which we adjust for the availability of data for the respondents in the outcome year.[12]

We start with the model predicting 1989 income for the 1980 (HSB) cohort, incrementing the set of traits as described. Model 1 simply recapitulates the results of table 6.6, showing that recent arrivals have higher income than third-plus generation individuals, the reference group. Model 2 adds age, the SES index, and measures of family structure that characterized the individual circumstance in high school, at about age seventeen. Several of these variables are quite powerful, as we might expect. In our 1980 cohort, each additional unit (standard deviation) of SES predicts another 5 percent in 1989 income. The effects of family structure are also powerful, with those who lived in family structures other than two-parent families when they were in high school experiencing lower income in young adulthood. Race-

Table 6.6   Median Earnings in Young Adulthood

Median Earnings	Male	Female
High School and Beyond cohort, 1989		
Generation status		
Recent arrivals	$32,000	$16,640
1.5 generation	24,320	19,200
Second generation	25,600	16,640
Third and higher generation	25,600	17,920
National Education Longitudinal cohort, 1999		
Generation status (third as ref.)		
Recent arrivals	30,000	30,000
1.5 generation	29,000	15,000
Second generation	31,500	21,000
Third and higher generation	27,000	19,000

Source: Authors' compilation of High School and Beyond data and National Educational Longitudinal Study data.
Notes: 1989 earnings are adjusted to 1999 dollars.
HS&B sophomore cohort (weighted) N = 5,049 males; 5,368 females.
NELS sophomore cohort (weighted) N = 4,873 males; 5,460 females.

ethnicity (model 3) introduces an additional effect, with those from black and other Hispanic backgrounds predicted to have statistically significant deficits in income, compared to otherwise equivalent young men. The effects of language are slight and not statistically significant.

Model 4 adds an indicator for receipt of the high school diploma, at least by 1986, within four years of expected graduation time for this cohort. High school completion is associated with an appreciable income premium. Finally, model 5 introduces income level two years before the 1990 survey (1989 income). Not surprisingly, those with greater earnings in 1987 are expected to show greater earnings in 1989. These are the outlines of various factors that influence status attainment (income) in our cohort. Immigrant status coefficients do not budge much from model 1 to model 5, and their level of statistical (non)significance also does not change.[13]

Model 3 and model 5 are worth a closer look. Model 3 takes into account all the background factors—family SES, family composition, home language environment, race-ethnicity—but nothing more. Model 5 does incorporate two critical intermediate measures of the trajectory, high school graduation and income two years prior. In both these comparisons, and after controlling for the selection process, we find no differences in the 1.5 and second generation from the third-plus generation.[14] We do find that recent immigrants in this cohort are predicted to have incomes greater than one would expect on the basis of these other background factors. We find that the receipt of a high school diploma is associated with an improvement in earnings, here about 13 percent. Earnings in 1987 also are strongly and positively associated with earnings in 1989. Even when we include covariates for receipt of high school diploma and for 1987 earnings, the picture regarding immigrant status changes very little. Young men of the first generation trace significantly superior earnings trajectories than one would expect on the basis of background traits alone.

For males in the more recent NELS cohort who graduated high school in about 1992 and were about age twenty-five at the time of the survey, the picture differs somewhat. Here, model 1 shows no differences from the third generation for any of the three other immigrant status groups. Additional controls, however, bring statistically significant differences in predicted income by immigrant status. Model 3, which includes all traits determined before age eighteen, exhibits only ethnic effects among these young men. Family socioeconomic status is not statistically significant here in part because of the number of young men in NELS from higher SES backgrounds who do not have valid earnings data for 1999. The direction of the SES effect, however, is consistent with the HS&B analyses and the results for women discussed below.

The most inclusive analysis, model 5, shows very strong effects of high school graduation, prior earnings, and several background traits. It indicates that NELS males of all immigrant groups do better than otherwise comparable natives of the third- and higher-order generations (the third generation). Newly arrived members of the first generation are expected to earn nearly 30 percent more than their more established native counterparts. Members of the second generation are expected to earn about 12 percent more. For the 1.5 generation (those who arrived before commencing school), there is a predicted higher level of earnings (about 6 percent), but this differential is not statistically significant.

We note that in this regression the receipt of a high school diploma is associated with about a 20 percent higher level of 1999 earnings. Income in 1997 is clearly and significantly associated with 1999 income. The results for this more recent NELS cohort, a decade younger than the HSB cohort, exhibit stronger returns to both high school graduation and earlier earnings than seen in model 5 of table 6.7, HSB cohort.

Results for Females

Table 6.8 presents the earnings regression results for women in the two cohorts. Recall that labor force participation was somewhat lower for women, but some 85 percent of women in the third-plus generation report being at work in the previous year.[15] High School and Beyond women (the 1980 co-hort) would be about fifteen in 1980 and about twenty-five in 1990. The story here is about what is not present. In our various models that include a selection correction and the addition of increasing numbers of covariates, we find almost no statistically significant differences across generations. Even in the basic model, no generational coefficient is significant statisti-cally, and the magnitude of any differences is at most a few percentage points. Introducing additional predictors does nothing to change this. In most models, including model 5, the most inclusive, the direction of the dif-ference tends to be negative, indicating that young first- and second-gener-ation female workers would be expected to earn a little less than third-gen-eration counterparts from similar backgrounds. Given that these results are not even borderline significant, it is difficult to make any conclusion other than the one of no difference across generations.

For women in the younger NELS cohort, we find statistical significant immigration status effects in all models ranging from model 1 with no other controls (except a selection adjustment) to model 5 with the full set of co-variates. In model 1, controlling for selection and nothing else, second-gen-eration women are seen to have incomes about 14 percent above the com-parison group of those in the third-plus generation. Again parallel to the case of men, women in the first generation are predicted to have higher in-comes than the comparison group. No difference is found for young women in the 1.5 generation.

These patterns hold up upon the introduction of further controls for fam-ily background and ethnicity. Model 2 points to very strong SES effects on women's earnings, and women are still differentiated by immigrant status. Model 4 indicates formidable predictive power for high school graduation and prior earnings (stronger effects than the corresponding equation for males), and the magnitude of immigrant status effects remains. In this most inclusive model, the second generation is indicated to have earnings about 15 percent above what would otherwise be anticipated on the basis of per-sonal traits. Recent immigrant (first-generation) women also show much higher earnings, but women who arrive in time to attend school (the 1.5 generation) do not differ. Women in the first generation are predicted to have earnings more than 40 percent higher than their third-generation counterparts. This differential seems extraordinarily high; it is most likely driven by gaps in background traits and the degree of labor market attach-ment between the two generations.[16]

We also estimated models (not shown) that split the sample by genera-tion. In these, we did not find statistically significant differences. The sam-ples are admittedly smaller for the first and second generation, but strong evidence of segmentation is difficult to see. Still, an overall race-ethnicity ef-fect in the pooled sample remains.

Table 6.7 Regression Models Predicting Earnings (Logged) in Young Adulthood, Males

High School and Beyond Cohort

	1	2	3	4	5
Generation status (third-plus as ref.)					
Recent arrivals	0.28**	0.32**	0.32**	0.32**	0.30***
1.5 generation	−0.01	0.00	0.01	0.01	0.03
Second generation	0.005	0.02	0.02	0.03	0.02
Age (age seventeen or over as ref.)		−0.09*	−0.08	−0.06	−0.05
SES		0.05***	0.04***	0.04**	0.05***
Family structure (both parents as ref.)					
Parent and partner		−0.15**	−0.14**	−0.13*	−0.13**
Single mother		−0.04	−0.02	−0.02	−0.02
Single father		−0.01	−0.01	0.00	−0.02
Neither parent		−0.13*	−0.09	−0.08	−0.08
Family size (one or two siblings as ref.)					
No siblings		0.02	0.02	0.02	0.02
Three or more siblings		0.07**	0.07**	0.07***	0.07**
Race-ethnicity (white as ref.)					
Non-Hispanic black			−0.16***	−0.16***	−0.15***
Mexican			−0.04	−0.02	−0.04
Puerto Rican			−0.01	0.00	−0.03
Other Hispanic			−0.13*	−0.12**	−0.13*
Asian			0.00	0.00	0.01
Language (English only as ref.)					
Non-english			−0.01	−0.01	−0.02
Bilingual, non-English dominant			0.01	0.00	0.01
Bilingual, English dominant			−0.01	−0.01	−0.01
High school graduation by 1986 (no grad as ref.)				0.14***	0.13**
Logged previous income in 1987					0.07***
Constant	9.90***	9.89***	9.90***	9.77***	9.09
Log pseudolikelihood	−5396.25	−5354.46	−5337.94	−5358.04	−5167.55
rho	−0.87	−0.87	−0.87	−0.86	−0.83
lambda	−0.56	−0.56	−0.56	−0.55	−0.51

(Table continues on p. 142.)

Table 6.7 (Continued)

National Education Longitudinal Cohort

	1	2	3	4	5
Generation status (third-plus as ref.)					
Recent arrivals	0.04	0.05	0.20*	0.20*	0.28*
1.5 generation	-0.04	-0.04	0.07	0.06	0.06
Second generation	0.06	0.06	0.13**	0.13**	0.12**
Age (age seventeen or over as ref.)	-0.05	-0.05	-0.05	-0.03	-0.01
SES		0.02	0.00	-0.01	0.02
Family structure (both parents as ref.)					
Parent and partner		-0.06	-0.07	-0.06	-0.05
Single mother		-0.10*	-0.07	-0.07	-0.08*
Single father		0.00	0.00	-0.01	-0.03
Neither parent		-0.19*	-0.14	-0.13	-0.06
Family size (one or two siblings as ref.)					
No siblings		0.00	0.01	0.04	0.06
Three or more siblings		-0.05	-0.03	-0.03	-0.01
Race-ethnicity (white as ref.)					
Non-Hispanic black			-0.24***	-0.24***	-0.11*
Mexican			-0.20**	-0.20**	-0.18**
Puerto Rican			0.12	0.15	0.19
Other Hispanic			-0.13	-0.14	-0.11
Asian			-0.23*	-0.24*	-0.14
Language (English only as ref.)					
Non-English			-0.01	-0.02	-0.02
Bilingual, non-English dominant			-0.09	-0.10	-0.09
Bilingual, English dominant			0.03	0.04	0.03
High school graduation by 1996 (no grad as ref.)				0.20***	0.19***
Logged previous income in 1997					0.09****
Constant	10.17***	10.25***	10.26***	10.07***	9.17***
Log pseudolikelihood	-5574.82	-5547.90	-5499.29	-5485.04	-5233.74
rho	-0.92	-0.92	-0.93	-0.93	-0.90
lambda	-0.66	-0.66	-0.66	-0.66	-0.60

Source: Authors' compilation of High School and Beyond data and National Educational Longitudinal Study data

Notes: Family structure and SES variables refer to conditions in sophomore year. Sample excludes Native Americans. HS&B sophomore cohort (weighted) N = 5,049. NELS sophomore cohort (weighted) N = 4,873.

Table 6.8 Regression Models Predicting Earnings (Logged) in Young Adulthood, Females

High School and Beyond Cohort

	1	2	3	4	5
Generation status (third-plus as ref.)					
Recent arrivals	0.03	0.07	0.01	0.01	0.03
1.5 generation	-0.02	-0.03	-0.06	-0.05	-0.03
Second generation	-0.03	-0.02	-0.03	-0.03	-0.04
Age (age seventeen or over as ref.)		-0.33*	-0.32*	-0.30	-0.18
SES		0.11***	0.11***	0.10***	0.10***
Family structure (both parents as ref.)					
Parent and partner		-0.04	-0.04	-0.03	-0.02
Single mother		0.06	0.06	0.06	0.06
Single father		-0.10	-0.10	-0.10	-0.13
Neither parent		0.12	0.13	0.14	0.16
Family size (one or two siblings as ref.)					
No siblings		0.09	0.09	0.09	0.07
Three or more siblings		0.00	0.01	0.01	0.01
Race-ethnicity (white as ref.)					
Non-Hispanic black			-0.01	-0.02	0.00
Mexican			-0.12	-0.12	-0.14*
Puerto Rican			-0.01	-0.02	0.05
Other Hispanic			0.11	0.10	0.07
Asian			0.16	0.16	0.16*
Language (English only as ref.)					
Non-English			0.09	0.09	0.12
Bilingual, non-English dominant			0.10	0.11	0.14
Bilingual, English dominant			0.02	0.02	0.02
High school graduation by 1986 (no grad as ref.)				0.14*	0.09
Logged previous income in 1987					0.09***
Constant	9.77***	9.76***	9.76***	9.62***	8.88***
Log pseudolikelihood	-7199.01	-7131.93	-7124.69	-7120.08	-6855.57
rho	-0.94	-0.93	-0.93	-0.93	-0.90
lambda	-0.83	-0.81	-0.81	-0.81	-0.72

(Table continues on p. 144.)

Table 6.8   (Continued)

National Education Longitudinal Cohort

	1	2	3	4	5
Generation status (third as ref.)					
Recent arrivals	0.23*	0.29*	0.26	0.23	0.35**
1.5 generation	0.03	0.05	0.04	0.05	−0.01
Second generation	0.14**	0.14**	0.15**	0.15**	0.14**
Age (age seventeen or over as ref.)		0.02	0.02	0.03	0.06
SES		0.09***	0.09***	0.07***	0.09***
Family structure (both parents as ref.)					
Parent and partner		−0.04	−0.03	−0.03	−0.03
Single mother		−0.10	−0.10	−0.09	−0.10
Single father		−0.23*	−0.22*	−0.21*	−0.17
Neither parent		−0.17	−0.17	−0.15	−0.05
Family size (one or two siblings as ref.)					
No siblings		−0.06	−0.06	−0.01	−0.01
Three or more siblings		0.02	0.02	0.03	0.02
Race-ethnicity (white as ref.)					
Non-Hispanic black			−0.03	−0.04	0.02
Mexican			−0.03	−0.05	−0.02
Puerto Rican			−0.17	−0.22	0.01
Other Hispanic			−0.01	−0.02	−0.04
Asian			0.02	−0.01	0.05
Language (English only as ref.)					
Non-English			0.05	0.06	0.09
Bilingual, non-English dominant			0.05	0.08	0.05
Bilingual, English dominant			−0.03	−0.02	−0.03
High school graduation by 1996 (no grad as ref.)				0.30*	0.22*
Logged previous income in 1997					0.09***
Constant	9.91***	9.94***	9.94***	9.64***	8.93***
Log pseudolikelihood	−6879.35	−6824.62	−6817.50	−6793.91	−6516.64
rho	−0.96	−0.96	−0.96	−0.96	−0.94
lambda	−0.91	−0.89	−0.89	−0.88	−0.80

Source: Authors' compilation of High School and Beyond data and National Educational Longitudinal Study data
Notes: Family structure and SES variables refer to conditions in sophomore year. Sample excludes Native Americans. HS&B sophomore cohort (weighted) N = 5,368. NELS sophomore cohort (weighted) N = 5,460.

Table 6.9   Simulations of Earnings in Young Adulthood

Scenarios	Male	Female
High School and Beyond Cohort, 1989		
Baseline model (white, English-only home, high school grade, dual-parent home, average age)	$19,930	$17,501
Lower SES	19,536	16,482
Old for grade, single mother, three or more siblings	19,341	13,360
Less than high school education	16,851	11,384
Mexican, second generation, non-English home	16,482	9,509
National Education Longitudinal Cohort, 1999		
Baseline model (white, English-only home, high school grade, dual-parent home, average age)	28,854	20,744
Lower SES	28,999	20,030
Old for grade, single mother, three or more siblings	25,463	19,438
Less than high school education	20,848	14,400
Mexican, second generation, non-English home	19,245	16,899

Source: Authors' compilation of High School and Beyond data and National Educational Longitudinal Study data.
Notes: HS&B sophomore cohort (weighted) N = 5,049 males; 5,368 females. NELS sophomore cohort (weighted) N = 4,873 males; 5,460 females.

The results for the two cohorts of HSB and NELS clearly show that eight years after high school, immigrants and the second generation fare no worse—and often better—than the otherwise comparable members of the third-generation comparison group. This should be seen in the context of overall achievement from youth into early adulthood. Family background and other traits—SES, family composition, race-ethnicity, age-for-grade— all matter. Once these are controlled, immigrant status carries little additional predictive power. Although language effects show up in many other studies, we find no independent effect of language background. One way to consider the relative contributions of background traits, generation status, and ethnicity to the earnings of the young adults is to simulate or predict earnings based on the final regression models. Table 6.9 does so by illustrating the changes in earnings predicted by changing the characteristics included. So, for example, using the reference categories for our variables to predict earnings for a white male with average SES and demographic profile (age, family structure) in the NELS sample, we obtain predicted earnings of approximately $29,000. These earnings drop, however, for those with more disadvantaged backgrounds. The decline in earnings, the penalty so to speak, is larger for completing less than a high school education than it is for considering ethnicity and generation status. (The last row of the table predicts earnings for a Mexican-origin male in the second generation as one illustration). Overall, then, the results here are more consistent with the standard status attainment model focused on earlier background and educational attainment than a model of negative or downward assimilation.

CONCLUSIONS

What can we say by way of summary about the labor market experience of immigrants? Do immigrants seek and achieve the American success story? Do they run the risk of falling into an underclass? And what about their children? How well does the second generation do? Our central finding is that immigrants and the second generation fare no worse than others who come from similar socioeconomic backgrounds. The reality of the immigrant experience is varied, and the extreme portrayals of success or failure do not characterize what happens for most. This carries over from our findings for the educational trajectories to complete the status attainment picture.

Crucial to understanding how well immigrants and their children do is the need to keep separate starting point and trajectory. A cross-sectional snapshot of how immigrants compare with natives today (or in any year) will give one picture. A series of frames over time, especially over the life of a cohort of individuals, will give another view of how the U.S. economic experience is unfolding for the first and second generation. The analysis has been built around this conceptual position.

In this chapter we looked through several windows on the immigrant experience. These views reveal a picture of the immigrant experience that starts with some disadvantage and improves gradually over time. We see that immigrants and the second generation show considerable attachment to the labor force. At the same time, snapshots from the census and major U.S. surveys show that members of the first generation have lower socioeconomic standing than the U.S. born. We show higher levels of poverty, occupational dissimilarity, and earnings differentials for the first and third generations, but note that these differences appear largest for the most recent arrival cohorts. Overall, we observe far fewer differences between the second and third generations in occupation, earnings, and poverty.

The simple aggregate snapshot shows higher poverty rates among immigrants than natives. But even peering a little bit more closely into this snapshot reveals some influences of composition. When the National Academy of Sciences looked at the poverty issue, it found that immigrant poverty rates were not especially high for those arriving from nonrefugee countries. Because of the special circumstances surrounding refugees, their poverty rates are usually much higher. Recent immigrants differ considerably from natives in their occupational distribution. When one looks at performance in the U.S. labor market, most researchers have found that immigrants admitted under the occupational skill categories do better than those admitted under other criteria, but both groups of immigrants gain with time in the United States. Our CPS-based results on occupational differentiation indicate that on average, immigrants become more similar to natives with time in the U.S. setting.

It is also quite clear from the CPS analysis of occupation and of median income that more recent arrivals exhibit the largest gap from the U.S. born. Approximately 25 percent of immigrants who arrived in the half decade immediately before the CPS would have to change occupation to match the distribution of the U.S. born. Immigrants with more time in the United States—some of whom arrived during or before the 1970s, for example—are of course closer to the U.S. born.

The declining cohort quality notion has also captured the attention of many analysts. Here, too, the evidence is not compelling. For example, those immigrants who arrived about fifteen to twenty years before the 1994 Current Population Survey show the same poverty rate as those who arrived about fifteen years before the 2004 survey. Moreover, men who immigrated in the 1990s and were twenty-five to forty-nine in the 2004 exhibited higher ratios of earnings (within age groups) to the men who immigrated in the 1980s and were twenty-five to forty-nine in 1994. Finally the social origins (family SES) and early economic attainment (median income at about age twenty-five) for our HSB and NELS cohorts show no evidence of deterioration in the ten year span. To be sure, recent immigrants are disadvantaged when compared to more established immigrants and the second generation, but there is strong evidence for improvement with time in the United States and little evidence that more recent immigrant waves start off any further down the ladder than earlier waves.

Consider again the hypothetical trajectories of chapter 3. Unlike some early research, which suggested that immigrants dramatically overcome early disadvantage and actually overtake natives, the picture that now matches best is a trajectory for immigrants that is displaced downwards but catches up modestly. Immigrants start with socioeconomic and other disadvantages. We see this in the highly aggregated statistics for income, for occupational status, and for the family SES starting points of our two longitudinal cohorts of youths.

Our longitudinal analysis of the two school-based cohorts (High School and Beyond and National Educational Longitudinal Study) had access to much more information than other sources. What we find is that well-known traits—family background, high school completion, and ethnicity—condition achievement in measurable ways. Beyond this, being a member of the first or 1.5 generation, as we describe here, or the second generation has very little more to say about life chances. In a few cases statistical coefficients are negative, and in a few cases positive. In no case is it strongly predicted that the first or second generation does appreciably less well than higher generations of natives.

Social science research has shown time and again that family background predicts achievement in school. Both school performance and family background (SES, parental availability) also predict outcomes after adolescence, which our results bear out. After controlling for these background traits, immigrants are not disadvantaged. To be sure, some of the effects of immigration are intertwined with language ability and ethnic background.[17] But even here some of these intertwined effects are sometimes overshadowed by socioeconomic and family structure effects. In the face of all these statistical controls, immigrants do no worse (and sometimes do better) than natives. All this is to say that immigrants with family structure and socioeconomic backgrounds similar to natives tend to trace similar earnings paths.

Recent discussions of immigrant paths have raised the specter of segmented assimilation, a topic we discussed earlier. Although conceptualizations vary, the general notion is one in which the experience of immigrants and the second generation is conditioned by race and ethnic relations in the host society. Only a few of our empirical findings are consistent with the picture of segmented assimilation. In some cases, race and ethnicity help predict 1989 or 1999 earnings. There is evidence for lower earnings for black males in both cohorts; for Latinos and Asians, the evidence is mixed. For young women in the labor force, there is really no support for systematic and persistent ethnic differentials, net of other traits. To provide a more direct examination of one version of the segmented assimilation paradigm, we estimated models that examined achievement separately by generation. In those models, we cannot statistically detect differential trajectories by race, an expectation from the segmentation model. To be sure, immigrants carry their racial or ethnic identity (and linguistic heritage) into the United States—or perhaps more accurately, the U.S. race-ethnic system helps determine this identity. Although there may be some evidence for segmentation in other studies, these other studies are often limited in representativeness, background information, or longitudinal structure. When one can take the longer view and get a better handle on both starting point and trajectory, the colors painted by the segmentation picture begin to fade.

Perhaps the first reality of the immigrant experience in America is its diversity, especially in the skills possessed by those coming to the United

States. This diversity is driven, not surprisingly, by U.S. immigration policy and by the attendant diversity in national origins and routes of entry. Immigrants are both more and less skilled than the U.S. labor force at large.[18] The attractiveness of the U.S. labor market to those without skills—particularly those from nearby countries—brings a steady stream of less skilled migrants through various routes, mostly family reunification. But some immigrants also arrive with considerable skills, either admitted directly for these skills or arriving by way of family reunification. On balance, in a simple snapshot, we would find immigrants to be less skilled than natives, but it is good to keep sight of the diversity.

Furthermore, our HSB and NELS panel analysis allows us to follow several thousand individuals from high school into their late twenties, where we get a better picture of the genuine trajectory and whether it differs for immigrants and the second generation. Again, the experience is diverse. Both composition and starting point matter in determining the trajectory. Family background, socioeconomic status, performance on tests and the like all have more to say about the likelihood of economic success in the early adult years than whether an individual was an immigrant or in the second generation. Those in the first generation who attend school only in the United States are more like the second generation than those who started school in another country. What does matter is that, on balance, immigrants start behind natives because immigrants come to the starting line with fewer socioeconomic resources. Once the race is on, immigrants run just about as fast, and sometimes faster, than others in the labor force. For the second generation, the starting point is closer still and the stride more evenly matched.

Chapter 7

Neighborhood: Residential Assimilation of Immigrants and Ethnic Groups

PATTERNS OF neighboring give us a particularly clear window into the process of adaptation, adjustment, and assimilation of immigrants and ethnic groups in American society. Although violent confrontation is relatively rare, tension over who lives next door speaks of the visceral importance of neighborhood in American society. Who one's neighbors are is important not only for social interaction, but also for a host of perceived material resources and concerns: public services, access to schools, property values. Neighborhoods provide friends and are a source of role models and socialization for children. We derive some of our social status from those with whom we share the surrounding streets. The expression "there goes the neighborhood," spoken sometimes in jest and other times in all seriousness, captures the importance of who lives among whom.

Neighboring patterns are particularly informative for the study of assimilation. Mary Waters and Tomás Jiménez, in their review, indeed identified spatial patterns as one of the four key dimensions of assimilation (2005).[1] First, everyone has to find a place in urban social (ecological) space, so residential patterns encompass all members of society. Second, there is an interesting asymmetry with respect to social policy and residential patterns, touched on in chapter 3. The civil rights era brought laws prohibiting discrimination in mortgage lending and renting and created an environment in which, at least in principle, individuals can seek housing wherever they prefer. Yet there is no affirmative policy in the United States to integrate neighborhoods. So for integration to take place, even in the absence of outright discrimination, the new residents have to desire to live among the old, and the old must elect to remain rather than leave. The socioeconomic attainment process, therefore, has a residential parallel. Most persons who improve their social status in their personal lives seek to manifest that gain in their neighborhood setting. In this sense, who one's neighbors are can tell a great deal about achievement and acceptance in American society.

The stakes are high. In a recent book on residential patterns in Chicago, William Wilson and Richard Taub concluded with skepticism, if not outright pessimism, about the promise of racial integration: "neighborhoods in urban America, especially in large metropolitan areas like Chicago, are likely to remain divided, racially and culturally" (2006, 161).[2]

This chapter examines residential patterns, looking at both ethnicity and nativity. Much sociological ink has been spilt on analyzing and debating the social meaning of ethnic groupings and attachments. The large literature on the mutability and even the arbitrariness of these labels notwithstanding, ethnic group membership forms a set of categories within which Americans operate (Waters 1990). We take that process as a given, and the census instrument as a manifestation of it. As with others who work with census materials, we examine residential intermingling once those groups have been defined.

Theoretical and empirical studies of segregation remain a major window on ethnic relations, even as the analysis of residential patterns has expanded from a relatively narrow and straightforward examination of blacks and whites alone, to a much more involved analysis and interpretation of a complicated ethnic mosaic (Lieberson 1980; Massey and Denton 1993; Farley and Frey 1994; Iceland 2004; White, Kim, and Glick 2005). Ethnic groups generally translate gains in socioeconomic status and experience in the United States into integration with Anglos and others (Alba and Logan 1993; Denton and Massey 1988; Ishizawa and Stevens 2007; Logan and Alba 1991; Massey and Mullan 1984; South, Crowder, and Chavez 2005a, 2005b; White, Biddlecom, and Guo 1993). Although segregation indices summarize in a single measure the outcome of several related processes, including discrimination, self-selection, and population composition, they provide key insights into social sorting through urban space from readily available data.

The limitations and history of measures of segregation are important to note. The segregation of the United States by ethnicity has been studied usually with reference to two or a few groups at a time. Historically, black-white residential segregation formed the core of concern (Taeuber and Taeuber 1965). This expanded in the 1970s and 1980s to studies of Asians and Latinos, for both of whom the immigration experience was more recent. Most recently, studies of segregation and residential assimilation have begun to examine subgroups within these broader categories. In the meantime there have always been parallel studies of white ethnics, those of European stock, dating from the 1950s. Lieberson offered a comparative analysis of the fortunes of blacks and white ethnics (1980), and many recent studies have looked a multiple panethnic groups, such as Latinos and Asians, as well as blacks. We offer a more direct focus on nativity and length of experience in the United States, and embed this in the more general concern with variegated ethnic segregation.

The study of ethnic and immigrant segregation speaks directly to theory. Residential outcomes are a key dimension on which to observe ethnic group competition and accommodation and, relatedly, the assimilation of ethnic groups. Most indicative, scholars of ethnic residential patterns use the terms *residential assimilation* or *spatial assimilation* to describe the process of increasing intermingling with non-Hispanic whites (and the middle class), borrowing directly and analogously from the usage so widespread in the study of immigrant fortunes. Typically, residential assimilation is taken to be associated with the development of social ties outside the ethnic community, and in turn, further structural assimilation. Some evidence supports this contention (Wierzbicki 2004).

In this as in our earlier empirical chapters, the conceptualization of time is important. We can often measure time relating to potential assimilation for the individual immigrant. In census data this is indicated by year of entry or period of arrival, and the measure figures prominently in our analyses to follow. We cannot directly measure generation status, as we did in the panel data for the schooling and labor market analyses, in census neighborhood data. We can speak generally, however, of the vintage of various ethnic groups. By vintage we mean the time since average arrival period for those from that origin over the history of U.S. immigration (White and Glick 1999). This has a rough parallel with the distinction often made between old and new groups in earlier immigration writing. Later in this chapter we discuss vintage as we look broadly at residential patterns, including studies beyond our own.

A straightforward application of the notion of residential assimilation would seem to accord best with the model of straight-line assimilation, described in chapter 3. But what of other modes of residential incorporation? How might segmented assimilation be manifest in the urban residential fabric? Although there is no clear consensus or benchmark, we suggest that the interpretation most consistent with segmentation is one in which certain minorities intermingle more slowly than others. Studies of residential patterns less often examine the segmented assimilation framework (Wierzbicki 2004). In one such effort, using longitudinal data on residence, Scott South and his coauthors found differences among Latino groups in the likelihood of intermingling with Anglos (South, Crowder, and Chavez 2005). In a study focused on the Mexican-origin population of Los Angeles, the intergenerational pattern of intermingling with Anglos was called delayed spatial assimilation (Brown 2007). Another recent investigation concluded that residential assimilation dynamics are, in fact, quite diverse and complicated. Zhou Yu and Dowell Myers found considerable variation in the residential assimilation outcomes across ethnic groups in Los Angeles, including continued ethnic clustering in the wake of socioeconomic success (Yu and Myers 2007). Such variation does not readily align with a standard forecast from the segmented assimilation model. Perhaps it could be that self-segregation linked to entrepreneurship might lead to both socioeconomic advancement and continued coethnic residential clustering and distance from other ethnic groups. Mary Fischer and Douglas Massey argued to the contrary (2000). They use census microdata to predict the likelihood of entrepreneurship from personal characteristics and metropolitan structural characteristics, including segregation levels. Although some results show curvilinear effects of segregation, Fischer and Massey, on examining more comprehensive models, came to argue that a high degree of residential segregation is actually more likely to limit business opportunities. They acknowledged that regional concentration of an ethnic group may enhance market opportunities for entrepreneurs, but neighborhood segregation seems not to do so.[3]

In the most extreme view of segmented residential assimilation, segregation would actually increase from time of first settlement, and more so for certain ethnic groups. Between these two views of segmentation and straight-line assimilation, the possibility of different ethnic (and for us, country of birth) segregation with parallel (or at least similar) patterns of integration with others in the host society is considerable. Some might classify any such continued ethnic separation also as a manifestation of segmented assimilation, but we would prefer to identify this in-between pattern distinctly. At a minimum, it indicates a weaker form of segmentation; more generally, it illustrates an operation of an overall residential assimilation dynamic embedded in a society pattern of ethnic stratification.

Another process is possible. We call it the immigrant entrepôt model, borrowing from the economic concept of the entrepôt as an intermediate point in the movement of goods, and extending it to international migrants. Here, in contrast to segregation on the basis of national origin or ethnicity, segregation is on the basis of nativity and time of arrival only. Under the entrepôt model, new arrivals are funneled to certain neighborhoods—immigrant ghettoes—and mixed in with others of the first generation, even those from different places of origin. These neighborhoods function as way stations. The entrepôt model posits that these immigrants will move on within and across generations. From time to time, writing—in urban studies, ethnic studies, immigration—has spoken of certain neighborhoods as occupied by (even teeming with) immigrants from diverse origins. The classic urban spatial schematic developed by Ernest Burgess can be seen in this light: immigrant groups identify distinct neighborhoods in the urban core, and then resettle outward with time (1967). Burgess even called some neighborhoods areas of second settlement. What remains to be seen, however, is the degree to which this clustering was on the basis of time and generations—all new immigrants, say, in the same neighborhood, regardless of origin, or immigrants from a particular national origin clumped together, regardless of time of arrival. Obviously both dimensions come into play, and thus an examination of segregation by nativity (including year of entry) and national origin will provide a better indication of how much, if at all, the entrepôt model applies.

This process of residential assimilation or any change over time raises the question of how newcomers from varying countries of origin are segregated in urban space to begin with. We know less about the process of initial immigrant urban settlement than we do about the snapshot of patterns identifiable at any census and the resulting dispersion (or lack thereof) with time. To be sure, networks (sources of social support from family and friends and links to potential jobs) play a role, in directing immigrants both to certain regions and metropolitan areas. The very identification of certain immigrant and ethnic groups with certain cities, both now and in the past—Irish in Boston, Jews in New York, Poles in Chicago, Arabs in Detroit, Cubans in Miami, Chinese in Seattle, Ethiopians in Washington, D.C.—speak to the net results of a clustering process. Undoubtedly, socioeconomic conditions sometimes linked to specific labor recruitment and opportunities also play a part in where the new arrivals live. For contemporary immigrants who arrive with modest economic resources (the case for many, not all), housing and living costs will help determine residential location. These facets are often mentioned in discussions of the origin and persistence of immigrant neighborhoods and ethnic communities (Logan, Alba, and Zhang 2002). Although unpacking the process of initial settlement is beyond our reach here, our window into the 2000 Census snapshot—looking at both country of origin and period of arrival—should help us sort out the relative influence of these two factors. Then, stepping back, we can place our view of current American urban patterns against the broader landscape of urban theory and historical patterns.

In this chapter we employ the index of dissimilarity, D, to examine residential segregation in 2000. This is the same measure we used in chapter 6 to describe occupational distributions. But it is, of course, also quite commonly used to represent residential distributions as well. Despite several weaknesses (White 1986), it is highly correlated with other indices, and is the most widely used and readily understood segregation measure (Massey, White, and Phua 1996). D varies between 0 (no segregation) and 1 (complete segregation). The value of 0 occurs when each neighborhood contains an equal share of the city's immigrant and native residents; the value of 1 (100 percent) occurs when each neighborhood contains exclusively immigrants or natives.

Our analyses use census tracts as the approximation of the neighborhood. Tracts are small spatial units developed for each decennial census. By design tracts are to be well delimited in urban space, to contain about 4,000 to 6,000 people, and to be relatively homogeneous with regard to housing stock. As such, they provide a reasonable approximation of the neighborhood (White 1986). Tracts have been used repeatedly in analyses of American residential segregation, including a recent comprehensive Census Bureau analysis of U.S. segregation patterns for the 2000 Census (Iceland, Weinberg, and Steinmetz 2002).[4]

Because our analysis (and that for most segregation studies) relies on aggregate census data, we look at tract tabulations for all people living within the tract. Because few multiple tabulations are available, we use cross-tabulations of the 2000 Census by year of entry (in grouped periods) and place of birth (POB). Within this cross-classification, further breakdown is not available. Thus we cannot isolate household heads from others, children from adults, and the like. All told, tract segregation analyses still give us a comprehensive picture of patterns of residential intermingling. These patterns, in turn, allow us to make inferences about the differential residential patterns across immigrant-ethnic groups, metropolitan areas, and the like.

D is always calculated in pairwise comparisons. In several analyses, we use U.S. born (natives) as the comparison group, determining D for immigrants (or year of entry group) versus U.S. natives. In some calculations, we examine the specific group from all other persons not in the group (versus all other), as appropriate. In calculations of residential segregation for the simultaneous classification of origin (place of birth) by year of entry, we used non-Hispanic whites (Anglos) as the reference group. In alternative calculations, using the U.S. born as the reference group, we saw much the same pattern. Despite the informative methodological debates over segregation, the indices themselves and the substantive story they tell are quite robust to alternative formulations.

SEGREGATION OF THE FOREIGN BORN IN 2000

Most social scientists and the general public draw on a model of residential assimilation in which new arrivals to a metropolitan area are clustered, that is, residentially segregated. Rarely, however, are segregation statistics calculated directly by nativity (U.S. born versus not U.S. born) or year of immigration. Rather, inferences are made from the segregation patterns exhibited by various ethnic groups.

In 2000, the mean value (weighted by metropolitan area size) of the segregation of the foreign born from the U.S. born is .35, implying that about 35 percent of immigrants would need to relocate to new neighborhoods

Figure 7.1   Comparative Segregation Levels by Ethnic Group and
Nativity, 2000

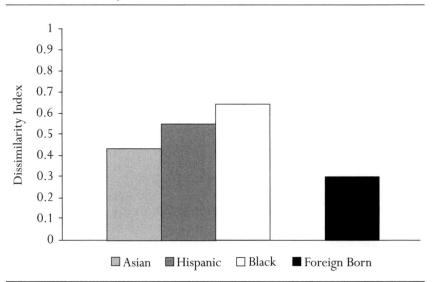

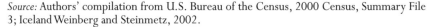

Source: Authors' compilation from U.S. Bureau of the Census, 2000 Census, Summary File 3; Iceland Weinberg and Steinmetz, 2002.

within their respective metropolitan area to produce an even distribution.[5] By way of comparison, figure 7.1 presents a bar chart showing weighted means across all metropolitan areas of immigrant-native segregation plus the level of segregation from non-Hispanic whites in 2000 reported for major census race-ethnic groups: Asians (mean $D = .41$), Hispanics (mean $D = .51$) and blacks (mean $D = .64$) (Iceland, Weinberg, and Steinmetz 2002). Immigrant segregation, without regard to specific national origin, is somewhat below that of Asians and Latinos.

Immigrant-native segregation is considerably below the level of black-white segregation. Although immigrants are, by definition, new arrivals, their residential intermingling is more extensive than that of major panethnic groups, even those including a substantial number of immigrants. The results suggest that neighborhood sorting takes place less along the lines of nativity than ethnicity, something we examine further.

We can also consider the distribution of immigrant-native D values for metropolitan areas in the United States in 2000. Fully half of metropolitan areas fall into the range (.25, .36).[6] This is a fairly narrow band, and indicates, as mentioned, that in many metropolitan areas, about one-third of the immigrant population would need to change neighborhoods to become evenly interspersed with the population born in the United States.

Immigrants are not evenly spread across metropolitan areas, as is well known. Reynolds Farley examined information for the 1990 Census and found that only eleven of thirty-eight large (population more than 1 million) U.S. metropolitan areas had immigrant fractions above 7.9 percent, the 1990 national average (Farley 1996). These eleven included several of the very largest metropolitan areas: New York, Los Angeles, Chicago, Houston, San Francisco, Boston, and Washington. Other metropolitan areas with large shares include Miami (more than 33 percent foreign born), San Diego, and Sacramento.

The immigrant share of the American population has been growing into the 2000s, but much of this immigration remains directed to a few key areas. Our tabulations of census data on consolidated metropolitan areas indicate that some 65 percent of the immigrant population in 2000 was concentrated in ten major metropolitan areas. These same ten areas contained 32.3 percent of the U.S.-born population. Some thirty-one metropolitan areas had immigrant proportions greater than the national average of 13 percent. Compared to Farley's 1990 results, this is evidence—consistent with other findings during the 1990s and since 2000—that the immigrant proportion is spreading more broadly through the United States, including both suburban and nonmetropolitan territory (Massey 2008; Singer 2004; Singer, Hardwick, and Brettell 2008). This spread has gathered attention among scholars and more generally in the media. Several states that were not traditionally seen as immigrant destinations (Georgia, Iowa, and North Carolina) experienced sizable growth in their immigrant populations. Within these states and others, the relative growth of the foreign born in certain rural areas has been quite large. William Kandel and Emilio Parrado documented the substantial rural growth of the foreign-born population in selected locations. They reported, for instance, that the growth of the Hispanic population from 1990 to 2000 was 66 percent and that Anglo growth in these areas was linked to labor market opportunities for immigrants in the meat packing industry (2005). At the same time, this growth most often took place on a small starting base, so the increment may look relatively dramatic compared to traditional immigrant receiving locations. The impact of this substantial relative influx of immigrants (and their children)—linguistic diversity, health-care needs, school enrollment—on new destinations, especially small communities, is likely to be substantial. Nevertheless, these instances should be seen in the context of overall immigration and population distribution. Thus, major metropolitan areas are still the field on which residential assimilation will play out.

We look first directly at the differential distribution of the foreign born across metropolitan areas. To gather more insight into the impact of clustering between areas, in addition to segregation within them, we can make an overall calculation of segregation across all U.S. metropolitan census tracts, that is, neighborhoods. A straightforward calculation of this overall immigrant-native dissimilarity for the United States as a whole yields a value of 0.48. This value was almost unchanged from the 1990 value of 0.49. The 2000 D value is based on 52,173 census tracts; the 1990 value is based on 45,510 tracts. This means that about half of the immigrants (or natives) would have to shift residences, not only within but among metropolitan areas, to produce an unsegregated distribution nationally. For this distribution in 2000, every neighborhood would have 13 percent foreign-born residents, matching the national average. This is a somewhat atypical use of a segregation statistic, but it does give a sense of overall settlement patterns.

Segregation by Year of Arrival

The standard picture of assimilation argues that as time passes, immigrants adapt and the host society accommodates. Thus, over time we would expect any group to experience residential assimilation and see its level of segregation decline. Within the population of immigrants, we would expect those with more time in the United States to be less segregated.

Figure 7.2 confirms that those who arrived in earlier decades are less segregated than more recent immigrants. The graph reveals a moderate decline of about 3 percentage points per decade, enough so that immigrants who arrived in the late 1960s are about 10 percentage points less segregated than those who arrived in the late 1990s.[7] We do not know for certain how much of this decline is attributable to integration of immigrants with time in the United States and how much to clustering of the newest immigrants, because these data are from a 2000 Census cross-section. Immigrants who arrived before 1965 are noticeably less segregated than those who came later. Although 1965 was a watershed year in immigration law, implementing the provisions took some time to influence the flow of people; thus pre-1965 immigrants certainly predate the redirection of the flow. This temporal pattern is also reminiscent of the argument about declining cohort quality versus genuine positive trajectory, an issue we discussed in relation to socioeconomic attainment. Here, the pattern of residential segregation by period of arrival is clearly consistent with a process of residential intermingling, but the changing composition of new U.S. arrivals probably plays a role as well.

Historical comparisons of immigrant segregation are limited, but the segregation value for the foreign born in the 1980 Census was just about the same as in 2000. In 1980, the dissimilarity index on a national sample of nineteen metropolitan areas stood at .29 (White 1987, table 5.4). A further comparison for several social characteristics indicated that, compared to race and housing type, segregation by nativity (along with some other social char-

Figure 7.2   Residential Dissimilarity from Natives by Year of Entry

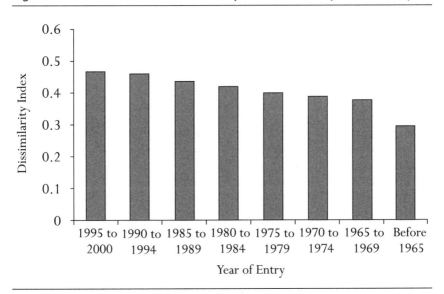

Source: Authors' compilation of U.S. Bureau of the Census, 2000 Census, Summary File 3.
Note: U.S. metro areas, weighted means.

acteristics) has been relatively modest in U.S. metropolitan areas. Nativity segregation also fluctuated somewhat (White 1987, 189).

Such findings suggest that a simplistic model of immigrant ghettoes is unlikely to be accurate. If the immigrant entrepôt model holds, those who arrived more than forty years ago should be quite segregated, in that their children would have aged out of their households and new immigrants would have replaced some of their neighbors. This seems not to be the case. Instead, immigrants who came some time ago are more residentially intermingled than those who arrived more recently. At least at this level of analysis, the ethnic residential assimilation model has some support.

ETHNIC ORIGIN, DURATION, AND RESIDENTIAL ASSIMILATION

We can open another window on residential assimilation by looking at the residential patterns of ancestry groups by year of immigration, and thus begin to disentangle the relative influence of ethnic background and timing arrival in the residential pattern. We expect more recent arrivals to be more residentially isolated. But in addition, a long history of research on ethnic residential patterns has found substantial ethnic variation in isolation. Although the notion of segmented assimilation is usually focused on socioeconomic outcomes, there is a testable extension with regard to residence. Those groups disadvantaged in the segmentation process (typically blacks) should be found to be more segregated and isolated than other groups, even if one accounts for the time the group has been in the United States. Strictly speaking, as we discussed at the outset of this chapter, the segmented assimilation idea goes further and suggests that a group's position within the racial-ethnic hierarchy comes to dominate other factors, such as arrival time, in determining residential outcomes. Thus, groups who are disadvantaged in this hierarchy are expected to become less integrated over time or even to be more segregated.

We examine these assertions directly by looking at 2000 Census tract data in detail. Whereas in the previous section we looked at segregation by year of immigration, now we look at segregation by both year of immigration and birthplace. The relative level of segregation for this two-dimensional classification will help illuminate the landscape of residential assimilation and integration. Because ethnic patterns are so distinctive for individual regions, the figures we show first are for selected large metropolitan areas. We then provide some summary information for all U.S. metropolitan areas. The results point to the importance of local context. At the same time, they indicate persistent patterns of residential sorting that hold across much of U.S. territory.

The standard straight-line assimilation model predicts that immigrants who have been in the United States longer should be less segregated, and that this intermingling should proceed for all groups. Alternatively, under a model of segmented residential assimilation, some ethnic groups will show much higher levels of segregation regardless of time in the United States, and will have lower rates of intermingling with time. The entrepôt model, in further contrast, would hold that residential duration would dominate birthplace in determining residential patterns. In other words, the entrepôt model would pose that recent arrivals would be heavily clustered, regardless of country of origin, and that long-term residents (or succeeding generations) would be intermingled regardless of ethnic identity.

Three Metropolitan Cases

We now present figures showing segregation by place of birth and period of entry for a few large metropolises.[8] In all cases, we restrict the presentation to several key geographic origins—Europe, Asia, Africa, Caribbean, Mexico, South America—and look at individuals who arrived in the 1990s, 1980s, and before 1980.[9] The categories are from the 2000 Census tabulations (SF3). The availability of two-way tabulations at the tract (neighborhood) level exacts a cost: we cannot get detailed country of origin by detailed year of entry, only the broad regional and temporal groupings we present here. We continue to use the index of dissimilarity for ease of exposition and interpretation.[10] Here the reference category for each of the several groups is the U.S.-born population; that is, we calculate the segregation level of the specific group, say Caribbean immigrants in the 1980s, from all U.S. natives resident in metropolitan area tracts in 2000. We define the dissimilarity calculation for metropolitan areas. Where defined, we use consolidated metropolitan areas, which represent more territory and thus a more inclusive housing market and social setting.

Figure 7.3 presents the birthplace by year-of-entry dissimilarity for the New York metropolitan area.[11] Consider first immigrants from Europe to New York in respect to U.S. natives. We find that the index for immigrants who arrived in the 1990s is .54. That for European immigrants who arrived in the 1980s is .46, and that for immigrants who arrived before 1980 is .33. The difference by period of immigration corresponds strongly to expectation under that conventional straight-line residential assimilation model. Those who have been in the United States longer (regardless of whether they immigrated to New York originally or came there only later) are less segregated. In fact, a comparison of the first two values, which correspond to strict ten-year intervals, suggest a decline of segregation on the order of 1 percentage point per year of U.S. residence.

Asian-origin immigrants are generally of more recent vintage, but the three period-of-arrival intervals at least partly control for timing. Recent arrivals from Asia have a dissimilarity index of .53, just about the same as those from Europe. Immigrants arriving in the 1980s are segregated at .50 and pre-1980 immigrants at .45. These two Asian arrival groups are more segregated than Europeans of corresponding arrival eras.

The flow of African immigrants to New York and the United States generally is more modest, but has been increasing over time. The New York metropolitan area in 2000 included about 169,000 residents born in Africa. African-origin immigrants are also interesting in that their arrival is more recent, yet they come into a country with a history of deep racial residential separation. African immigrants are themselves diverse, coming from a wide range of countries and with only about half of the 2000 Census immigrants from Africa identifying their race as black. African immigrants reveal the standard pattern for duration: those with more U.S. experience are less segregated. The comparison with immigrants from Asia and Europe is instructive, however. For each of the three arrival periods, African immigrants are more segregated than Asians; in fact, the differential is on the order of 10 percentage points for all three periods. Given that this difference holds for immigrants arriving in the 1990s and 1980s, it is not likely to be simply a compositional effect of differential arrival time within the decade.

Figure 7.3   Residential Dissimilarity, New York Metropolitan Area, 2000

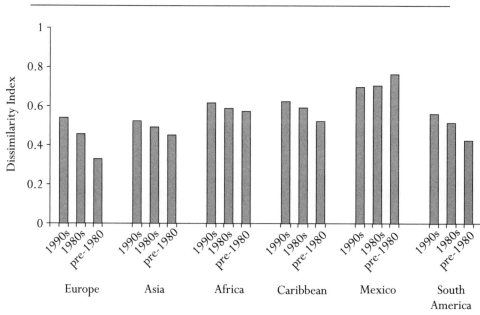

Source: Authors' compilation of U.S. Bureau of the Census, 2000 Census, Summary File 3.
Note: Dissimilarity values calculated for the group versus all other groups. Weighted means.

Caribbean immigrants in the New York metropolitan region exhibit a segregation pattern by arrival time quite similar to those from Africa. It is quite striking, in fact, that 1980s and 1990s Caribbean and African immigrants have about the same level of dissimilarity. Immigrants from the Caribbean who came before 1980 are segregated at a level that is intermediate between Africans and Asians. The total number of Caribbean immigrants in the New York region is quite large—1,238,902, of whom 402,130 came before 1980.[12] Thus, we see descriptive support for the assertion that race may matter more for some immigrants.

Mexico is the largest single country of origin for immigrants to the United States over the past few decades. Mexican-origin immigrants and their descendants make up large portions of several major metropolitan areas, though to a lesser extent in New York. By contrast, it is likely, though there is little direct evidence, that immigrants from Mexico in the New York

Figure 7.4   Residential Dissimilarity, Los Angeles Metropolitan
                 Area, 2000

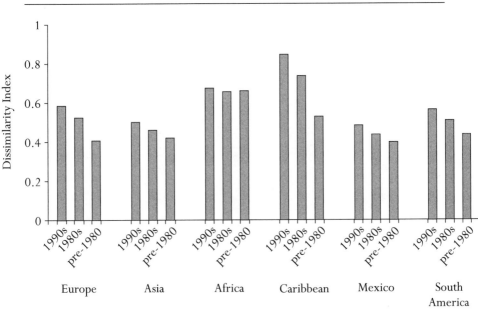

Source: Authors' compilation of U.S. Bureau of the Census, 2000 Census, Summary File 3.
Note: Dissimilarity values calculated for the group versus all other groups. Weighted means.

area in 2000 are likely to have first settled—and perhaps for an appreciable time—elsewhere in the United States. Mexican immigrants in the New York area do not show the expected pattern of residential segregation by duration. Rather, pre-1980 Mexican immigrants are the most segregated in New York, with a dissimilarity index of about .75, above Europeans, Asians, and Africans from that arrival period. Immigrants who arrived in the 1980s and 1990s have dissimilarity levels on the order of .70, still above those for other origin groups we have discussed.

Los Angeles and Chicago, the next two largest metropolitan areas, provide evidence of ethnic and immigrant clustering that broadly reaffirms the results for the New York region, but in which some distinctive aspects of the local setting show through. Figure 7.4 presents results for Los Angeles and figure 7.5 for Chicago.

In Los Angeles the general pattern holds for declining segregation with increasing U.S. residence. Most noteworthy are Asian and Mexican immi-

Figure 7.5   Residential Dissimilarity, Chicago Metropolitan Area, 2000

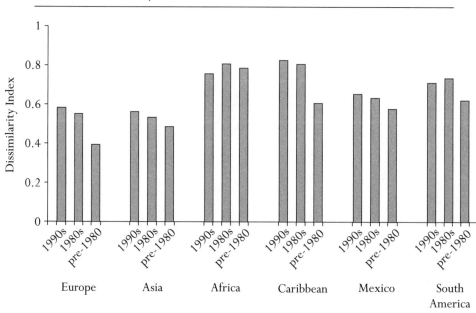

Source: Authors' compilation of U.S. Bureau of the Census, 2000 Census, Summary File 3.
Note: Dissimilarity values calculated for the group versus all other groups. Weighted means.

grants who not only make up substantial proportions of the Los Angeles population, but for whom that metropolitan area is the major entrepôt. In Los Angeles, Asian and Mexican immigrants who have lived in the United States for twenty years or more as of the 2000 Census are clearly less segregated than the most recent arrivals, about 10 percentage points. This sharp pattern, consistent with the straight-line assimilation model, applies to European, Caribbean, and South American immigrants in Los Angeles. The one group for which the model fails is African immigrants, for whom no residence-related pattern can be discerned.

In Chicago, too, the conventional pattern holds. For immigrants from Europe, Asia, Mexico, and the Caribbean, residential intermingling increases (segregation decreases) with time in the United States. Conversely, the residential assimilation pattern is not apparent for immigrants from Africa, and here, too, immigrants from South America fail to follow any clear pattern of time in the United States.

A National Summary of Year-of-Entry by Place of Birth Segregation

These three cases are for major U.S. metropolitan areas that have been traditional immigrant-receiving regions, and continue to receive a substantial number of the most recent waves of immigrants. In the current wave, the foreign born have spread out throughout the United States, through several re-emerging gateways and several new ones (Singer 2004). We therefore expand our view beyond the largest cities. To do so, we conduct a statistical analysis of such data for all metropolitan areas. That is, we made the same calculation for all U.S. metropolitan areas from the 2000 Census Summary File 3 data that we made for New York, Los Angeles, and Chicago. We also turn to disentangling, at least in part, the relative impact of arrival period (1990s, 1980s, pre-1980) and place of birth (Asia, Africa, Mexico, and so on) on the degree of group residential separation, which is apparent in residential segregation statistics.

Our approach is to pool the dissimilarity results for each combination of city, origin, and year of arrival. The combination of eight origins, three arrival periods, and 280 metropolitan areas means 7,560 values. We stack these values and conduct a regression, predicting the level of segregation (D from the white population) as a function of metropolitan area population and dummy variables for place of birth (POB) and year of entry (YOE) into the United States. The regression results (summarized with simulation results) indicate that we can predict about 17 percent of the national variation in segregation from measures of population clusters of place of birth and entry period indicators. All these indicators contribute statistically significant predictions of segregation. Most important is that place of birth trumps year of entry in predicting the level of segregation exhibited by a group.[13] Although statistically significant the measures for YOE add only about another percentage point to explained variance once POB and metropolitan population are controlled. We also find a strong effect of city size. A hypothetical increase of metropolitan population from 1 million to 10 million is associated with a predicted increase of dissimilarity of 3 points.

We present these results in figures 7.6 and 7.7. By design, these are simulated values, predicting the levels of segregation for particular combinations of birthplace and arrival period, holding constant city size at its mean. The simulations help us see the magnitude of birthplace or arrival period, holding other traits constant. Figure 7.6 shows sizable differences across origin in the predicted value of group segregation, holding constant arrival

Figure 7.6   Predicted Residential Dissimilarity by Origin

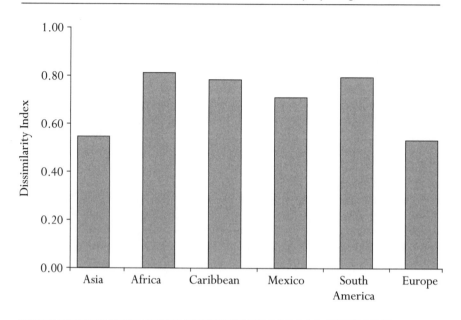

Source: Authors' compilation from U.S. Bureau of the Census, 2000 Census, Summary File 3.
Note: U.S. metro areas, weighted means. 1980s arrival cohort, referenced to non-Hispanic whites.

period and urban area population. Immigrants from Asia and Europe are far less segregated, given their year of entry and the size of the city in which they live, than immigrants from other origins. By contrast, immigrants from Africa are more segregated than any other group. Immigrants from the Caribbean, Central America, and South America are only slightly less segregated.[14]

Figure 7.7 takes up the case of segregation by year of entry, that is, period of arrival. Again these are simulated values, based on the same underlying regression equation. Consistent with our statistical findings, the difference in predicted values across the bar graph is modest. We simulate results for hypothetical case of immigrants from Mexico, but—precisely because this is a simulation on the basis of a linear regression equation—the period-by-period pattern would hold for any origin group.[15] Immigrants who arrived in the 1970s and earlier are predicted to have dissimilarity values about 5

Figure 7.7   Predicted Residential Dissimilarity by Arrival Cohort

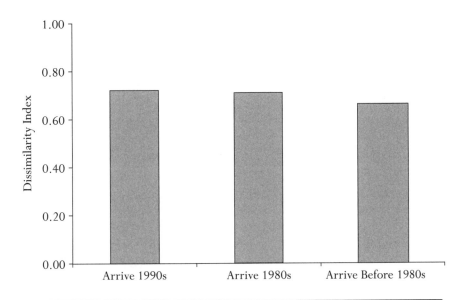

Source: Authors' compilation from U.S. Bureau of the Census, 2000 Census, Summary File 3.
Note: U.S. metro areas, weighted means. Adjusted for country of birth and size of metropolitan area.

percentage points lower than those arriving the 1990s. Immigrants in the 1980s are predicted to exhibit segregation just about 1 point lower than the most recent immigrants. These effects are surely in the direction of the residential assimilation hypothesis, but are modest when placed alongside the differentials exhibited across place of origin.

We know that immigrants tend to be concentrated in the larger metropolitan areas, even though the foreign born have been dispersing throughout American territory. Aware of this big-city concentration, we repeated our analysis for subsamples of metropolitan areas that were limited to those with populations of 500,000 or more, and then to those with million-plus populations. In general, when we limit the analysis to these larger metropolises, we find results consistent with those just presented. Larger metropolises are more segregated, as our coefficient on population indicated. Beyond that, differences are modest. We find, for instance, that Asian and European immigrants are a couple percentage points less segregated in million-plus metropolitan areas (versus the full sample), whereas Mexican migrants are a couple points more segregated. In one additional subsequent test, we took a close look at recent Mexican immigrants because that group constitutes such a large and controversial flow of the foreign born. We added an interaction term (Mexican nativity and entry in the 1990s) to the model behind figures 7.6 and 7.7. We find that recent Mexican immigrants are actually less segregated than one would predict from other characteristics included in such a model.

CONCLUSION

In this chapter we have examined residential patterns as a window on the adaptation of new groups in American society. Residential assimilation is played out in a world where ethnicity matters, especially given that immigration generates ethnicity. Some particularly useful insights come from residential segregation values. Our first finding is that the overall residential segregation of immigrants is modest, at least by conventional standards of research on American ethnic residential segregation. Segregation by nativity is lower than most forms of segregation that major panethnic groups, such as blacks, Asians, and Hispanics, experience.[16] Although lower levels may be less surprising, or even less intrinsically interesting, nativity segregation does give us the comparative window on the sources of residential clustering. It also sheds light on competing hypotheses about this clustering.

Our second finding is one of residential assimilation over time. We find that the level of segregation—across all the foreign born, from natives—declines steadily with time. Our results, presented in figure 7.2, indicate that pre-1965 immigrants exhibit about 40 percent less segregation than those who arrived in the 1990s. This is consistent with an individual-level process in which time in the United States leads to residential intermingling. Decennial census data cannot follow individuals over time, but these results accord with such a view.

Our third finding concerns the relative impact of period of arrival and place of birth. It shows that immigrant segregation takes place in the context of a society with significant ethnic residential separation. Whether looking at large receiving metropolitan areas—New York, Los Angeles, Chicago—or adjusted summary statistics for all metropolitan areas and ethnic groups pooled together, we find that place of birth trumps arrival period in determining segregation. There is less evidence for the entrepôt model of segregation, in which immigrants, new arrivals especially, are clustered regardless of place of origin.

At the outset of this chapter, we discussed residential assimilation. Simply stated, individuals are expected to show more residential integration with time. Our results are consistent with residential assimilation, but not as an inexorable unitary force. Ethnicity and other traits matter. Our own results clearly point to country or region of origin, so closely linked to ethnicity, as differentiating residential outcomes. Averaging across the experience of U.S. metropolitan areas, most groups do show increasing intermingling over time, but ethnic (place of origin) background still conveys a major off-set in residential location.

We can back up and see where our picture with 2000 Census data fits in with other work. The relationship of vintage—a group's average arrival time—to residential intermingling is also consistent with residential assim-ilation (White and Glick 1999). Contemporary descendants of older-ethnic stock—that is, whose ancestors arrived on average at earlier times—are less segregated. Vintage is far from a perfect predictor of residential intermin-gling, however, and many groups are found off the line. Notably, in our ear-lier work, we found several racial groups to be segregated far more than their time in the United States would predict. Moreover, many segregation studies have found excess segregation—even hypersegregation—for the African American population (Wilkes and Iceland 2004). Ethnic stratifica-tion, then, still operates powerfully to separate Americans in urban space.

In most other related research, socioeconomic well-being (of individuals and households) and ethnic context are clearly shown to matter as well. This comes through clearly when research can rely on contextual microdata, in which individual information has been merged with neighborhood informa-tion, so that neighborhood outcomes such as ethnic composition can be pre-dicted from a variety of personal traits. Results of such statistical analyses indicate that the several measures of immigrant status (nativity, year of im-migration, citizenship) are relatively unimportant in determining the likeli-hood of living near a non-Hispanic white, once ethnic background and household socioeconomic status are taken into account. Again, physiognomy and history matter, because groups with substantial African heritage are found to be much less intermingled with whites, net of these personal traits (White and Sassler 1998). The general picture from these studies and others (Logan et al. 1996; Massey and Denton 1993; South, Crowder, and Chavez 2005a, 2005b) is consistent with several aspects of general assimilation models. Most groups translate personal socioeconomic gain into both prox-imity to whites and neighborhood status. This means that structural (eco-nomic) assimilation in the wider society becomes manifest in neighborhood integration as well.

Is there evidence of segmentation? The concept of segmented assimilation has had a powerful influence on the discourse in immigration studies, as we have discussed elsewhere in this volume. The notion of segmented assimila-tion raises the specter of differential paths for different ethnic or country-of-origin groups, especially according to race. What about residential outcomes? Although the theory regarding segmentation assimilation has not really been developed for residential patterns, a reasonable extension would posit that minority or disadvantaged groups would experience less residential assimilation with time than others.

Are our results consistent with segmented assimilation? Only partly so. The strong interpretation of the segmented assimilation notion would point to weaker trajectories of residential integration among blacks (and selected others) with time. Consider immigrants from Africa and the Caribbean, and perhaps Mexico. Our examination of residential segregation jointly by birthplace and entry period in the largest metropolitan areas (with enough immigrants) suggests less progression over time for these minority groups than for others. By contrast, most cities show marked declines in segregation for Europeans, Asians, and immigrants from other places. They also show declines across time for Mexican immigrants. For Caribbeans, the picture is also mixed, with some cities exhibiting clear declines in residential segregation with time, and others showing no change. To be sure, this differential—even inconsistent—pattern of residential trajectory sits on top of major differences at any point in time. As our results clearly showed, country of origin differences are marked for all decades of immigrant arrivals. Segmented assimilation may help offer—after the fact—a description of the differential cross-sectional outcomes of nation origin groups; the jury is still out on whether the over-time trajectories take on decidedly different paths for immigrants of different national origins.

Another important interpretation follows. There is at best faint evidence that immigration per se is segregating American society. By contrast, these results demonstrate the powerful and variegated influence ethnic background exerts on residential outcomes in American society. The declining cohort quality argument posits that the skills of recent immigrant cohorts have been deteriorating. This in turn raises concerns about the ability of recent immigrants to adapt. Failure to adapt would suggest that immigrant ghettoes would form. Yet, our analysis of chapters 5 and 6 cast doubt on the empirical premise of declining cohort quality, and the longitudinal analysis pointed to successful structural assimilation. It is true that immigrant neighborhoods are evident now in major metropolitan areas, just as they have been during previous eras. The story that emerges from the social science evidence, however, is that these immigrant clusters will decrease with time. As time in the United States increases, both for the individual and the ethnic group, integration proceeds.

Chapter 8

Conclusion: Immigrant Assimilation and Social Policy

PERHAPS ONE of the most enduring images of American culture is that of near-penniless immigrants arriving at Ellis Island and, through dint of hard work, clambering their way up the ladder of success in the land of opportunity. No one doubts the power of this image, but how accurate is it? Do those who now come through the nation's jetways or across the land border match the myth developed from the experience of those who, several generations ago, walked down the nation's gangplanks? Do today's immigrants lift themselves by their bootstraps? Do they adjust, adapt, accommodate, assimilate?

Unlike many nations, the United States considers itself a country of immigration. However vocal, almost all partisans in the current debate about immigration acknowledge a positive contribution of immigrants—through a variety of routes—to American society. The issue is more often *how many* rather than *if any* immigrants. Not far below the surface of the debate is a set of perceptions about how well immigrants do in American society. We have perspectives on immigrants of earlier eras and others about how well today's arrivals are faring. Do today's immigrants advance quickly, or do they and their children fail to push forward in their new society? To some there may be even the specter of an immigrant underclass (Clark 2001). More pertinent, the debate about admission criteria and policy constantly invokes questions about who gets in. The balance between skills-based immigration (and adopting a point system like other countries to recognize this) versus family unification and diversity immigration remain topics of debate in the U.S. Congress and in the nation's op-ed pages.

Our task in this book has been to examine structural assimilation, that is, patterns of adaptation linked to socioeconomic position in American society. Our analyses are a response to recent debates over the degree to which immigrants and their descendants successfully make their way in the United States. To put it simply, we address the question of how well immigrants and their children do. As we argued throughout this book, how we conceptualize time and the suitability of data to capture these concepts are critical to our understanding of contemporary immigration. All notions of immigrant assimilation invoke time. Time can be traced both within the life cycle of individuals and across generations, from first to second to third and higher. And time is often, sometimes explicitly, sometimes implicitly, in the background of comparisons of ethnic groups who arrive in different immigration eras.

We selected three windows through which to observe the structural assimilation of America's new faces: school achievement (chapter 5), labor market adjustment (chapter 6), and residential intermingling (chapter 7). Findings from each of these realms can help us think about policy issues, both the large-scale questions about how many new arrivals and with what characteristics the United States will accept, and more detailed questions about that value and kind of interventions, if any, to consider in these three areas. In each chapter, we exploited nationally representative data about the experience of immigrants and their descendants. Where possible, we introduced multivariate controls to assess the effect of immigration—generation status—net of other factors.

We began our empirical analysis with school achievement, because schools are both a crucible for assimilation and a major conduit by which opportunities for the later society are realized. Because one in five children in primary and secondary school are first or second generation (Jamieson, Curry, and Martinez 2001), it is worth understanding how generation status predicts performance in secondary school, high school graduation, and enrollment in higher education. As our theoretical review indicates, this is a particularly relevant setting in which to look for the possible alternative paths of assimilation. These vary in contemporary theoretical formulations among straight-line, super achievement, and segmentation. In particular, the specter of segmented assimilation—divergent paths of assimilation—is driven in part by the ethnic or racial stratification of the wider society. A careful analysis of schooling, including analysis that can draw on the life experience of individuals, forces the social scientist and policy analyst to specify more concretely the models of paths and the alternative interpretations of results.

Labor market adaptation is the most extensively studied of the three by social scientists. These earlier studies have alternately found superior and inferior labor market performance of immigrants (or the second generation, both compared to natives) depending on alternative conceptualizations and the newest rounds of data. We take advantage of the opportunity to exploit cohort comparisons over a decade in poverty and earnings using nationally representative data. We then dig deeper and use high-quality longitudinal data for individuals and take differing origins (family background) into account to examine starting point and trajectory in the paths of immigrants, the second generation, and others in their early labor market outcomes.

The final area we focus on is the residential setting. We give special attention to residential segregation, because the intermingling of immigrants and their ethnic descendants in neighborhoods can be seen as a benchmark of social integration.[1] Immigration generates ethnic diversity, and residential integration is key for those who wish to think about the accommodation of multiple groups in a diverse society. Residential patterns—who lives next to whom—indicate powerfully the joint effects of nativity, ethnicity, and class. What is in our view particularly noteworthy about these patterns is that the neighborhood environment is one of the most intimate areas of social life into which government policy intrudes (though it does so only asymmetrically). Equal opportunity policy, at least on paper, proscribes discrimination in the housing market, yet households are free to re-sort themselves into communities through the means of their own residential mobility. (The degree to which the government is active in housing enforcement is another debate.) Residential patterns offer some of the best evidence we have on who accepts whom in American society and the extent to which these patterns are distinguished by nativity or by other traits.

A REVIEW OF OUR MAJOR FINDINGS

Here we recapitulate our longitudinal framework and summarize our key findings in our three structural assimilation realms: schooling, labor market, and neighborhood. We then go beyond our own empirical work to point to other realms of immigrant adaptation and discuss several implications for contemporary social science theory regarding assimilation. Finally, we return to policy, one of the motivating forces behind this book, to offer thoughts about what our research has to say about contemporary immigration debate, a debate whose arguments will be with us for some time to come.

The Starting Point and Trajectory

Part of the mythology of American immigration is that new arrivals have a strong work ethic that, despite whatever shortcomings they may have in educational preparation or language skills, leads to greater economic progress over time with greater educational achievement across generations. There is another picture of immigration, however, that asserts that the United States is less well positioned to absorb immigrants and maintain high educational and employment levels. Concerns about a U.S. economic retrenchment in 2008 and 2009 reinforce such a position. The concerns about assimilability range from economic progress to cultural adaptation. But, whether positive or negative, many of these views of immigration are based on simple, contrasting snapshots of immigrants and natives on a variety of characteristics. Theoretically, however, it is much more useful to consider both the starting point and the trajectory as elements of immigrant incorporation or adaptation. This dynamic framework is a useful way to evaluate the state of knowledge about immigration.

For example, the socioeconomic starting point for most foreign-born individuals is below that for the average U.S.-born student. It is true that immigrants, the 1.5 generation, and the second generation show lower initial scores on most standardized achievement indicators in our study. At the same time, immigrants and children of immigrants come from households with lower socioeconomic status than their peers. Simple cross-sectional snapshots of education point to lower educational achievement for immigrants and little or modest differences between the second and three-plus generations. This cross-sectional view has the advantage of comparing immigrants of all ages and with varying lengths of time in the United States.

Masked in such comparisons, of course, is the evaluation of starting point and trajectory that our longitudinal approach enables. We are able to get more information about starting point and trajectory in our analysis of schooling and labor market. One insight into immigrant outcomes over time comes from tracing cohorts through the 1994 and 2004 Current Population Survey. Another insight comes from tracing the same individuals over time in panel microdata: the High School and Beyond (HSB) survey and the National Education Longitudinal Study (NELS). Although HSB and NELS are confined to an examination of immigrants who arrive at fairly young ages, these longitudinal data do allow us to see the starting point (family of origin) of immigrants and the second generation, and compare their trajectories to peers in the third and higher generations.

Educational Achievement

It is in the arena of public education that great concern, even alarm, arises about the introduction of first and second generation pupils. How well do they fare? Our basic answer is that once one takes into account other socioeconomic factors, immigrant and second-generation pupils fare much the same in their school achievement as other students. When we use the 1994 and 2004 CPS data to take comparative snapshots of education across generations, we find that the second generation looks very much like the third and higher-order generations. First-generation Americans in every age group (who may have arrived at any time) are less likely to have completed high school. Many, of course, came to the United States as adults with only a primary or partial secondary education. We find, interestingly, that in the 2004 (though not in the 1994) data the second generation was more likely to complete a baccalaureate degree than their counterparts of either the first or third and higher generations.[2] The more nuanced view comes with the HSB and the NELS surveys.

Overall analyses or trajectories from panel data point to few major alterations in the path by immigrant status. Some other traits are predictive, however, and some are not. We find strong effects of family socioeconomic background, so the extent to which immigrants and second-generation children carry their family background through their schooling, they will face some obstacles, just like other Americans. We find virtually no effect of language on the sophomore-senior trajectory; if anything, our results suggest superior outcomes for students from non-English or dual language backgrounds, once other characteristics are controlled.

Race-ethnicity is a complicating factor here, just as in the other realms of adaptation analyzed in this volume. We find some differences in standardized score trajectory by race-ethnicity. Specifically, black and Mexican-origin students score below what one would predict on the basis of other characteristics. We find no differences for students of Asian, Puerto Rican, or other Hispanic origin. The source of this apparent lower performance (through lack of resources, parental aspirations, or discrimination) remains a question. The degree to which immigrants are subsumed in these ethnic categories may have implications for achievement. Recent analyses of even younger children in school suggest these racial and ethnic disparities emerge long before students reach high school (Glick and Hohmann-Marriott 2007). Overall, barriers to achievement seem much more predicated on racial or ethnic identity across all generations (first, second, and third or higher) than on traits directly linked to immigrant status. Further, if one shifts focus to high school graduation and postsecondary schooling, one finds that blacks and some other minority ethnic group members are more likely to complete secondary schooling and go on to further education.

That basic snapshots indicate that immigrants have lower education levels than natives is an incomplete picture. Some of that differential is explained by the adult immigrants who received less formal schooling in their origin countries. Some additional portion is attributable to the difference in SES and other traits at the starting line that tends to disadvantage immigrants. The statistical analysis of the panel data helps complete the picture. Immigrants and natives who are on the same footing—that is, they are enrolled in the sophomore year of high school—do about equally well getting through school and graduating.

The Labor Market

The sphere of earnings has been most extensively studied for immigrant so-cioeconomic attainment, again revealing the tendency to focus on pecuniary outcomes. As we have discussed, many early studies in this area found that immigrant earnings trajectories rose quickly to meet or exceed those for na-tives. Subsequent studies tempered that finding, and still more recent stud-ies revived the view that immigrants do quite well, all told. One important consideration in the comparison concerns the starting point itself. The par-ticular concern is about declining cohort quality (Borjas 1999), in which more recent immigrants arrive with fewer skills. There is some evidence to support the declining cohort quality notion and even more evidence for the heterogeneity of immigrant skills.[3] For us, a key aspect of the picture is—once again—the trajectory immigrants and their children trace.

Our first round of insights in chapter 6 comes from generational compar-isons in the Current Population Survey. These cross-sectional results point to higher levels of poverty, occupational dissimilarity, and earnings gaps in the first generation compared to the third. The CPS snapshot shows that gaps are larger for more recent arrivals than those who came before 1970, consistent with previous research (Bean and Stevens 2003). Overall, we ob-serve far fewer differences between the second and third-plus generations in occupation, earnings, or poverty status. We do not find compelling evidence for declining cohort quality, either. Our key finding from comparing labor force surveys a decade apart is that immigrants of more recent vintage tend to catch up to natives in terms of occupational status and other indicators of achievement. The second generation differs modestly from higher-order generations.

Chapter 6 relies on longitudinal comparisons to trace achievement in the labor market for persons early in their working careers. We turn again to the longitudinal educational surveys (HSB and NELS). We get a much richer picture, one that allows us to examine the relative impact of a host of traits not available in the CPS data and, more important, trace the achievement trajectories of the same people over several years (the same, in fact, as those observed for education in chapter 5), a perspective more closely in tune with models of assimilation. In addition, we include extensive controls for background, with test scores and family SES being particularly important indicators not available in the labor force survey. Echoing decades of social science research, our longitudinal study finds that family background, high school completion, and race-ethnicity all condition labor market achieve-ment in measurable ways. From these panel data, the central finding is that immigrants fare no worse than natives who come from similar socioeco-nomic backgrounds.

All is of course not equal for immigrants, and our findings do show that earlier socioeconomic disadvantages—lower SES, upbringing in a nonintact family, poor earlier academic performance—all can cumulate to influence labor market outcomes. Immigrants also carry their race and ethnicity into the American context. In several of our longitudinal analyses, we detect lower earnings for minority groups (often for blacks, sometimes for Mexicans and other groups) net of the other background traits. This raises the specter of segmented assimilation. Beyond this, however, being a member of the first or second generation has little more to say about life chances.

Immigrants and the second generation show high levels of labor force attachment in our study. Most have incomes that would place them within the American mainstream. Once their somewhat disadvantaged starting point is taken into account, they have a trajectory that takes them on a parallel path to natives. Many start with some disadvantage: limited English language proficiency, less human capital, less cultural familiarity with U.S. institutions and labor markets. This certainly works to counterbalance any sharper trajectory, motivation, and other gainful traits. If one takes the results of this study in tandem with the findings of a growing body of labor market studies, one concludes that most immigrants succeed in American society.

Residential Patterns

The urban residential mosaic provides a great deal of information about how the U.S. social system operates. In opinion surveys, questions about whether one would accept a person (usually an ethnic minority group member) in the neighborhood tap sentiments about social proximity. The neighborhood is one of the most intimate areas in which the government does intervene, at least in the form of legal strictures against housing discrimination.[4]

Chapter 7 offers insights into the way in which time, within and across generations, operates to erode immigrant and ethnic clustering. Although we cannot use panel data to trace residential life histories of individuals, we can examine arrival cohort and look broadly at the vintage of various ethnic groups. First, the notion of cities being divided into immigrant ghettos, clusters of residential areas with immigrants of diverse origins, is as inaccurate a picture as it is persistent. Unquestionably, immigrants are segregated. About one-third of immigrants would have to move to new neighborhoods within their metropolitan area to produce an even distribution with respect to natives, but segregation also declines measurably with time in country. In analysis of data from the 2000 Census, we found that pre-1965 immigrants are about 40 percent less segregated than those who arrived in the 1990s. As chapter 7 discussed, groups of older vintage persons, whose ancestors arrived in earlier epochs, are less segregated. Irish and German Americans, for example, are less segregated than Greeks and Portuguese. Similarly, Vietnamese and Salvadoran Americans are more segregated than Asian and Latin

American immigrants. Thus, both individual and group intermingling with time is evident.

With time, immigrants and their descendants mix, but it is equally clear that residential fissures persist between subgroups. We find clear evidence that place of birth overshadows arrival period in determining residential patterns. Whether we look at individual large cities or an average over metropolitan areas, immigrants are more clustered by their origins than by when they arrived. What may be important about these findings is that some arrival cohort effects show through in individual cities, though it is often modest next to nativity effects.

Evidence for residential segmentation in our results is modest. We have already seen that place of birth more strongly separates neighborhood than period of arrival. What is more, our results suggest that there is further differentiation for major panethnic or racial groups. Immigrants from Asia and Europe are far less segregated, given their period of arrival and the size of the city in which they live, than immigrants from other origins. By contrast, immigrants from Africa are more segregated than any other group. Immigrants from the Caribbean, Central America, and South America are only slightly less segregated than Africans. Mexican immigrants are more segregated than Asian immigrants but less so than African immigrants. Stronger evidence for residential segmentation would have to come in the form of a strict residential hierarchy based on race (and relatedly skin color), regardless of origin. We observe this only in part.

Accumulated social science research, some of which we discussed in earlier chapters, indicates that those with more resources (household income, education, and so on) live nearer to native whites. We cannot readily ascertain the degree to which such better-off minority households consciously seek this proximity to gain access to public resources (schools, parks, lower crime rates) versus the desire to have white or mixed-ethnicity neighbors per se. Although we cannot rule out a role for self-segregation, a wealth of independent evidence points to discrimination and ethnic stratification for producing the residential separation we see.

In sum, a study of structural assimilation confronts many myths about immigration. One powerful and persistent image is that of the "up by bootstraps" story.[5] Surely we find evidence consistent with this, at least in the sense that immigrants arrive (in school) with more modest means and begin to climb the ladder both in school and in the labor market. A second compelling image has been the melting pot notion, in which all immigrants have similar opportunities to become part of the American scene. The immigrant flow to the United States is actually quite diverse not only by national origin, but also skills and training. Immigrants and their children start off with a disadvantage in climbing the socioeconomic ladder. They are neither a nascent underclass nor super-achievers, and racial-ethnic differences persist across generations. The residential segregation of immigrants does decline with time, both within the first and across subsequent generations. But here again there is reason to temper the melting pot image: the difference between contemporary Asian and African immigrant residential patterns is probably the starkest indicator that not all is equal. Immigrants arrive not into a blank slate, but into a complex society with an array of social institutions: the context of reception. This context matters in that race and ethnic background (separate from immigrant status) help predict educational, labor market, and residential outcomes.

OTHER REALMS OF ASSIMILIATION

Our presentation has concentrated on labor force, schooling, and neighborhood, dimensions of structural assimilation that are closely linked to economic well-being of individuals and the broader society. Clearly the range of traits or dimension on which adaptation might be measured is extensive. A large body of research is devoted to these other dimensions of assimilation and acculturation. We take here only a brief look at a few areas of structural assimilation that have attracted considerable social science research: language acquisition, naturalization and political incorporation, childbearing and family patterns, and intermarriage.

Language Acquisition

Language is sometimes contested territory in the realm of immigration and immigrant policy. Samuel Huntington, whose views we discussed at the outset of this volume, has raised particular concern about language (and cultural) transition of the large contemporary flow of immigrants from Latin America (2004). Despite the concerns about English language acquisition and use—occasionally even seen in the flare-up to designate English as the official language of the United States or an individual state or a municipality—the transition to English language proficiency is manifest. In a comprehensive study, Richard Alba and his coauthors found that "the majority of third- and later-generation children speak only English at home, which implies that, with probably limited exceptions, they will grow up to be English monolinguals who have at most fragmentary knowledge of a mother tongue" (Alba et al. 2002, 480). At the same time, these authors found somewhat lower rates of conversion to English-only for those whose origins are in Spanish-speaking nations. After conducting a multigenerational survival analysis of home country languages from a broad array of origins, Ruben Rumbaut, Douglas Massey, and Frank Bean concluded, a bit impishly, that, "like taxes and biological death, linguistic death seems to be a sure thing in the United States, even for Mexicans living in Los Angeles, a city with one of the largest Spanish-speaking urban populations in the world" (2006). In their comprehensive review, Waters and Jimenez summarize the state of language assimilation as one in which the immigrant generation makes some progress in English; the second generation is often bilingual, and the third generation is predominantly English-only (2005). With time, a generation or two, language acquisition seems to be an almost inexorable process.

Citizenship and Naturalization

Naturalization is keenly watched as an indicator of conscious adoption of and commitment to the American setting. And beyond naturalization, voting is a key indicator of more general political incorporation—assimilation—into the receiving society. Predictors of naturalization rates, by country of origin and characteristics of the individual, are scrutinized for the information they might convey about long-term settlement, the future composition of the American electorate, and demands on public sector resources. Of course, because the United States has birthright citizenship, all those born in U.S. territory are citizens, so the American naturalization process, unlike some European immigrant-receiving states, applies principally to the first generation. Commitment to stay is of course a major reason to naturalize, but there are instrumental reasons as well. Beyond the political rights and access to social provision guaranteed through citizenship, a naturalized immigrant (as opposed to a noncitizen permanent resident, a green-card holder) can bring in other immediate family members under the exempt admission categories. These several variables, again including both individual traits and country of origin, help predict voting turnout as well (Bueker 2005).

Immigrants naturalize at widely varying rates by country of origin. A host of factors are involved in predicting these rates, and include origin country proximity to the United States, income, education, and length of eligible residence time in the United States (Bueker 2005). Country of origin matters, even after controlling for personal traits. For much of the latter decades of the twentieth century, immigrants from U.S. neighbors Mexico and Canada were much less likely to naturalize; by contrast, immigrants from China and Cuba did so at comparatively high rates (Liang 1994). Although it is difficult to tell definitively from the kinds of data used in many naturalization studies, the general thinking would be that immigrants with relative ease of circulation across the border and those from less economically and politically fettered societies are less likely to naturalize. Presumably this is because they are less likely to perceive their move to the United States as irreversible. Clearly, international migrants are embedded in a social process and network. Irene Bloemraad has examined patterns of citizenship acquisition in the United States and Canada. She argued that citizenship acquisition and political incorporation more generally are decidedly social processes where friends, family, and community organizations play an important role in encouraging or facilitating the change, a process she describes as structured mobilization (2006).

Complications of status (and acquisition) and the prevalence of mixed-status families—some members in legal status, some illegal—feed directly into policy concerns. Michael Fix and Wendy Zimmerman pointed out, for instance, that changes in the ease and routes to legal status, could "increase the number of mixed-status families whose members could face divided fates as the parents are locked into illegal status while their children are born as citizens" (2001, 398).

Family Formation

How immigrants and their descendants build families has long-term consequences for the receiving society. Many American immigrants tend to come from areas of the world that have higher fertility rates than the United States, though once again the perception of the scale of these differentials may outrun the reality. At the same time, immigrants are usually a selective subset of those populations—younger, highly motivated, sometimes higher in socioeconomic status, sometimes lower.

U.S. Census Bureau data for 2006 show that U.S.-native women completing their childbearing (ages forty to forty-four) have 1.82 children on average. Foreign-born women in the same age group have 2.05 children, with a negligible difference between naturalized and noncitizen immigrants (U.S. Bureau of the Census 2007a). Unfortunately, these data are unable to differentiate where the childbearing took place. Thus, it is not a simple matter to determine how birth rates change with migration to the United States. Persistent high fertility within and across generations in the United States has implications for population growth and probably also for rates of assimilation. Larger families imply great competition for household resources. This may in turn depress the opportunity for translating effort in the current generation into gains for the subsequent generation. Kenneth Johnson and Daniel Lichter pointed out the potential for demographic transformation in new immigrant growth areas, often predominantly rural or small-town in character and receiving large numbers of new Hispanic immigrants (2008).

The evidence accumulated to date, however, suggests that aggregate native-immigrant fertility differentials are modest, as noted above. Within these broad classifications birth rates do vary by country of origin and other background characteristics of the women (Ford 1985; Kahn 1994; Pagnini 1997). Our own work on family-building patterns—again using these longitudinal school-based data—points to the continuing importance of race and ethnic differentials in the timing of marriage and first birth (Glick et al.

2006). Our results also point to the important intertwining of the timing of human capital formation and family formation. Adolescent females, across all ethnic groups and regardless of generation, whose academic careers are supported and rewarded are also likely to have slower family formation. At the same time, this research provides some support for the minority group status hypothesis, wherein minority group members (here immigrants) pursue higher socioeconomic status through schooling, and thus delay family formation.

Moreover, fertility rates in several major sending countries are quite low now. This is especially noteworthy for the largest sending country, Mexico, where the total fertility rate (TFR), at 2.4, is only modestly above replacement (Bean and Stevens 2003, 63). Two major East Asian–origin sending countries, China (1.6) and South Korea (1.1), are well below replacement, with Cuba, Colombia, and Jamaica all exhibiting recent fertility near replacement levels. Above-replacement TFR values are found for the Dominican Republic (2.9), India (2.9), and the Philippines (3.4), all significant sending countries, but even these are not high fertility settings (Population Reference Bureau 2007). The overall message, then, is that the family-building patterns of the most recent wave of immigrants fall within the U.S. range.

Intermarriage

Marriage across social groups is perhaps the ultimate indicator of admixture into American society. For sociologists, intermarriage has always been a powerful measure of individual and group acceptance, and the study of marriage patterns, along ethnic and other lines, is extensive. Certainly Milton Gordon and many who have come since have seen intermarriage in this way; in fact Gordon takes intermarriage to be a separate dimension of assimilation distinct from structural assimilation (1964, 71). Intermarriage also gives rise to children of dual or multiple ancestries, and so directly stirs the melting pot.

Studies of intermarriage reveal widely varying rates by nationality, ethnicity, and socioeconomic grouping. As with other analyses of adaptation, how one defines the relevant groups determines a bit about what one sees in the way of little or much intermarriage. Most of the study of intermarriage has concentrated on ethnic groups, with the study of intermarriage rates by nativity and generation lagging behind.

Overall, intermarriage in the United States is increasing. Black-white intermarriage rose sharply during the 1970s and the 1980s (Farley 1996, 262) and continues to increase. Intermarriage rates for other groups are much higher. Citing Frank Bean and Gillian Stevens (2003), Jennifer Lee and Frank Bean observed that "the percentages of Asian or Latino husbands or wives having spouses of another race or ethnicity exceeded 30 percent by the late 1990s, with the vast majority married to a white partner" (2004, 195). This has implications for identity, particularly multiple ancestry identity. One recent projection placed the multiple ancestry share of the U.S. population at 2050 at 21 percent under medium assumptions for immigration and intermarriage (Waters 2000a).

Most of these analyses and projections use broad racial and ethnic categories and have little to say directly about nativity. Bean and Stevens pointed out the importance of cross-nativity marriages in the immigrant flow itself (2003). Zhenchao Qian and Daniel Lichter did look directly at the role of nativity (immigrant versus U.S. born) in intermarriage across broad racial lines. They found greater propensity for intermarriage among Latinos and Asians than among blacks (2001). More important for assimilation study, they found that intermarriage increased in later generations. In the end, they placed more weight on racial differences than on nativity itself. This, then, is the consistent finding across the many realms of adaptation, those we investigate in this volume and those addressed by others: racial and ethnic differences override those based on nativity alone.

IMPLICATIONS FOR ADAPTATION AND ASSIMILATION THEORY

Our overarching results offer some implications for theories about immigrant assimilation. The stream of immigrants to the United States has been so large and diverse in the last few decades as to defy generalization. Still, the public debate inevitably speaks of immigration and changes in policy, whether alterations to categories of admission or redistribution of resources for instruction in the primary grades will affect a huge swath of potential and actual new arrivals.

Our findings cast an uneven light on assimilation theory. Theoretical perspectives regarding immigrant adaptation have evolved considerably over the last half-century. Early thinking, often identified with Milton Gordon, has been tagged straight-line assimilation or the melting pot model (1964). Other writing challenged the melting pot and offered the alternative metaphors of stewpot or salad bowl. In the 1990s, the segmented assimilation perspective gained increasing currency, with scholars suggesting that alternative paths, linked closely to racial and ethnic background in the particular American setting, arose for members of the second generation (Portes and Zhou 1993; Portes and Rumbaut 2001). Some still more recent writing can be interpreted as again supportive of more of the conventional straight-line perspective (Alba and Nee 2003). We would agree with Alba and Nee that "there is no reason to believe that assimilation is inevitable" (2003, 275). Thus, evidence for any assimilation is important, and moreover, evidence for the kinds of assimilation under way is of particular interest.

One of our major arguments is not so much about assimilation, per se, but how to look at it. Our approach, particularly in chapters 5 and 6, is to invoke the notion of the starting line and trajectory. Only by looking at both can we properly understand the path immigrants travel in the United States. Because historical and contemporary immigrants often arrive with less (money and skills), comparisons over time are crucial. Most snapshots will show immigrants at a disadvantage, but do not tell us whether the path traced over time is one of success or failure.

Overall, our results indicate that immigrants and the second generation do succeed, tracing an upward socioeconomic trajectory parallel to that of the third-plus generation. If they face barriers, the barriers are similar to those their counterparts faced. In particular, race and ethnicity still matter; they condition assimilation but do not dominate it. The strong view of segmented assimilation theory would hold that with time (again, within and across generations) immigrants and their minority group descendants would fall further behind and become more isolated. Our results do not match this scenario. In some of our results, even after controlling for a host of characteristics, certain minority group members do realize fewer returns to their schooling or workplace effort than others. We do find this evidence of racial and ethnicity conditioning outcomes in school, workforce, and neighborhood, but the patterns are variable across groups and intertwined with other strong forces. Further, the similar persistence of family background and race as predictive across generations casts some doubt on any hegemonic view of segmentation. Proponents of segmented assimilation have made it clear, however, that immigrants are absorbed into a host society with a racial-ethnic system that affects immigrants' chances, no matter their origin. Our results come closer to supporting the straight-line assimilation pattern than they do the strong segmentation pattern.

NEW FACES: IMMIGRATION AND IMMIGRANT POLICY

The United States is experiencing a large, new wave of immigration, but it is not a tidal wave. Its size as a proportion of the U.S. population is not yet as large as it was a century ago, and is in fact on the order of only half its historical peak. Still, many wonder whether the United States can successfully absorb a million or so new residents per year. That dozens of thousands of those new arrivals come into the country without authorization only fans the flames of contentious debate.

The foreign born constitute a large influx into the American labor market. Immigrants make up 15.4 percent of the 2006 U.S. workforce.[6] As we pointed out in chapter 1, the U.S. labor force in 2000 included about 22 million more workers than it would have done had women remained at

1960 participation rates, an increment about the same as the foreign-born civilian labor force in 2000 (U.S. Bureau of the Census 2007a). Many economies strain somewhat under the pressure of adding large ranks of new workers. Without a doubt, receiving and hiring individuals who arrive with less skill, speak another language, and perhaps entered illegally presents a different set of challenges, but the comparison provides a useful numerical perspective on the scale of the change.

Immigration, Social Science, and the Policy Circuit

Americans, many of themselves recently descended from immigrants, express some reservations about increasing the annual number of new admissions, but overall they approach immigration with considerable equanimity. Even in the 2006 and 2007 marches and contentious debates about immigration, much of the discourse has preserved the view that the United States remains a country of immigration, a haven and a golden door to many, and a country that values peoples of diverse origins. At least that is the public rhetoric. The complaints tend to hinge on the total number of immigrants, chalenge of undocumented immigration, and the value of particular categories ofadmission.

Compared to a century ago, U.S. immigration today takes place in a context of a highly technological (and highly skilled) economy and a global market (Massey, Durand, and Malone 2002; Stalker 2000). These characterizations influence debate about immigration. Particularly with regard to immigration, the pattern of economic growth prompts some to consider more skills-based immigration and perhaps a point system (Borjas 1999). Such a call not only aligns with immigrant policy in some other countries, but also echoes the discussion and recommendation of the National Commission on Immigration Reform at work more than a decade ago.

Are these the right policy levers to push? What will be the implications for the size, growth, and diversity of the American population? Can these immigrants adapt and be absorbed into American society? What are the implications for social welfare policies and government services? These are difficult questions that immigration pushes to the fore.

We have distinguished immigration policy from immigrant policy. Immigration policy concerns itself with the number and composition of new arrivals to the United States. Immigrant policy concerns itself with the treatment of those who have already arrived. The two are closely intertwined and sometimes, as in treatment of undocumented immigrants, blurred. We conclude with several thoughts about where this research leads us with regard to immigration and immigrant policy.

Many of the policy choices the nation faces depend on the articulation of our values, rather than on any engineering guided by findings from social science. Decisions about the ethnic diversity of the society and the balance between family reunification, refugees, and skill-based immigration can be informed by social science, but can also go beyond it.

Number and Composition of Immigrants

It is probably impossible to determine an optimal flow of immigrants. The number of persons entering the United States is, ultimately, a choice that our society wishes to make. Can we absorb the current flow of about 800,000 per year? Probably yes. The number is high, but as we state, not out of bounds with historical experience.

Immigration policy is one of the few areas—arguably the sole area—in which American society gets to set explicit policy about the kinds of people who can join. Since the 1965 revisions to the immigration law, U.S. immigration policy has favored family connections, with additional provisions for skilled workers and refugees. In 1994, 58 percent of all legal immigrants to the United States came through family reunification channels (U.S. Immigration and Naturalization Service 1996). By 2004, 66 percent of legal immigration was family-based (U.S. Department of Homeland Security 2005). It is difficult to foresee circumstances that would substantially curtail these family-based admissions. These admissions have been running at over 200,000 persons annually.

Recent policy has, in fact, shifted the balance toward skills. The number of employment-based immigrants more than doubled between 1996 and 2005. The fact that immigrants do about as well as natives, once the starting point is taken into account, confirms the salutary effect of the diverse American immigrant pool. The second generation also does as well as the others. It would be true that more skilled immigrants would earn more and perhaps have a greater impact on national income (gross domestic product, or GDP), yet there is no evidence that immigrants, per se, are a drain on the economy or fall increasingly behind natives over the working life.

Affirmative Action and Antidiscrimination Policies

For many years Americans have been in the grips of a wrenching debate about affirmative action and ethnically based policies.[7] And legal scholar Peter Schuck writes, "affirmative action policy is even more divisive and unsettled today than at its inception" (2003, 134). These battles have been fought in state voter referenda, among them California in 1996 and Michigan in 2006. U.S. Supreme Court decisions from the 1954 Brown v. Board of Education case through the 1978 Bakke case regarding reverse discrimination, to the 2007 Seattle public schools case regarding intervention to achieve diversity or ethnic balance in public schools have reset the parameters of public policy. Immigration stirs the ethnic pot and thus complicates the issue. It is fair to say that much of U.S. civil rights policy was carved out on the presumption of a black and white world. From the vantage point of U.S. history in the mid-twentieth century, perhaps this was appropriate, but it is no longer.

Who has standing? Even in the black-white world of conventional affirmative action discussion, questions have been raised about the right to redress across generations: the claims of those originally wronged versus their descendants. The arguments are many and varied (Edley 1996). This is not the place to review them all, but Peter Schuck's argument is noteworthy; he has argued that contemporary immigration, among other factors, is undermining the conceptual and normative underpinnings of affirmative action (2003). For their part, several demographers have pointed out how rapidly immigration is changing the picture, both by adding new ethnic groups and through intermarriage generating subsequent generations of mixed ancestry (Bean and Stevens 2003, 195). Do recent immigrants from the Caribbean or Africa have as much claim to government action or preferences—to remedy—as those whose ancestors were enslaved in the eighteenth- and nineteenth-century United States? There is every bit of evidence that the nineteenth-century treatment of Chinese labor recruits was viciously discriminatory (Lieberson 1980). Do new immigrants from China have claim? What about descendants of the 1940s Japanese Americans who were interned in the Manzanar Camp in the Sierra foothills of California and other places? What about immigrants who come today from a country with a standard of living matching that of the United States but are admittedly ethnic minorities?

The results of our research do argue for stronger antidiscrimination policies. We still observe different outcomes on the basis of ethnic heritage, outcomes that are difficult to wave away as mere group predictions or culture. At the same time, the demise of the two-group world of American civil rights policy calls for some rethinking. Disparate outcome—discrimination—has not disappeared from American society, as many housing, employment and consumer audit studies have shown (Yinger 1995; Pager 2007). The increasingly diverse origins of new immigrants, arriving now after the great waves of civil rights legislation of the 1960s, may call on us to think creatively about how to make those dreams of a society of equal opportunity come true. Although criticized on some points of implementation, the stated goals of the No Child Left Behind policy suggest a national focus on ameliorating just those racial and ethnic disparities in education that we have found are the greatest barriers to subsequent achievement.

Immigrant Adaptation Policy

What policy for immigrants? Need there be a policy expressly for immigrants, separate from policies for which people are eligible on the basis of other criteria? The major message of the research on immigrant adaptation is that only modest immigrant policies need to be adopted, but some of these might be quite helpful in speeding the adjustment of immigrants to American society. (Policies are already in place for refugees; this discussion pertains to other immigrants.) There are two aspects of immigrant policies: eligibility for programs and specific training.

Likely policy revisions would include eligibility criteria, waiting periods, and sponsorships. For several key programs, fewer immigrants are deemed eligible than comparable natives, but research confirms variation across programs and that socioeconomic composition matters appreciably (Van Hook, Glick, and Bean 1999). Efforts to restrict access of U.S.-born children to benefits, such as education, are totally miscast. Public expenditures are an investment in the future. Occasionally a flag is raised to limit immigrant access to health care, but usually such proposals are denied on humanitarian grounds.

We might think more generally about social welfare provision, especially education. Many have pointed out that the United States lags behind many of its high-income peers in providing social welfare (Esping-Anderson 2007; Skocpol 1995). Gøsta Esping-Anderson, among others, has argued for redistribution of U.S. welfare state resources toward children (2007). This argument is based, in part, on increasing evidence that early childhood investments pay long term dividends, coupled with the observation of the higher level of inequality, for children as well as adults, in the United States (Heckman, Krueger, and Friedman 2003).

Immigration—both immigration policy and immigrant policy—is part of these discussions. Our work shows that on average immigrants arrive with fewer resources than higher-order generations. At the same time, immigrants and their children do well in their trajectory. Policies to improve socioeconomic conditions and early life opportunities will benefit all, and especially the first two generations.

The most important specific social policy for which the public sector should contribute is language training. Language proficiency clearly plays into school performance and later job performance. Students do better on substantive and achievement tests, and because school performance is cumulative, better skills at the outset indicate high trajectories later. Not too much intervention is really needed for children. The work on language assimilation we reviewed and our own analysis of in-school performance suggest that children of the second and the 1.5 generation adapt quite quickly. Guiding and encouraging the natural proclivity to adopt the host language might be enough. For older persons, particularly adults already in the labor force, more aggressive intervention may be useful. Here individuals will be rewarded with better abilities to negotiate their local American community, and the society as a whole may be spared more of the agonizing tension over multilinguality. There is probably no way that the United States in its public countenance can adequately accommodate (officially, in schools, on ballots, in workplaces, in public settings) all the languages spoken by immigrants. The fiercest battle will be fought—and has already seen several skirmishes in several states in recent years—over bilingual education. On this front, it will be most difficult to strike a balance between the needs of new Americans and the demand for a simple coherent society as exemplified by having all instruction in the historically dominant language.

CONCLUSION

The current round of immigration puts stress on American society, just as previous waves brought debate and contention, policy and backlash. It is a measure of the American success story that the nation continues to perceive itself as a country of immigration. In all likelihood, both immigrants and the nation will succeed in the wake of the movement of many new faces to America's shores.

CHAPTER 1

1. Writers vary here, some preferring *illegal*, others *undocumented* or *unauthorized*. It is important to note that of the illegal (unauthorized) population in the United States at any one time, the routes of entry vary. Some in this group, such as the substantial number who overstay visas, arrive legally and then transition to unauthorized or illegal status.

2. We have used this conceptualization in our own earlier work. Similar approaches have been taken by others (Perlmann 2005; Rumbaut 1999; Kasnitz, Mollenkopf, and Waters 2004).

3. We will speak of the *vintage* of various ethnic groups, and by this we mean the general arrival time (era) of their immigrant forbears (White and Glick 1999).

CHAPTER 2

1. Although the number of undocumented migrants is notoriously difficulty to determine, especially between censuses, Jeffrey Passel placed the unauthorized flow at 450,000 annually between 1990 and 1994 and 750,000 annually between 1995 and 1999 (Passel 2005).

2. The 1990s decade was not aberrant in this regard. Companion calculations for the 1980s indicate that births over the decade added 16.8 percent to the 1980 population, and that documented immigration added 3.2 percent. For the 2001 to 2004 interval, births added 6.1 percent and documented immigration 1.9 percent to the resident U.S.

population. The scale of adjustment for the immigration contribution for the 1980s and the early 2000s would likely be comparable to that for the 1990s.

3. These would include immigration during the 1960s, 1970s, and 1980s of 3.7, 7.7, and 10.0 million, respectively, with about 10 million in the simulation for the 1990s. A full description of the method is included in a paper Barry Edmonston and Jeffrey Passel presented at the 1994 Annual Meeting of the Population Association of America. These authors also applied the procedure historically. They calculated that the 1990 population of the United States would be about 174 million had there been no immigration since 1900 (Edmonston and Passel 1994). They did not provide the companion fertility scenarios.

4. In 2000, the labor force participation rate of the foreign born was 67.7 percent (U.S. Bureau of the Census 2007a). Between 1960 and 2000, immigrants added another 32 million to the pool—about 24 million legal and 8.4 million undocumented (Passel 2005).

5. Douglas Massey and Chiara Capoferro have pointed out that the 1986 Immigration Reform and Control Act legalization program may have flooded some labor markets with newly authorized workers even as it gave these workers the means to move legally elsewhere (2008).

6. These recent Census Bureau estimates reflect 2006 metropolitan boundary redefinition and are extensive territories. Comparable values of this sort for the broader period 1960 to the present are not uniformly available.

7. These values are from the Census Bureau's *State and Metropolitan Area Data Book 1997*, table B1. Values for net domestic migration are calculated from other columns. We use here data for primary metropolitan statistical areas.

8. This positive sentiment in New York (and a number of other places) is fairly longstanding across the political spectrum. It is worth noting that both Jack Kemp (the 1996 Republican vice presidential nominee) from New York and Mario Cuomo (Democrat, the former governor of New York) supported immigration. Of course mayors and governors of other areas have expressed alternative views. Smaller places might not be as receptive to significant influxes of new immigrants. Charles Hirschman and Douglas Massey have suggested that initial tensions, uncertainty, and ambivalence among small town residents can be observed, but that these can also give way to acceptance (2008).

9. Metropolitan areas were not defined for 1910, though the municipal boundaries (city) assuredly captured a very large proportion of the population than might be regarded as metropolitan. The 2000 data for this figure refer to primary metropolitan statistical areas. In some areas, such as New York and Philadelphia, consolidated metropolitan statistical areas would be more extensive and contain more people than the PMSAs, but the story would remain much the same. Data for 2000 come from the 2001 Current Population Survey.

10. We use the data for the core metropolitan division; the broader Miami–Ft. Lauderdale–Miami Beach area records 35 percent foreign born (U.S. Bureau of the Census 2006, table B4).

11. These immigrants' descendants would be ethnic group members of older and newer vintage, respectively.

12. Joel Perlmann captured this comparison, perhaps most succinctly and cleverly, in his title *Italians Then, Mexicans Now,* though his study looks at a varying and wider array of immigrant and ethnic groups (2005).

13. In the 1951 to 1960 interval, the leading Pacific origins included Japan, Hong Kong, and the Philippines. Israel sent more immigrants than these last two countries, and is classified as an Asian origin in INS statistics.

14. These numbers have been calculated from Paul Demeny (1986) and U.S. Bureau of the Census (2007a), and Homeland Security Office of Immigration statistics data from 2000, 2003, and 2005. We take the ratio of the number of immigrants to the United States during the period divided by the total world population estimate for that period. The simple approximation is taken as the average annual migration for the decade following the year in the figure (1850, 1900, 1950, and 1990). For the final entry, we have taken U.S. immigration from 1990 to 1999 to calculate the annual average, and include an estimate of undocumented migration over the decade of 5.8 million (Passell 2005). These calculations remove the United States from the world population in the denominator.

CHAPTER 3

1. Brubaker also made an enumerated point that "the unit within which the change occurs—the unit that undergoes assimilation—is not the person but a multi-generational population" (2001, 543). This is perceptive and provocative. We may differ slightly in that our analysis, especially of schooling and labor market, will measure outcomes for in-

dividuals, and statistical results will of course necessarily aggregate these (for covariates). The interpretation is best seen as multilevel, where individual processes and circumstances are partly driven by aggregates (state policy, group affiliation). These effects are manifest at the individual level and are aggregated to group outcomes.

2.   Although Greenman and Xie offered many pertinent observations and useful empirical analysis of longitudinal data, our approach (and that of many others, we suggest) would differ conceptually from theirs. Where they labeled various measures of duration assimilation, that is de facto, we take these indicators to be predictors of assimilation, which is itself better indicated by socioeconomic outcomes.

3.   Greenman and Xie's usage of *negative* is somewhat different than that of Chiswick and Miller, mentioned earlier.

4.   Their study included students who had already met the test of admission to an elite post-secondary institution. It is not clear what the comparable data and analysis would show at an earlier educational stage.

5.   For ease of exposition, we will often speak simply of the third generation.

6.   Immigrants, grouped by period of arrival, can be termed arrival cohorts. Thus, Borjas is speaking of more recent cohorts (arriving groups of immigrants) as less skilled, on average, than earlier cohorts. If this holds, it can give rise to an apparent immigrant labor market success when analyzed with cross-sectional data. Such a possibility provides all the more argument for empirical analysis tracing the longitudinal experience of individuals.

7.   The same can be said about residential patterns outside of urban areas. Neighborhood data limited to metropolitan areas confine our analysis to these larger agglomerations. Statistical information of residential segregation, the outcome we examine here, is much more limited for nonmetropolitan areas. Still, there are efforts to examine the spatial incorporation of immigrants in small town and rural America as well (Massey 2008).

8.   To restate the contention, ethnic groups A and B might be segregated somewhat from one another overall, but after controlling for duration in the country (and the income differences associated with duration), there is no additional predictive power offered by ethnic group. Obviously this statement reasserts the intertwining of the dimensions of assimilation first considered by Gordon and refined by others since.

9.   White and Glick operationalized vintage to be the median year of ar-

rival of all recorded immigrants from that national origin. Although certainly approximate, it does provide a numerical value and wider range for what in other contexts were simply called old and new immigrants (1999).

CHAPTER 4

1. The 1940s Bracero Program and the 1952 Texas Proviso, which provided a loophole making it easier for employers to hire undocumented aliens (Calavita 1994), and various temporary agricultural visa programs, provide such examples.

2. Although much of the debate is cast in terms of illegal versus legal immigration, the data to which we have access do not measure legal status. For second-generation people in our analysis, almost all will be legal (citizens) because they were born on U.S. soil, regardless of the legal status of their parents.

3. The 1921 act based admissions quotas on the 1910 Census population; the 1924 act set the categories back to the 1890 Census (Jasso and Rosenzweig 1990).

4. The Bracero Program actually included nationals from several Western Hemisphere nations, but more than 70 percent of Braceros were Mexican. In additional to this fact, David Reimers points out that temporary U.S. guestworker programs date as far back as 1917 (1985).

5. Ethnocentricism and ethnic prejudice are undoubtedly part of the picture. Both Reimers (1985) and Stanley Lieberson (1980) have described hostility toward various groups, particularly Asians, in this era.

6. Amnesty also presumably reduces the constraints on the newly legalized migrants, enabling further migration and occupational change within the United States. We can only acknowledge here also the wide-ranging discussion of the relatively free movement of labor versus capital in a globalizing economy.

7. In a parallel case about a decade earlier, the U.S. Supreme Court struck down a provision of Texas law that allowed the state to withhold funding from local districts for the education of illegal immigrants (Plyler v. Doe 457 U.S. 202 (1982), available at: http://www.oyez.org/cases/1980-1989/1981-1981_80_1538/).

8. George Borjas argued that immigrants also responded by increasing their labor supply in ways that made them eligible for employer-sponsored health care benefits (2003).

9. The Immigration Act of 1990 (PL 101–649) established the commission, along with introducing revisions to U.S. legal immigration. The commission's mandate required it "to examine and make recommendations regarding the implementation and impact of U.S. immigration policy" (USCIR 1994, preface).

10. Despite that fact that the Social Security Act of 1935 is often taken to be the signal event placing the United States on the road to the social welfare state, the picture is considerably more complicated. Not only was some form of social welfare well-ingrained much earlier—at the turn of the twentieth century, the U.S. government spent about one-fourth of its income on Civil War pensions—the American style itself always differed from some European nations, and it evolved over the twentieth century (Skocpol 1995).

11. The National Academy of Sciences panel has pointed out the substantial variation in types of programs in which immigrants and natives participate (Smith and Edmonston 1997).

12. Of course, international migration has been linked to trade and technology in other eras (Chiswick and Hatton 2002), even as it picked up pace over the twentieth century and into the twenty-first (Castles and Miller 1993).

13. The U.S. Census Bureau reported a 10 percent rise in the Gini index of income inequality over ten years, to a value of 0.469 in 2005 (De-Navas-Walt, Proctor, and Lee 2006).

CHAPTER 5

1. Myers showed how important these effects are for CPS measures of educational attainment of California Latinos (Myers 2007).

2. HSB is probably most notable for its link to the controversy regarding public versus private school, and particularly for how the impact of school type differed by ethnicity and socioeconomic disadvantage (Coleman, Hoffer, and Kilgore 1982; Coleman and Hoffer 1987). A considerable literature relating ethnic group characteristics and school and employment outcomes has accumulated through the HSB study. HSB has been used to show that white and Cuban recent immigrants are less likely to drop out and that Chicanos and Puerto Ricans are more likely to do so (Velez 1989). Other HSB analyses have been used to examine the relative influence of tracking within school and differences across school environments (Gamoran and Mare 1989).

3. Sample weights are recalculated on the basis of attrition (those lost to follow-up receive a weight of zero but remain in the data), and we estimate with both weighted and unweighted data.

4. The NELS contains an oversample of Asians, and the sampling strategy across schools varies as well.

5. A more detailed comparison (Bonferroni pairwise comparisons of means) indicates that all pairwise differences of means are significantly different ($p < 0.05$), except the comparison between preschool immigrants and the second generation.

6. We also repeated these same comparisons with unweighted data (as some analysts might prefer). In the unweighted test, the mean test gain for English speakers is 0.71 points, while the gain for non-English speakers is 1.27 points. Tests for both weighted and unweighted data were highly significant ($p < 0.001$).

7. Recall that Portes and Rumbaut reported substantial variation across nativity-ethnicity-language groups in grade point average (Portes and Rumbaut 1990). Of course, those results were limited to student achievement in San Diego, but it seems quite plausible, given the wide variety of origins and routes to the United States.

CHAPTER 6

1. Of course, a complementary economic viewpoint on immigration examines the impact of new workers through immigration on the labor market outcomes of natives and other immigrants, as seen in the assessment of the National Academy of Sciences (Smith and Edmonston 1997).

2. Because it is designed to cover the entire noninstitutional U.S. population, the Current Population Survey data represents all resident immigrants, including refugees and the undocumented. Highly transient and unauthorized populations might be expected to have higher undercoverage rates, but all residents are included.

3. Like all conclusions drawn from similar data, these results are for immigrants who remain in the United States and exclude those who leave within the ten-year interval.

4. The dissimilarity index is a commonly used tool to illustrate the relative distribution of two groups across occupations, neighborhoods or other indicators. It is simply calculated as: $\frac{1}{2} \Sigma \, |(n/N)\text{-}(i/I)|$, where n/N refers to the proportion of natives in a particular occupation and i/I refers to the proportion of immigrants in the same occupation.

5. Myers assigns prestige scores developed and maintained by the National Opinion Research Center. These scores, used by many social scientists, translate a numerical census occupation code from the census into a prestige value between 0 and 100 (actual range is 9 to 82).

6. In theory, selective emigration of the less successful could play a role. The size of the CPS cohort populations across time suggests that any role would be minor. Unfortunately, the United States does not maintain definitive data on emigration.

7. We have conducted a companion double-cohort analysis from the 1990 and 2000 Census. The larger samples in the census data allow us to also adjust for age (birth cohort) as well as immigration arrival cohort (for an application of this technique to immigrants, see Myers and Cranford 1998). These census results are consistent with what we show from the CPS. In most cases, for each birth cohort the decade of change is accompanied by a decline in the poverty rate for the immigrant cohort. The most dramatic declines are found in the younger ages. The elderly, or those aging into the elder bracket over the decade, experienced only moderate declines.

8. These are results from Current Population Survey March Supplement files from the respective years. Income statistics are for the previous calendar year. While the overall pattern for females is quite similar to that for males, women show, as expected, lower incomes among both natives and immigrants. Data are sometimes not enough to support reliable income statistics for recent immigrant women.

9. Technically, 17 percent of either immigrant or native workers would have to make this hypothetical change. The dissimilarity index is symmetric in this regard.

10. Male naturalized citizens are employed in management positions only at very slightly lower rates than U.S.-born males, and the immigrant citizen representation in professional occupations is almost 3 percentage points higher than the U.S.-born male workers (tables not shown). This significantly higher representation in the professional and managerial occupations among immigrant citizens is likely attributable not only to greater U.S. familiarity (minimum duration and language ability for citizenship eligibility), but also to the recruiting networks (business and spouses of U.S. citizens) that would bring in individuals of higher skill who would also be more likely to become citizens.

11. Data for income are presented in constant dollars to adjust for inflation differences between the two surveys.

12. We use the Heckman selection procedure available in STATA9. The se-

lection procedure models the presence of any income in the calendar year before the survey. The regressors included in the probit model for the NELS selection include: dummy variable for old age for grade, living with neither parent, language (three dummy contrasts), dummy for member of the freshened sample, parental data missing. married in 1994, and handicapped. Our HSB approach used similar variables.

13. The introduction of high school graduation does not alter coefficients much, and in fact is offset mostly by a shift in the constant.

14. In fact, one observes very few dramatic shifts in covariates with other variables introduced to the model.

15. Some 71 percent of women in the third-plus generation report being full-time workers in the NELS survey. Second-generation women participate at 68.92 percent. Women in the 1.5 generation report a full-time participation rate of 57.94 percent, and those in the first generation who arrived after schooling had begun report full-time work at 73.38 percent. These are proportions of women reporting one of three categories: unemployed (both not in labor force and looking for work), employed part-time, and employed full-time. Women in the 1.5 generation report higher rates of nonemployment, 25.18 percent versus about 15 percent for the other three generations.

16. The selection equation is of some relevance here. In the Heckman selection estimation we find that married women are much less likely to report earnings in 1999. Those with less ability in English, who are old for their grade in their school, and are raised without either parent present are also less likely to report any earnings.

17. The lack of systematic effects for language ability in our findings is noteworthy.

18. In fiscal years 2000 through 2002, 63.3 percent of all immigrants were family sponsored. Of those admitted under employment-based preferences (16.4 percent), 8.3 percent were skilled-unskilled workers or professionals, and 4.2 percent were professionals with advanced degrees or exceptional ability (U.S. Department of Homeland Security 2003).

CHAPTER 7

1. They emphasize interregional population distribution in their discussion. Issues of proximity are meaningful in any residential environment. Our analysis concentrates on intra-urban residential patterns, a long-standing window on group accommodation.

2. Wilson and Taub, we note, titled their book *There Goes the Neighborhood*. William Clark drew attention to the sharp variation in interpretation regarding segregation, the degree to which racial segregation is attributable to racial discrimination versus compositional variation in income and other socioeconomic traits (2007, n. 1).

3. In work on Australia, Mariah Evans (2004) found that less linguistically proficient workers seem to benefit from linguistic isolation and concentration in ethnic enclaves. Although limited to blacks and whites, Gregory Fairchild's work with U.S. Census microdata lends support to the view of Fischer and Massey that residential segregation is unlikely to be beneficial for minority entrepreneurship (2008).

4. Other studies have used alternative geographic small-area units, mostly block groups (smaller than tracts, but limited in census sample data) and zip code areas (larger than tracts and less consistently defined). The tract is the most common unit used.

5. Coresidence of immigrants with their U.S.-born children, a necessary limitation of calculation from summary file data, will depress segregation values calculated by nativity. Total immigrant-native segregation and that limited to the population of adults track quite closely. Our analyses, which look at both nativity, year of arrival, and ethnicity provide some improvement on such broad calculations.

6. This is the range of unweighted values; if one weights by metropolitan population size, the range is (.31, .38).

7. Here we use the weighted mean dissimilarity of immigrants versus nonimmigrants for the set of all U.S. metropolitan areas. Weighted and unweighted means and the median values are very close.

8. All our data in this chapter are for metropolitan areas. Here we use the term *city* interchangeably.

9. We do not show Oceania, Other Central America, and North America. Because Mexico is tabulated separately, Canada is most of this last category.

10. We have also replicated these analyses with the increasingly used entropy index, and results are much the same.

11. We omit from the display the Other North America (mostly Canada) category, although these values were calculated.

12. Caribbean immigrants may be of any racial-ethnic group; many are of African heritage. Available at: http://factfinder.census.gov2000_SF3 _PCT019 and PCT020, accessed on January 21, 2007.

13. We have confirmed this with a decomposition analysis of place of birth versus year of entry. We thank Weiwei Zhang for assistance with this calculation.

14. For the sake of legibility we exclude from the figure Oceania, for which the simulated value is .73. For Other Central America the value is .80.

15. This is because by design we do not introduce interactions or estimate separate models by origin.

16. Moreover, the modest level of segregation appears—given that the segregation of adult immigrants from adult U.S. born is also modest—to be attributable not simply to the second-generation effect.

CHAPTER 8

1. As Antonio McDaniel and others have pointed out, the intermingling is not a simple admixture and it takes place within a context of dynamic racial classification and social relations (1995).

2. We really cannot look profitably at cohort progression in these data, even though we do have age, since more education was completed following ages we observe.

3. There is also discussion of a bimodal skill distribution of immigrants in high-income receiving societies (Kahn 2004), and an hourglass-shaped skill distribution of receiving economies (Portes and Zhou 1993).

4. To be sure, some state and national policies—directly regarding same-sex unions and indirectly regarding programs surrounding sexual behavior and childbearing—would involve more intimate spheres.

5. Consider the emotional reaction of wrestler Henry Cejudo, son of illegal immigrants from Mexico, on his gold medal victory in the 2008 Olympics for the United States: "I'm living the American dream. . . . The United States is the land of opportunity, so I'm glad I can represent it" (Kevin Baxter, "Henry Cejudo Captures Gold and a Piece of the American Dream," *Los Angeles Times*, August 20, 2008).

6. This number represents the proportion of the employed civilian population that is foreign born in 2006.

7. Affirmative action spans more than ethnically based characteristics, but those are the ones of particular relevance to immigration.

REFERENCES

Akresh, Ilana R. 2006. "Occupational Mobility Among Legal Immigrants to the United States." *International Migration Review* 40(4): 854–84.

Alba, Richard. 1990. *Ethnic Identity: The Transformation of White America*. New Haven, Conn.: Yale University Press.

———. 2005. "Bright vs. Blurred Boundaries: Second-Generation Assimilation and Exclusion in France, Germany, and the United States." *Ethnic and Racial Studies* 28(1): 20–49.

Alba, Richard, and John R. Logan. 1993. "Minority Proximity to Whites in Suburbs: An Individual-Level Analysis of Segregation." *American Journal of Sociology* 98(May): 1388–427.

Alba, Richard, John Logan, Amy Lutz, and Brian Stults. 2002. "Only English by the Third Generation? Loss and Preservation of the Mother Tongue Among the Grandchildren of Contemporary Immigrants." *Demography* 39(3): 467–84.

Alba, Richard, and Victor Nee. 1997. "Rethinking Assimilation Theory for a New Era of Immigration." *The International Migration Review* 31(4): 826–74.

———. 2003. *Remaking the American Mainstream: Assimilation and Contemporary Immigration*. Cambridge, Mass.: Harvard University Press.

Alderson, Arthur S., and Francois Nielsen. 2002. "Globalization and the Great-Turn: Income Inequality Trends in 16 OECD Countries." *American Journal of Sociology* 107(5): 1244–299.

Allensworth, Elaine M. 1997. "Earnings Mobility of First and 1.5 Generation Mexican-Origin Women and Men: A Comparison with U.S.-Born Mexican Americans and Non-Hispanic Whites." *International Migration Review* 31(2): 386–410.

Anderton, Douglas L., Richard E. Barrett, and Donald J. Bogue. 1997. *The Population of the United States*, 3d ed. New York: Free Press.

Antecol, Heather, Deborah A. Cobb-Clark, and Stephen J. Trejo. 2001. "Immigration Policy and the Skills of Immigrants to Australia, Canada, and the United States." *IZA* Discussion Paper 363. Bonn: Institute for the Study of Labor.

Bankston, Carl L., and Stephen Caldas. 1996. "Majority African American Schools and Social Injustice: The Influence of De Facto Segregation on Academic Achievement." *Social Forces* 75(2): 535–55.

Bankston, Carl L., and Min Zhou. 1995. "Effects of Minority-Language Literacy on the Academic Achievement of Vietnamese Youths in New Orleans." *Sociology of Education* 68(1): 1–17.

Bartel, Ann P., and Marianne J. Koch. 1991. "Internal Migration of U.S. Immigrants." In *Immigration, Trade, and the Labor Market*, edited by John M. Abowd and Richard B. Freeman. Chicago: University of Chicago Press.

Bean, Frank D., Barry Edmonston, and Jeffrey S. Passel, eds. 1990. *Undocumented Migration to the United States: IRCA and the Experience of the 1980s.* Santa Monica, Calif., and Washington, D.C.: Rand Corporation and Urban Institute Press.

Bean, Frank D., and Gillian Stevens. 2003. *America's Newcomers and the Dynamics of Diversity*. New York: Russell Sage Foundation.

Bean, Frank D., and Marta Tienda. 1987. *The Hispanic Population of the United States.* New York: Russell Sage Foundation.

Becker, Gary S., and Nigel Tomes. 1986. "Human Capital and the Rise and Fall of Families." *Journal of Labor Economics* 4(S3): 1.

Blau, Peter M., and Otis Dudley Duncan. 1967. *The American Occupational Structure.* New York: Wiley.

Bleakley, Hoyt, and Aimee Chin. 2004. "Language Skills and Earnings: Evidence from Childhood Immigrants." *Review of Economics and Statistics* 86(2): 481–96.

Bloemraad, Irene. 2006. "Becoming a Citizen in the United States and Canada: Structured Mobilization and Immigrant Political Incorporation." *Social Forces* 85(2): 667–95.

Borjas, George J. 1985. "Assimilation, Changes in Cohort Quality, and the Earnings of Immigrants." *Journal of Labor Economics* 4(3): 463–89.

———. 1999. *Heaven's Door: Immigration Policy and the American Economy.* Princeton, N.J.: Princeton University Press.

———. 2003. "Welfare Reform, Labor Supply, and Health Insurance in the Immigrant Population." *Journal of Health Economics* 22(6): 933–58.

Borjas, George J., and Rachel M. Friedberg. 2007. "The Immigrant Earnings Turnaround of the 1990s." Paper presented at the annual meeting of The Society of Labor Economists. Chicago (May 5). Available at: http://client.norc.org/jole/SOLEweb/780.pdf (accessed May 30, 2007).

Bos, Eduard. 1984. "Estimates of the Number of Illegal Aliens: Analysis of the Sources of Disagreement." *Population Research and Policy Review* 3(3): 239–54.

Brown, Susan K. 2007. "Delayed Spatial Assimilation: Multigenerational Incorporation of the Mexican-Origin Population of Los Angeles." *City and Community* 6(September): 193–210.

Brubaker, Rogers. 1992. *Citizenship and Nationhood in France and Germany*. Cambridge, Mass.: Harvard University Press.

———. 2001. "The Return of Assimilation? Changing Perspectives on Immigration and Its Sequels in France, Germany, and the United States." *Ethnic and Racial Studies* 24(4): 531–48.

Bueker, Catherine S. 2005. "Political Incorporation Among Immigrants from Ten Areas of Origin: The Persistence of Source Country Effects." *International Migration Review* 39(1): 103–40

Burgess, Ernest W. 1967. "The Growth of the City." In *The City*, edited by R. E. Park, E. W. Burgess, and R. D. McKenzie. Chicago: University of Chicago Press.

Calavita, Kitty. 1994. "U.S. Immigration and Policy Responses: The Limits of Legislation." In *Controlling Immigration: A Global Perspective*, edited by Stephen Castles and Mark Miller. New York: The Guilford Press.

Card, David. 2005. "Is the New Immigration Really So Bad?" *Economic Journal* 115(November): F300–23.

Castles, Stephen, and Mark J. Miller. 2003. *The Age of Migration*. 3d ed. New York: Guilford Press.

Charles, Camille Z. 2003. "The Dynamics of Racial Residential Segregation." *Annual Reviews in Sociology* 29(1): 167–207.

———. 2006. *Won't You Be My Neighbor? Race, Class, and Residence in Los Angeles*. New York: Russell Sage Foundation.

Chiswick, Barry R. 1978. "The Effect of Americanization on the Earnings of Foreign Born Men." *Journal of Political Economy* 85(October): 897–921.

Chiswick, Barry R., and Timothy J. Hatton. 2002. "International Migration and the Integration of Labour Markets." IZA Discussion Paper 559. Bonn: Institute for the Study of Labor (IZA).

Chiswick, Barry R., and Paul W. Miller. 2008. "Why Is the Payoff to Schooling Smaller for Immigrants?" *Labour Economics* 15(6): 1317–340.

Clark, William A. V. 2001. "The Geography of Immigrant Poverty: Selective Evidence of an Immigrant Underclass." In *Strangers at the Gates: New Immigrants in Urban America*, edited by Roger Waldinger. Berkeley and Los Angeles: University of California Press.

———. 2007. "Race, Class, and Place: Evaluating Mobility Outcomes for African Americas." *Urban Affairs Review* 42(January): 295–314.

Clark, Mary A., and David A. Jaeger. 2006. "Natives, the Foreign-Born and High School Equivalents: New Evidence on the Returns to the GED." *Journal of Population Economics* 19(4): 769–93.

Coleman, James S., and Thomas Hoffer. 1987. *Public and Private High Schools: The Impact of Communities*. New York: Basic Books.

Coleman, James S., Thomas Hoffer, and Sally Kilgore. 1982. *High School*

Achievement: Public, Catholic and Private Schools Compared. New York: Basic Books.

Cornelius, Wayne A., and Marc R. Rosenblum. 2005. "Immigration and Politics." *Annual Review of Political Science* 8(June): 99–119.

Cranford, Cynthia J. 2005. "Networks of Exploitation: Immigrant Labor and the Restructuring of the Los Angeles Janitorial Industry." *Social Problems* 52(3): 379–97.

Day, Jennifer Cheeseman, and Eric C. Newberger. 2002. "The Big Payoff: Educational Attainment and Synthetic Estimates of Work-Life Earnings." *Current Population Reports*, series P-23, no. 210. Washington: U.S. Government Printing Office.

De Jong, Gordon F., and Quynh-Giang Tran. 2001. "Warm Welcome, Cool Welcome: Mapping Receptivity Toward Immigrants in the U.S." *Population Today* 29(8): 1–4.

Demeny, Paul. 1986. "The World Demographic Situation." In *World Population and U.S. Policy*, edited by J. Menken. New York: W. W. Norton.

DeNavas-Walt, Carmen, Bernadette D. Proctor, and Cheryl Hill Lee. 2006. "Income, Poverty, and Health Insurance in the United States: 2005." *Current Population Reports* P60–231. Washington: U.S. Government Printing Office.

Denton, Nancy A., and Douglas S. Massey. 1988. "Residential Segregation of Blacks, Hispanics, and Asians by Socioeconomic Status and Generation." *Social Science Quarterly* 69(December): 797–817.

Dobson, William J. 2006. "The Day Nothing Much Changed." *Foreign Policy-Washington* 156(September–October): 22.

Donato, Katharine M., Charles Tolbert, Alfred Nucci, and Yukio Kawano. 2008. "Changing Faces, Changing Places: The Emergence of New Nonmetropolitan Immigrant Gateways." In *New Faces in New Places*, edited by Douglas S. Massey. New York: Russell Sage Foundation.

Edelman, Peter. 1997. "The Worst Thing Bill Clinton Has Done." *Atlantic Monthly* 279(March): 43.

Edley, Christopher, Jr. 1996. *Not All Black and White: Affirmative Action, Race, and American Values.* New York: Hill and Wang.

Edmonston, Barry, and Jeffrey S. Passel. 1994. "Ethnicity, Ancestry, and Exogamy in U.S. Population Projections." Paper presented at the 1994 annual meeting of the Population Association of America. Miami (May 5).

Espenshade, Thomas J., and Haishan Fu. 1997. "An Analysis of English-Language Proficiency Among U.S. Immigrants." *American Sociological Review* 62(2): 287–305.

Espenshade, Thomas J., and Katherine Hempstead. 1996. "Contemporary American Attitudes Toward U.S. Immigration." *International Migration Review* 30(2): 535–70.

Esping-Andersen, Gøsta. 2007. "Equal Opportunities and the Welfare State." *Contexts* 6(3): 23–27.

Espino, Rodolfo, and M. M. Franz. 2002. "Latino Phenotypic Discrimination Revisited: The Impact of Skin Color on Occupational Status." *Social Science Quarterly* 83(2): 612–23.

Evans, Mariah D. R. 2004. "Do Ethnic Enclaves Benefit or Harm Linguistically Isolated Employees?" *Research in Social Stratification and Mobility* 22: 281–318.

Fairchild, Gregory B. 2008. "Residential Segregation Influences on the Likelihood of Black and White Self-Employment." *Journal of Business Venturing* 23(1): 46–47.

Farkas, George. 1996. *Human Capital or Cultural Capital? Ethnicity and Poverty Groups in an Urban School District*. New York: Aldine de Gruyter.

Farley, Reynolds. 1996. *The New American Reality: Who We Are, How We Got Here, Where We Are Going*. New York: Russell Sage Foundation.

Farley, Reynolds, and Richard Alba. 2002. "The New Second Generation in the United States." *International Migration Review* 36(3): 669–701.

Farley, Reynolds, and William H. Frey. 1994. "Changes in the Segregation of Whites from Blacks During the 1980s: Small Steps Toward a More Integrated Society." *American Sociological Review* 59(1): 23–45.

Feliciano, Cynthia. 2006. *Unequal Origins: Immigrant Selection and the Education of the Second Generation*. New York: LFB Scholarly Pub.

Fennelly, Katherine. 2008. "Prejudice Toward Immigrants in the Midwest." In *New Faces in New Places*, edited by Douglas S. Massey. New York: Russell Sage Foundation.

Fischer, David H. 1989. *Albion's Seed: Four British Folkways in America*. New York: Oxford University Press.

Fischer, Mary J., and Douglas S. Massey. 2000. "Residential Segregation and Ethnic Enterprise in U.S. Metropolitan Areas." *Social Problems* 47(3): 408–24.

Fix, Michael E., and Jeffrey S. Passel. 1994. *Immigration and Immigrants: Setting the Record Straight*. Washington, D.C.: Urban Institute Press.

Fix, Michael E., and Wendy Zimmermann. 2001. "All Under One Roof: Mixed-Status Families in an Era of Reform." *International Migration Review* 35(2): 397–419.

Ford, Kathleen. 1985. "Declining Fertility Rates of Immigrants to the United States (with Some Exceptions)." *Sociology and Social Research* 70(1): 68–70.

Freeman, Richard B. 2004. "Trade Wars: The Exaggerated Impact of Trade in Economic Debate." *The World Economy* 27(1): 1–23.

Frey, William H., and Kao-Lee Liaw. 1998. "The Impact of Recent Immigration on Population Redistribution within the United States." In *The Immigration Debate: Studies of Economic, Demographic and Fiscal Effects of Immigration*, edited by James P. Smith and Barry Edmonston. Washington: National Academies Press.

Frey, William H., and Alden Speare, Jr. 1988. *Regional and Metropolitan Growth and Decline in the United States*. New York: Russell Sage Foundation.

Gallup Organization. 2008. *Gallup's Pulse of Democracy, Immigration*. Available at: www.gallup.com/poll/1660/Immigration.aspx (accessed December 2008).

Gamoran, Adam, and Robert D. Mare. 1989. "Secondary School Tracking and Education Inequality: Compensation, Reinforcement, or Neutrality?" *American Journal of Sociology* 94(March): 1146–183.

Gans, Herbert J. 1992. "Ethnic Invention and Acculturation, a Bumpy-Line Approach." *Journal of American Ethnic History* 12(1): 42.

Gibson, Margaret A., and John Ogbu, eds. 1991. *Minority Status and Schooling: A Comparative Study of Immigrant and Involuntary Minorities*. New York: Garland Press.

Glenn, Susan A. 1990. *Daughters of the Shtetl: Life and Labor in the Immigrant Generation*. Ithaca, N.Y.: Cornell University Press.

Glick, Jennifer E., and Bryndl Hohmann-Marriott. 2007. "Academic Performance of Young Children in Immigrant Families: The Significance of Race, Ethnicity and National Origins." *International Migration Review* 41(2): 371–402.

Glick, Jennifer E., Stacey D. Ruf, Michael J. White, and Frances K. Goldscheider. 2006. "Educational Engagement and Early Family Formation: Differences by Ethnicity and Generation." *Social Forces* 84(March): 1391–415.

Glick, Jennifer E., and Michael J. White. 2003. "The Academic Trajectories of Immigrant Youths: Analysis Within and Across Cohorts." *Demography* 40(3): 589–603.

———. 2004. "Post-Secondary School Participation of Immigrant and Native Youth: The Role of Familial Resources and Educational Expectations." *Social Science Research* 33(2):272–99.

Gonzalez, Arturo. 2003. "The Education and Wages of Immigrant Children: The Impact of Age at Arrival." *Economics of Education Review* 22(2): 203–12.

Gonzalez, Virginia M., Rita Brusca-Vega, and Thomas D. Yawkey. 1997. *Assessment and Instruction of Culturally and Linguistically Diverse Students with or At-Risk of Learning Problems: From Research to Practice*. Boston: Allyn & Bacon.

Gordon, Milton M. 1964. *Assimilation in American Life*. New York: Oxford University Press.

Greeley, Andrew M. and William C. McCready. 1974. *Ethnicity in the United States: A Preliminary Reconnaissance*. New York: Wiley.

Greenblatt, Alan. 2008. "Immigration Debate." *CQ Researcher* 18(5): 99–118.

Greenman, Emily, and Yu Xie. 2008. "Is Assimilation Theory Dead? The Effect of Assimilation on Adolescent Well-Being." *Social Science Research* 37(1): 109–37.

Hagan, J. M. 1998. "Social Networks, Gender, and Immigrant Incorporation: Resources and Constraints." *American Sociological Review* 63(1): 55–67.

Hao, Lingxin, and Melissa Bonstead-Bruns. 1998. "Parent-Child Difference in Educational Expectations and Academic Achievement of Immigrant and Native Students." *Sociology of Education* 71(3): 175–98.

Heckman, James J., Alan B. Krueger, and Benjamin M. Friedman. 2003. *Inequality in America: What Role for Human Capital Policies?* Cambridge, Mass.: MIT Press.

Hirschman, Charles. 1983. "America's Melting Pot Reconsidered." *Annual Review of Sociology* 9: 399.

Hirschman, Charles, Philip Kasinitz, and Josh DeWind, eds. 1999. *The Handbook of International Migration: The American Experience.* New York: Russell Sage Foundation.

Hirschman, Charles, and Douglas S. Massey. 2008. "Places and Peoples: The New American Mosaic." In *Changing Faces, Changing Places*, edited by Douglas S. Massey. New York: Russell Sage Foundation.

Hogan, Dennis P. 1981. *Transitions and Social Change: The Early Lives of American Men.* New York: Academic Press.

Huntington, Samuel P. 2004. *Who Are We? The Challenge to America's National Identity.* New York: Simon and Schuster.

Hutchinson, Edward P. 1949. "Immigration Policy Since World War I." *Annals of the American Academy of Political and Social Sciences* 262(1): 15–21.

Iceland, John. 2004. "Beyond Black and White: Metropolitan Residential Segregation in Multi-Ethnic America." *Social Science Research* 33(June): 248–71.

Iceland, John, Daniel H. Weinberg, and Erika H. Steinmetz. 2002. *Racial and Ethnic Residential Segregation in the United States, 1980–2000.* U.S. Census Bureau Series CENSR-3. Washington: U.S. Government Printing Office.

Ishizawa, Hiromi, and Gillian Stevens. 2007. "Non-English Language Neighborhoods in Chicago, Illinois: 2000." *Social Science Research* 36(September): 1042–1064.

Jaeger, David A., and Marianne E. Page. 1996. "Degrees Matter: New Evidence on Sheepskin Effects in the Returns to Education." *Review of Economics and Statistics* 78(3): 733–39.

Jamieson, Amie, Andrea Curry, and Gladys Martinez. 2001. "School Enrollment in the United States—Social and Economic Characteristics of Students." *Current Population Reports*, series P-20, no. 533. Washington: U.S. Government Printing Office.

Jasso, Guillermina, and Mark R. Rosenzweig. 1990. *The New Chosen People: Immigrants in the United States.* New York: Russell Sage Foundation.

Jasso, Guillermina, Mark R. Rosenzweig, and James P. Smith. 2000. "The Changing Skill of New Immigrants to the United States: Recent Trends and Their Determinants." In *Issues in the Economics of Immigration*, edited by George J. Borjas. Chicago: University of Chicago Press.

Jencks, Christopher, Susan Bartlett, Mary Corcoran, James Crouse, David Eaglesfield, Gregory Jackson, Kent McClelland, Peter Mueser, Michael Olneck, Joseph Schwartz, Sherry Ward, and Jill Williams. 1979. *Who Gets Ahead? The Determinants of Economic Success in America*. New York: Basic Books.

Johnson, Kenneth M., and Daniel T. Lichter. 2008. "Natural Increase: A New Source of Population Growth in Emerging Hispanic Destinations in the United States." *Population and Development Review* 34(2): 327–46.

Kahn, Joan R. 1994. "Immigrant and Native Fertility During the 1980s: Adaptation and Expectations for the Future." *International Migration Review* 28(3): 501–19.

Kahn, Lawrence M. 2004. "Immigration, Skills and the Labor Market: International Evidence." *Journal of Population Economics* 17(3):501–34.

Kandel, William, and Emilio A. Parrado. 2005. "Restructuring of the U.S. Meat Processing Industry and New Hispanic Migrant Destinations." *Population and Development Review* 31(3): 447–71.

Kao, Grace, and Marta Tienda. 1995. "Optimism and Achievement: The Educational Performance of Immigrant Youth." *Social Science Quarterly* 76(1): 1–19.

———. 1998. "Educational Aspirations of Minority Youth." *American Journal of Education* 106(3): 349–84.

Kasinitz, Philip, John H. Mollenkopf, and Mary C. Waters. 2004. *Becoming New Yorkers: Ethnographies of the New Second Generation*. New York: Russell Sage Foundation.

Kollwelter, Serge. 2007. "Immigration in Luxembourg: New Challenges for an Old Country." Washington, D.C.: Migration Policy Institute. Available at: http://www.migrationinformation.org/Profiles/display.cfm?id=587 (accessed August 1, 2008).

Lamont, Michele, and Virag Molnar. 2002. "The Study of Boundaries in the Social Sciences." *Annual Review of Sociology* 28(1): 167–95.

Larsen, Luke J. 2004. "The Foreign-Born Population in the United States: 2003." *Current Population Reports* P20–551. Washington: U.S. Bureau of the Census.

Lee, Jennifer, and Frank D. Bean. 2004. "America's Changing Color Lines: Immigration, Race/Ethnicity, and Multiracial Identification." *Annual Review of Sociology* 30(August): 221–42.

Levitt, Peggy. 2007. *God Needs No Passport: Immigrants and the Changing American Religious Landscape*. New York: New Press.

Levitt, Peggy, and Mary C. Waters. 2002. *The Changing Face of Home: The Transnational Lives of the Second Generation*. New York: Russell Sage Foundation.

Liang, Zai. 1994. "Social Contact, Social Capital, and the Naturalization Process: Evidence from Six Immigrant Groups." *Social Science Research* 23(4): 407–37.

Lichter, Daniel T., and Kenneth M. Johnson. 2006. "Emerging Rural Settlement Patterns and the Geographic Redistribution of America's New Immigrants." *Rural Sociology* 71(1): 109–31.

Lieberson, Stanley. 1963. *Ethnic Patterns in American Cities*. New York: The Free Press of Glencoe.

————. 1980. *A Piece of the Pie: Blacks and White Immigrants Since 1880*. Berkeley: University of California Press.

Lieberson, Stanley, and Mary C. Waters. 1988. *From Many Strands: Ethnic and Racial Groups in Contemporary America*. New York: Russell Sage Foundation.

Lindholm, Kathryn, and Zierlein Aclan. 1991. "Bilingual Proficiency as a Bridge to Academic Achievement: Results from Bilingual/Immersion Programs." *Journal of Education* 173(2): 99–113.

Lofstrom, Magnus, and Frank D. Bean. 2002. "Assessing Immigrant Policy Options: Labor Market Conditions and Postreform Declines in Immigrants' Receipt of Welfare." *Demography* 39(4): 617–37.

Logan, John R., and Richard D. Alba. 1991. "Variations on Two Themes: Racial and Ethnic Patterns in the Attainment of Suburban Residence." *Demography* 28(3): 431–53.

Logan, John R., Richard D. Alba, Tom McNulty, and Brian Fisher. 1996. "Making a Place in the Metropolis: Locational Attainment in Cities and Suburbs." *Demography* 33(November): 443–53.

Logan, John R., Richard D. Alba, and Wenquan Zhang. 2002. "Immigrant Enclaves and Ethnic Communities in New York and Los Angeles." *American Sociological Review* 67(2): 299–322.

Lubotsky, Darren. 2007. "Chutes or Ladders? A Longitudinal Analysis of Immigrant Earnings." *Journal of Political Economy* 115(5): 820–67.

Martin, Philip, and Elizabeth Midgley. 2006. "Immigration: Shaping and Reshaping America," 2d ed. *Population Bulletin* 61(4): 1–32.

Martin, Susan. 2003. "The Politics of U.S. Immigration Reform." *The Political Quarterly* 74(S10): 132–49.

Massey, Douglas S. 1995. "The New Immigration and Ethnicity in the United States." *Population and Development Review* 21(3): 631–52.

————. 2008. *New Faces in New Places: The Changing Geography of American Immigration*. New York: Russell Sage Foundation.

Massey, Douglas S., and Chiara Capoferro. 2008. "The Geographic Diversification of American Immigration." In *New Faces, New Places*, edited by Douglas S. Massey. New York: Russell Sage Foundation.

Massey, Douglas S., Gretchen A. Condran, and Nancy A. Denton. 1987. "The Effect of Residential Segregation on Black Social and Economic Well-Being." *Social Forces* 66(4): 29.

Massey, Douglas S., and Nancy A. Denton. 1993. *American Apartheid: Segregation and the Making of the Underclass*. Cambridge, Mass.: Harvard University Press.

Massey, Douglas S., Jorge Durand, and Nolan J. Malone. 2002. *Beyond Smoke and Mirrors: Mexican Immigration in an Era of Economic Integration*. New York: Russell Sage Foundation.

Massey, Douglas S., Margarita Mooney, Kimberly C. Torres, and Camille Z.

Charles. 2007. "Black Immigrants and Black Natives Attending Selective Colleges and Universities in the United States." *American Journal of Education* 113(2): 243–71.

Massey, Douglas S., and Brendan P. Mullan. 1984. "Processes of Hispanic and Black Spatial Assimilation." *American Journal of Sociology* 89(4): 836–73.

Massey, Douglas S., Michael J. White, and Voon-Chin Phua. 1996. "The Dimensions of Segregation Revisited." *Sociological Methods & Research* 25(2): 172.

Mayda, Anna M. 2006. "Who Is Against Immigration? A Cross-Country Investigation of Individual Attitudes toward Immigrants." *Review of Economics and Statistics* 88(3): 510–30.

McDaniel, Antonio. 1995. "The Dynamic Racial Composition of the United States." *Daedalus* 124(1): 179–98.

Migration Policy Institute. 2008. "Foreign Born Population as a Percent of the Total Population." Washington, D.C.: Migration Policy Institute. Available at: http://www.migrationinformation.org/DataHub/charts/1.1.shtml (accessed November 27, 2007).

Montero, Darrel, and Ronald Tsukashima. 1977. "Assimilation and Educational Achievement: The Case of the Second Generation Japanese-American." *Sociological Quarterly* 18(4): 490–503.

Mouw, Theodore, and Yue Xie. 1999. "Bilingualism and the Academic Achievement of Asian Immigrants: Accommodation with or without Assimilation?" *American Sociological Review* 64(2): 232–53.

Myers, Dowell. 1995. *The Changing Immigrants of Southern California*. Research Report LCRI-95–04R. Los Angeles: University of Southern California, Lusk Center Research Institute.

———. 2007. *Immigrants and Boomers: Forging a New Social Contract for the Future of America*. New York: Russell Sage Foundation.

Myers, Dowell, and Cynthia J. Cranford. 1998. "Temporal Differentiation in the Occupational Mobility of Immigrant and Native-Born Latina Workers." *American Sociological Review* 63(1): 68–93.

National Center for Educational Statistics, *High School and Beyond*. Available at: http://nces.ed.gov/surveys/hsb.

National Center for Educational Statistics, *National Educational Longitudinal Study of 1988* [NELS88]. Available at: http://nces.ed.gov/surveys/nels88.

Neckerman, Kathryn M., Prudence Carter, and Jennifer Lee. 1999. "Segmented Assimilation and Minority Cultures of Mobility." *Ethnic and Racial Studies.* 22(6): 945–65.

Neidert, Lisa J., and Reynolds Farley. 1985. "Assimilation in the United States: An Analysis of Ethnic and Generation Differences in Status and Achievement." *American Sociological Review* 50(6): 840.

Neumann, Gerald L. 1996. *Strangers to the Constitution: Immigrants, Borders, and Fundamental Law*. Princeton, N.J.: Princeton University Press.

Nielsen, Francois, and Steven J. Lerner. 1986. "Language Skills and School Achievement of Bilingual Hispanics." *Social Science Research* 15(3): 209–40.

Novak, Michael. 1996. *Unmeltable Ethnics*. New Brunswick, N.J.: Transaction.

Owen, Carolyn A., Howard C. Eisner, and Thomas R. McFaul. 1981. "A Half-Century of Social Distance Research: National Replication of the Bogardus Studies." *Sociology and Social Research* 66(1): 80–98.

Pager, Devah. 2007. "The Use of Field Experiments for Studies of Employment Discrimination: Contributions, Critiques, and Directions for the Future." *The Annals of the American Academy of Political and Social Science* 609(1): 104–33.

Pagnini, Deanna. 1997. "Immigration and Fertility in New Jersey: A Comparison of Native and Foreign-Born Women." In *Keys to Successful Immigration: Implications of the New Jersey Experience,* edited by Thomas J. Espenshade. Washington, D.C.: Urban Institute Press.

Park, Robert E. 1924. "The Concept of Social Distance As Applied to the Study of Racial Attitudes and Racial Relations." *Journal of Applied Sociology* 8: 339–44.

———. 1950. *The Collected Papers of Robert Ezra Park*, edited by E. Hughes. Glencoe, Ill.: Free Press.

Parrado, Emilio A., and William Kandel. 2008. "New Hispanic Migrant Destinations: A Tale of Two Industries." In *New Faces in New Places*, edited by Douglas S. Massey. New York: Russell Sage Foundation.

Passel, Jeffrey S. 2005. *Unauthorized Migrants: Numbers and Characteristics*. Washington, D.C.: Pew Hispanic Center.

Perlmann, Joel. 2005. *Italians Then, Mexicans Now: Immigrant Origins and Second-Generation Progress, 1890 to 2000*. New York: Russell Sage Foundation.

Pew Research Center. 2007. *World Publics Welcome Trade – But Not Immigration*. Washington, D.C.: Pew Global Attitudes Project. Available at: http://pewglobal.org/reports/display.php?ReportID=258 (accessed October 4–16, 2007).

Population Reference Bureau. 2007. "World Population Data Sheet, 2007." Washington, D.C.: Population Reference Bureau.

Portes, Alejandro. 1995. *The Economic Sociology of Immigration: Essays on Networks, Ethnicity, and Entrepreneurship*. New York: Russell Sage Foundation.

Portes, Alejandro, and Jozsef Borocz. 1989. "Contemporary Immigration: Theoretical Perspectives on Its Determinants and Modes of Incorporation." *The International Migration Review* 23(3): 606–30.

Portes, Alejandro, and Rubén G. Rumbaut. 1990. *Immigrant America: A Portrait*. Berkeley: University of California Press.

———. 2001. *Legacies: The Story of the Immigrant Second Generation*. Berkeley: University of California Press.

Portes, Alejandro, and Richard Schauffler. 1994. "Language and the Second

Generation: Bilingualism Yesterday and Today." *International Migration Review* 108(4): 7.

Portes, Alejandro, and Min Zhou. 1993. "The New Second Generation: Segmented Assimilation and Its Variants Among Post-1965 Immigrant Youth." *Annals of the American Academy of Political and Social Science* 530(November): 74–96.

Qian, Zhenchao C., and Daniel T. Lichter. 2001. "Measuring Marital Assimilation: Intermarriage Among Natives and Immigrants." *Social Science Research* 30(2): 289–312.

―――――. 2007. "Social Boundaries and Marital Assimilation: Interpreting Trends in Racial and Ethnic Intermarriage." *American Sociological Review* 72(February): 68–94.

Regets, Mark C. 2001. "Research and Policy Issues in High-Skilled International Migration: A Perspective with Data from the United States." IZA Discussion Paper 366. Bonn: Institute for the Study of Labor. Available at: http://ssrn.com/abstract=285424 (accessed December 12, 2008).

Reimers, David M. 1985. *Still the Golden Door: The Third World Comes to America*. New York: Columbia University Press.

Rosenfeld, Michael J., and Marta Tienda. 1999. "Mexican Immigration, Occupational Niches, and Labor Market Competition: Evidence from Los Angeles, Chicago, and Atlanta, 1970–1990." In *Immigration and Opportunity: Race, Ethnicity, and Employment in the United States*, edited by Frank D. Bean and Susan Bell-Rose. New York: Russell Sage Foundation.

Rumbaut, Rubén G. 1994a. "Origins and Destinies: Immigration to the United States Since World War II." *Sociological Forum* 9(4): 583–621.

―――――. 1994b. "The Crucible Within: Ethnic Identity, Self Esteem, and Segmented Assimilation Among Children of Immigrants." *International Migration Review* 28(4): 748–94.

―――――. 1995. "The New Californians: Comparative Research Findings on the Educational Progress of Immigrant Children." In *California's Immigrant Children*, edited by Rubén G. Rumbaut and W. A. Cornelius. San Diego: University of California at San Diego, Center for U. S.-Mexican Studies.

―――――. 1996. "The Crucible Within: Ethnic Identity, Self-Esteem, and Segmented Assimilation Among Children of Immigrants." In *The New Second Generation*, edited by Alejandro Portes. New York: Russell Sage Foundation.

―――――. 1999. "Assimilation and Its Discontents: Ironies and Paradoxes." Pp. 172–195 in *The Handbook of International Migration: The American Experience*. New York: Russell Sage Foundation.

―――――. 2004. "Ages, Life Stages, and Generations Cohorts: Decomposing the Immigrant First and Second Generations in the United States." *International Migration Review* 38(3): 1160–205.

Rumbaut, Rubén G., Douglas S. Massey, and Frank D. Bean. 2006. "Linguistic Life Expectancies: Immigrant Language Retention in Southern California." *Population and Development Review* 32(3): 447–60.

Rumbaut, Rubén G., and Alejandro Portes. 2001a. "Ethnogenesis: Coming of Age in Immigrant America." In *Ethnicities*, edited by Rubén G. Rumbaut and Alejandro Portes. New York: Russell Sage Foundation.

———, eds. 2001b. *Ethnicities*. New York: Russell Sage Foundation.

Salins, Peter D. 1997. *Assimilation, American Style*. New York: Basic Books.

Sanders, Jimy, Victor Nee, and Scott Sernau. 2002. "Asian Immigrants' Reliance on Social Ties in a Multiethnic Labor Market." *Social Forces* 81(1): 281.

Sassler, Sharon. 1995. "Trade-Offs in the Family: Sibling Effects on Daughters' Activities in 1910." *Demography* 32(4): 557–75.

Scheve, Kenneth F., and Matthew J. Slaughter. 2001. "Labor Market Competition and Individual Preferences over Immigration Policy." *Review of Economics and Statistics* 83(1): 133–45.

Schmidley, Diane. 2001. "Profile of the Foreign-Born Population in the United States: 2000." *Current Population Reports*, Series P23–206. Washington: U.S. Government Printing Office.

Schuck, Peter H. 2003. *Diversity in America: Keeping Government at a Safe Distance*. Cambridge, Mass.: Belknap Press of Harvard University Press.

See, Catherine O., and William J. Wilson. 1988. "Race and Ethnicity." In *Handbook of Sociology*, edited by Neil J. Smelser. Newbury Park, Calif.: Sage Publications.

Sewell, William H., Robert M. Hauser, and David L. Featherman. 1976. *Schooling and Achievement in American Society*. New York: Academic Press.

Singer, Audrey. 2002. "Immigrants, Welfare Reform and the Coming Reauthorization Vote." Available at: http://www.migrationinformation.org/U.S.focus/eligibility_chart.shtml (accessed October 2, 2007).

———. 2004. "The Rise of New Immigrant Gateways." *Living Cities Census Series*. Washington, D.C.: Brookings Institution Press. Available at: http://www.brookings.edu/urban/pubs/20040301_gateways.pdf (accessed June 28, 2008).

Singer, Audrey, Susan W. Hardwick, and Caroline B. Brettell. 2008. *Twenty-First-Century Gateways: Immigrant Incorporation in Suburban America*. Washington, D.C.: Brookings Institution Press.

Skocpol, Theda. 1995. "State Formation and Social Policy in the United States." In *Social Policy in the United States: Future Possibilities in Historical Perspective*. Princeton, N.J.: Princeton University Press.

Small, Mario L., and Katherine Newman. 2001. "Urban Poverty after the Truly Disadvantaged." *Annual Review of Sociology* 27(August): 23–45.

Smith, James P., and Barry Edmonston. 1997. *The New Americans: Economic,*

Demographic, and Fiscal Effects of Immigration. Washington, D.C.: National Academy Press.

Smith, James P., and Finis R. Welch. 1986. *Closing the Gap: Forty Years of Economic Progress for Blacks*. Rand Report R-3330-DOL. Santa Monica, Calif.: Rand Corporation.

South, Scott J., Kyle Crowder, and Erick Chavez. 2005a. "Migration and Spatial Assimilation Among U.S. Latinos: Classical Versus Segmented Trajectories." *Demography* 42(August): 497–521.

———. 2005b. "Geographic Mobility and Spatial Assimilation among U.S. Latino Immigrants." *International Migration Review* 39(3): 577–607.

Stalker, Peter. 2000. *Workers Without Frontiers: The Impact of Globalization on International Migration*. Boulder, Colo.: Lynne Rienner.

Stanton-Salazar, Ricardo D. 1997. "A Social Capital Framework for Understanding the Socialization of Racial Minority Children and Youths." *Harvard Educational Review* 67(1): 1–40.

Stolzenberg, Ross M. 1990. "Ethnicity, Geography, and Occupational Achievement of Hispanic Men in the United States." *American Sociological Review* 55(February): 143–54.

Suarez-Orozco, Marcelo M., ed. 1991. "Migration, Minority Status, and Education: European Dilemmas and Responses in the 1990s." *Anthropology and Education Quarterly* 22(2): 99–120.

Taeuber, Karl, and Alma Taeuber. 1965. *Negroes in Cities*. Chicago: Aldine.

Telles, Edward E., and Edward Murguía. 1990. "Phenotypic Discrimination and Income Differences among Mexican Americans." *Social Science Quarterly* 71(4): 682–97.

———. 1992. "The Continuing Significance of Phenotype Among Mexican Americans." *Social Science Quarterly* 73(1): 120–23.

Tienda, Marta, and Faith Mitchell, eds. 2006. *Multiple Origins, Uncertain Destinies: Hispanics and the American Future*. Washington, D.C.: National Academies Press.

Trueba, Henry T. 1988. "Culturally Based Explanations of Minority Students' Academic Achievement." *Anthropology and Education Quarterly* 19(3): 270–87.

United Nations, Population Division. 2006. *Trends in Total Migrant Stock: The 2005 Revision*. POP/DB/MIG/Rev.2005/Doc. New York: United Nations. Available at: http://www.un.org/esa/population/publications/migration/UN_Migrant_Stock_Documentation_2005.pdf (accessed October 26, 2008).

U.S. Bureau of the Census. 1976. *Historical Statistics of the United States, Colonial Times to 1970*. Washington: U.S. Dept. of Commerce.

———. 2006. *State and Metropolitan Area Data Book 2006*. Washington: U.S. Government Printing Office. Available at: http://www.census.gov/prod/2006pubs/smadb/smadb-06.pdf (accessed November 17, 2008).

———. 2007a. *Statistical Abstract of the United States 2007*. Washington:

U.S. Government Printing Office. Available at: http://www.census.gov (accessed September 3, 2008).

————. 2007b. "Cumulative Estimates of the Components of Population Change for Metropolitan and Micropolitan Statistical Areas." Washington: U.S. Government Printing Office. Available at: http://www.census.gov/population/www/estimates/Estimates%20pages_final.html (accessed August 31, 2008).

U.S. Bureau of the Census, Census of Population and Housing 2000, Summary File 3, extracted via the Interuniversity Consortium for Political and Social Research (ICPSR), University of Michigan. Available at: http://www.census.gov/Press-Release/www/2002/sumfile3.html and http://www.icpsr.umich.edu/CENSUS2000/.

U.S. Bureau of the Census, Current Population Survey, March 1994, extracted via DataFerret. Available at: http://www.census.gov/cps.

U.S. Bureau of the Census, Current Population Survey, March 2004, extracted via DataFerret. Available at: http://www.census.gov/cps.

U.S. Commission on Immigration Reform (USCIR). 1994. *U.S. Immigration Policy: Restoring Credibility*. Washington: U.S. Government Printing Office.

————. 1995. *Legal Immigration: Setting Priorities*. Washington: U.S. Government Printing Office.

————. 1997. *Becoming an American: Immigration and Immigrant Policy*. Washington: U.S. Government Printing Office.

U.S. Department of Homeland Security, Office of Immigration Statistics. 2000. *2000 Yearbook of Immigration Statistics*. Washington: U.S. Government Printing Office.

————. 2003. *2003 Yearbook of Immigration Statistics*. Washington: U.S. Government Printing Office.

————. 2005. *2005 Yearbook of Immigration Statistics*. Washington: U.S. Government Printing Office.

U.S. Immigration and Naturalization Service. 1996. *Immigration to the United States in the Fiscal Year 1995*. Washington: U.S. Government Printing Office.

Van Hook, Jennifer, Jennifer E. Glick, and Frank D. Bean. 1999. "Public Assistance Receipt Among Immigrants and Natives: How the Unit of Analysis Affects Research Findings." *Demography* 36(1): 111–20.

Velez, William. 1989. "High School Attrition Among Hispanic and Non-Hispanic White Youths." *Sociology of Education* 62(2): 119–33.

Waldinger, Roger. 1995. "When the Melting Pot Boils Over: The Irish, Jews, Blacks, and Koreans of New York." In *The Bubbling Cauldron: Race, Ethnicity, and the Urban Crisis*, edited by Michael Peter Smith and Joe R. Faegin. Minneapolis: University of Minnesota Press.

————. 2003. "The Sociology of Immigration: Second Thoughts and Reconsiderations." In *Host Societies and the Reception of Immigrants*, edited by Jeffrey G. Reitz. Boulder, Colo.: Lynne Rienner Publishers.

Waters, Mary C. 1990. *Ethnic Options: Choosing Identities in America*. Berkeley: University of California Press.

———. 2000a. "Immigration, Intermarriage, and the Challenges of Measuring Racial/Ethnic Identities." *American Journal of Public Health* 90(September): 1735–173.

———. 2000b. "The Sociological Roots and Multidisciplinary Future of Immigration Research." In *Immigrant Research for a New Century: Multidisciplinary Perspectives*, edited by Nancy Foner, Rubén Rumbaut, and Steven J. Gold. New York: Russell Sage Foundation.

Waters, Mary C., and Tomás R. Jiménez. 2005. "Assessing Immigrant Assimilation: New Empirical and Theoretical Challenges." *Annual Review of Sociology* 31(August): 105–25.

White, Michael J. 1986. "Segregation and Diversity Measures in Population Distribution." *Population Index* 52(2 sw): 198–221.

———. 1987. *American Neighborhoods and Residential Differentiation*. New York: Russell Sage Foundation.

———. 1997. "Language Proficiency, Schooling, and the Achievement of Immigrants." Report prepared for the U.S. Department of Labor.

White, Michael J., Ann E. Biddlecom, and Shenyan Guo. 1993. "Immigration, Naturalization, and Residential Assimilation among Asian Americans in 1980." *Social Forces* 72(1): 93–117.

White, Michael J., Robert F. Dymowski, and Shilian Wang. 1994. "Ethnic Neighbors and Ethnic Myths: An Examination of Residential Segregation in 1910." In *After Ellis Island*, edited by Susan C. Watkins. New York: Russell Sage Foundation.

White, Michael J., and Jennifer E. Glick. 1999. "The Impact of Immigration on Residential Segregation." In *Immigration and Opportunity*, edited by Frank D. Bean and Susan Bell-Rose. New York: Russell Sage Foundation.

———. 2000. "Generation Status, Social Capital and the Routes out of High School." *Sociological Forum* 15(4): 671–191.

White, Michael J., and Gayle Kaufman. 1997. "Language Usage, Social Capital, and School Completion among Immigrants and Native-Born Ethnic Groups." *Social Science Quarterly* 78(2): 385–98.

White, Michael J., Ann H. Kim, and Jennifer E. Glick. 2005. "Mapping Social Distance: Ethnic Residential Segregation in a Multiethnic Metro." *Sociological Methods and Research* 34(2): 173–203.

White, Michael J., and Peter R. Mueser. 1994. "Changes in the Demographic Determinants of U.S. Population Mobility: 1940–80." *The Review of Regional Studies* 24(winter): 245–64.

White, Michael J., and Sharon Sassler. 2000. "Judging Not Only by Color: Ethnicity, Nativity, and Neighborhood Attainment." *Social Science Quarterly* 81(4): 997–1013.

Wierzbicki, Susan K. 2004. *Beyond the Immigrant Enclave*. New York: LFB Scholarly Publishing.

Wilkes, Rima, and John Iceland. 2004. "Hypersegregation in the Twenty-First Century." *Demography* 41(1): 23–36.

Wilson, Franklin D. 2003. "Ethnic Niching and Metropolitan Labor Markets." *Social Science Research*. 32(3): 429–66.

Wilson, William J., and Richard P. Taub. 2006. *There Goes the Neighborhood: Racial, Ethnic, and Class Tensions in Four Chicago Neighborhoods and Their Meaning for America*. New York: Alfred A. Knopf.

Wittke, Carl. 1949. "Immigration Policy Prior to World War I." *Annals of the American Academy of Political and Social Science* 262(March): 5–14.

Woodrow, Karen A., and Jeffrey S. Passel. 1990. "Post-IRCA Undocumented Immigration to the United States: An Assessment Based on the June 1988 CPS." In *Undocumented Migration to the United States: IRCA and the Experience of the 1980s*, edited by Frank D. Bean, Barry Edmonston, and Jeffrey S. Passel. Santa Monica, Calif., and Washington, D.C.: Rand Corporation and Urban Institute Press.

Yinger, John. 1995. *Closed Doors, Opportunities Lost*. New York: Russell Sage Foundation.

Yu, Zhou, and Dowell Myers. 2007. "Convergence or Divergence in Los Angeles: Three Distinctive Ethnic Patterns of Immigrant Residential Assimilation." *Social Science Research* 36(March): 254–85.

Zeng, Zhen, and Yu Xie. 2004. "Asian-Americans' Earnings Disadvantage Reexamined: The Role of Place of Education." *American Journal of Sociology* 109(5): 1075–108.

Zhou, Min. 1997. *Chinatown: The Socioeconomic Potential of an Urban Enclave*. Philadelphia: Temple University Press.

———. 1999. "Segmented Assimilation: Issues, Controversies, and Recent Research on the New Second Generation." In *The Handbook of International Migration: The American Experience*, edited by Charles Hirschman, Philip Kasinitz, and Josh Dewind. New York: Russell Sage Foundation.

Zhou, Min, and Carl L. Bankston. 1994. "Social Capital and the Adaptation of the Second Generation: The Case of Vietnamese Youth in New Orleans." *International Migration Review* 108(4): 197–220.

Zimmerman, Wendy, and Karen C. Tumlin. 1999. "Patchwork Policies: State Assistance for Immigrants under Welfare Reform." *Assessing the New Federalism*. Occasional Paper. Washington, D.C.: Urban Institute Press.

Zolberg, Aristide R. 2006. *A Nation by Design: Immigration Policy in the Fashioning of America*. New York and Cambridge, Mass.: Russell Sage Foundation and Harvard University Press.

Zsembik, Barbara A., and Daniel Llanes. 1996. "Generational Differences in Educational Attainment Among Mexican Americans." *Social Science Quarterly* 77(2): 363–74.

INDEX

Boldface numbers refer to figures and tables.

Panel on Hispanics in the United States
(National Academy of Sciences), 4
Park, Robert, 35, 49
Parrado, Emilio, 20, 157
Passel, Jeffrey S., 9, 62, 191*n*1, 192*n*3
Patriot Act of 2001, 68, 73
Perlmann, Joel, 193*n*12
Personal Responsibility and Work Opportunity Reconciliation Act of 1996, 62,
66
Plyler v. Doe, 195*n*7
population: components of change in metropolitan areas, 2000 to 2006, **16–17**;
contribution of fertility and immigration to growth of, 11–13, 191–92*n*2;
metropolitan distribution of foreign
born and total, **14**; proportion of immigrants in U.S., 26–27
Portes, Alejandro, 32, 38, 40, 85, 197*n*7
poverty among immigrants: by arrival year,
120–22; by generation status, 128–29;
by refugee/nonrefugee status, 146–47
public opinion, on immigration, 60, 62–66
public policy, immigration. *See* immigration policy

Qian, Zhenchao, 183

race. *See* ethnicity
Reimers, David, 59–60, 195*n*4–5
residential patterns (assimilation/segrega-
tion), 150–51, 173; analysis of, approach to, 154–55; assimilation, as a
stage of, 76; conclusions regarding,
168–70, 177–79; ethnicity and, 51–53,
151–52; immigrants and ethnic groups
in, 6–7; initial settlement, process of,
154; measuring, 50–51; models of,
152–54; residential assimilation defined,
50, 152; residential dissimilarity in the
Chicago metropolitan area, **164**; residential dissimilarity in the Los Angeles

metropolitan area, **163**; residential dissimilarity in the New York metropolitan
area, **162**; segmented assimilation and,
152–53, 160, 169–70; segregation by
year of arrival, 158–59; segregation by
year of arrival and birthplace, 159–61;
segregation by year of arrival and birthplace, national summary of, 165–68;
segregation by year of arrival and birthplace in three metropolitan areas,
161–65; segregation of the foreign born
in 2000, 155–58
Rosenblum, Marc, 57
Rosenzweig, Mark, 59
Rumbaut, Rubén G., 32–33, 38, 40, 85,
179, 197*n*7

Salins, Peter, 36
scale of immigration, 8–11, 25–27,
184–85; demographic dynamics and,
11–13; the global context, 23–27; historical trends, 9–10, **11**; national origins, shift in, 20–23; urban concentration of immigrant populations and,
13–20
Schuck, Peter, 186–87
segmented assimilation: as assimilation trajectory, 45–46; educational achievement
and, 83; ethnic discrimination and, 71;
labor market outcomes and, 148; residential patterns and, 152–53, 160,
169–70; results of longitudinal analysis
and, 184; theory of, 29, 37–40, 79–80
segmented identificational assimilation, 33
segregation, residential. *See* residential patterns (assimilation/segregation)
selective acculturation, 32, 40
Simpson, Alan, 56
Small, Mario, 39
Social Security Act of 1935, 196*n*10
socioeconomic outcomes. *See* early adult
earnings; earnings; labor markets